POSITIVE DISCIPLINE:

THE FIRST THREE YEARS

ALSO IN THE POSITIVE DISCIPLINE SERIES

Positive Discipline
Jane Nelsen

Positive Discipline A–Z
Jane Nelsen, Lynn Lott, and H. Stephen Glenn

Positive Discipline for Preschoolers
Jane Nelsen, Cheryl Erwin, and Roslyn Duffy

Positive Discipline for Teenagers
Jane Nelsen and Lynn Lott

Positive Discipline in the Classroom
Jane Nelsen, Lynn Lott, and H. Stephen Glenn

Positive Discipline: A Teacher's A–Z Guide
Jane Nelsen, Roslyn Duffy, Linda Escobar, Kate Ortolano, and
Debbie Owen-Sohocki

Positive Discipline for Single Parents
Jane Nelsen, Cheryl Erwin, and Carol Delzer

Positive Discipline for Your Stepfamily
Jane Nelsen, Cheryl Erwin, and H. Stephen Glenn

Positive Discipline for Parenting in Recovery
Jane Nelsen, Riki Intner, and Lynn Lott

Positive Discipline for Childcare Providers
Jane Nelsen and Cheryl Erwin

Positive Discipline for Working Parents
Jane Nelsen and Lisa Larson

Positive Discipline in the Christian Home
Jane Nelsen, Cheryl Erwin, Michael L. Brock, and Mary L. Hughes

POSITIVE DISCIPLINE

THE FIRST THREE YEARS

From Infant to Toddler—
Laying the Foundation for Raising a
Capable, Confident Child

Completely Revised and Expanded 2nd Edition

JANE NELSEN, ED.D., CHERYL ERWIN, M.A., AND ROSLYN ANN DUFFY

THREE RIVERS PRESS · NEW YORK

Originally published in different form by Prima Publishing, Roseville,
California, in 1998.

Interior illustrations by Paula Gray

Library of Congress Cataloging-in-Publication Data
Nelsen, Jane.
Positive discipline : the first three years : from infant to toddler—laying the
foundation for raising a capable, confident child / Jane Nelsen, Cheryl
Erwin, and Roslyn Duffy—Rev. and updated 2nd ed.
   p. cm.
Includes index.
1. Discipline of children. 2. Discipline of infants. 3. Infants.
4. Toddlers. 5. Child rearing. 6. Child development.
I. Erwin, Cheryl. II. Duffy, Roslyn. III. Title.
HQ770.4.N437 2007
649'.122—dc22   2006025805

ISBN 978-0-307-34159-4

Printed in the United States of America

Design by Cynthia Dunne

10

Second Edition

CONTENTS

CONTENTS

INTRODUCTION

PARENTS HAVE BEEN raising children since the dawn of time. But through our studies and work with families, we've found that in the eight short years since *Positive Discipline: The First Three Years* was originally published, much of what we know and understand about young children has grown and changed. Oh, some things will always be the same: young children will always need unconditional love, encouragement, skills, supervision—and lots of patience. In other areas, however, we are still learning. New research about the human brain has allowed us to understand more about what all humans truly need to be capable, competent, happy people. Parents have shared new stories with us—and we are happy to share them with you. We are grateful to have the opportunity to update and revise this book so it can be even more useful to parents just setting out on this amazing and challenging journey.

Some parents have commented over the years on the title of this book. "How," they ask, "can you even talk about discipline in the first year or two of life? Why would parents need to punish infants and toddlers?" As you read, you will discover that we do not advocate punishment at all, for any age. Instead, we believe in *discipline* that teaches young children in a kind, respectful, and gentle manner, discipline that imparts valuable social and life skills as a foundation for success in relationships and in life itself.

Above all, we believe in relationship, in the enduring bond between a parent and his or her child. The connection you create with your little one is by far your most valuable parenting tool; everything else depends on the quality of the relationship you share together. As parents who have raised families and watched our children embark on their own lives and journeys, we can tell you that what remains after all the tantrums, sleepless nights, mistakes, and worries that come with raising little ones are done is *love*. When all else fails and you don't know what to do, fall back on love. Love and your own inner wisdom will always help you decide what to do.

It is our hope that this book will become a valuable friend and teacher as you share these busy and exciting years with your child. It takes courage to raise a child; it also takes courage to *be* one. Take time to savor these first three wonderful years; they will pass all too quickly.

POSITIVE DISCIPLINE:

THE FIRST THREE YEARS

PROLOGUE:
BY THE CHILDREN

"I am Serena. I am three months old. I know my mother's voice and I am really happy when she picks me up. I like to drink my milk. I get really upset when they aren't ready to give me my milk on time. When my mother rocks me to sleep, I like to look around. I like to take my bath but I don't like it when they wash my hair or face. I like it when people talk to me, laugh out loud, and play with me. I want to hold my toys—but I can't. I like to go out every day because I want to know what is going on. I watch everything."

"I'm James. I just turned two in December. I want to do everything myself. I don't want any help. I like to do things my own way, even if it takes longer, and if you try to help we have to start all over. If you try putting on my sock, I have to pull it off and do it myself. That is much more important to me than whether I got it on backwards. I keep wishing everybody 'Happy Birthday.' Sometimes I scream. I can't talk too well—I have a hard time getting everything out. But I've learned one word that is very powerful: No!"

"Me is Billy. Me like dinos. Big loud dinos. Move their heads. Rex is meanest. Me eighteen months. Mine Mommy. Mine brother. Me walk. Me drink. Me fast. Me want it now!"

"I am Jose. Next month I will be one year old. I laugh all the *time. I like my way. I love to eat. Food is my favorite thing—especially big people's food, but I don't like squash. I am learning to walk. I get a lot of bumps and bruises. I like to chase my cat around the house. Maybe I love him too tight, because he bit my hand yesterday. My favorite words are 'ma-ma,' 'da-da,' 'good,' and 'baby.' "*

"My name is Bonnie and I am eight months old today. I have two teeth and an older sister. I love to flap my arms when I am happy. I invented a fun game. My mom gives me paper and I eat it up, and then she has to fish it out of my mouth. Then I grin. We play this game with lots of things. We played this game all the time with the pebbles at the beach. Mommy stays real busy searching my mouth. It is fun."

We are babies and toddlers. This book is all about us. Maybe the children you know are like us in some ways. This book takes a peek into our world—or what the world looks like as we lie on tables getting our diapers changed. It's about what we might be thinking when we grab for the shiny things on store shelves, or why we sometimes refuse to go to sleep at night, eat our peas, or use the potty. Learning to understand our world will give you lots of ideas about how to help us grow and how to encourage and teach us. We're newcomers in this world and we need your help all the time. We are lovable, time-consuming, and often messy. And there is no one like us in the whole world. This book is for those who love us most.

POSITIVE DISCIPLINE PRINCIPLES FOR YOUR FAMILY

It's probably safe to say that some of what you will read in this book is a bit different from the rules of parenting your parents knew. Kindness *and* firmness? Long-range parenting? Whatever happened to good old-fashioned discipline? After reading this book, you will have a new concept of discipline—one that helps even very young children develop a sense of their own self-worth, capability, and social and life skills, rather than the sense of doubt and shame that comes from punishment.

ADLER AND DREIKURS: PIONEERS IN PARENTING

Positive Discipline is based on the work of Alfred Adler and one of his colleagues, Rudolf Dreikurs. Adler was a Viennese psychiatrist and a contemporary of Sigmund Freud's—but he and Freud disagreed about almost everything. Adler believed that human behavior is motivated by a desire for belonging, significance, connection, and worth, a desire that is influenced by our early decisions about ourselves, others, and the world around us. Interestingly, recent research tells us that children are "hardwired" from birth to seek connection with others, and that children who feel a sense of connection to their families, schools, and communities are less likely to misbehave. All Positive Discipline methods help children achieve that sense of connection.

Dreikurs was also a Viennese psychiatrist; he immigrated to the United States before World War II. Dreikurs was a passionate advocate of the need for dignity and mutual respect in *all* relationships—including the family—and wrote books about teaching and parenting that are still widely read, including the classic *Children: The Challenge,* by Rudolf Dreikurs, with Vicki Soltz (New York: Plume Books, 1990).

WHAT IS DISCIPLINE?

Many have wondered what "discipline" could possibly mean for infants and very young children. Positive Discipline is effective with children birth to three because it is different from conventional discipline. It has nothing to do with punishment (which many people think is synonymous with discipline) and everything to do with teaching and guidance. As you will learn, much of what your little one does in these early years has more to do with emotional, physical, and cognitive development and age-appropriate behavior than it does with "misbehavior." Babies and toddlers need nonpunitive discipline that enhances their development—not blame, shame, and pain.

Discipline with very young children is mostly about deciding what *you* will do (and kindly and firmly following through) than with what you expect your *child* to do. And it's never too early to lay a foundation for respectful, effective parenting. The principles of Positive Discipline will help you build a relationship of love and respect with your child and will help you live and solve problems together for many years to come.

Not so long ago (and quite often today), when people talked about "discipline" they often meant "punishment," usually because they believed the two are one and the same. Real discipline, however, involves teaching; in fact, the word itself comes from the Latin root *disciplina*, which means "teaching; learning." Positive Discipline is about teaching, understanding, encouraging, and communicating—not about punishing.

Most of us absorbed our ideas about discipline from our own parents, our society, and years of tradition and assumptions. Many believe that children must suffer (at least a little) or they won't learn anything. But many things have changed in the past few decades (for example, our society and culture as a whole, and our understanding of how children grow and learn), and the ways we teach children to be capable, responsible, confident people must change as well. Punishment may seem to "work" in the short term. But over time, we know that it creates rebellion, resistance, and children who just don't believe in their own worth. There is a better way, and this book is devoted to helping parents discover it.

WHY SOME PARENTS DON'T ACCEPT NONPUNITIVE METHODS

Because all children (and all parents) are unique individuals, there are usually several nonpunitive solutions to any problem. Some of the parents we meet at lectures and parenting classes don't immediately understand or accept these solutions; indeed, Positive Discipline requires a "paradigm shift"—a radically different way of thinking about discipline. Parents who are hooked on punishment are often asking the wrong questions. They usually want to know:

- How do I make my child mind?

- How do I make my child understand "no"?

- How do I get my child to listen to me?

- How do I make this problem go away?

Most frazzled parents want answers to these questions at one time or another, but these questions are based on short-term thinking. Parents will be eager for nonpunitive alternatives when they ask the following questions—and see the results this change in approach creates for them and their children:

- How do I help my child learn respect, cooperation, and problem-solving skills?

- How do I help my child feel capable?

- How do I help my child feel belonging and significance?

- How do I get into my child's world and understand his developmental process?

- How can I use problems as opportunities for learning—for my child and for me?

These questions address the big picture and are based on long-term thinking. We have found that when parents find answers to the long-term questions, the short-term questions take care of themselves: Children do "mind" and cooperate (at least, most of the time) when they're involved in finding solutions to problems; they will understand "no" when they are developmentally ready; and they listen when parents listen to them and talk in ways that invite listening. Problems are solved more easily when parents use kind and firm guidance until children are old enough to be involved in the process of creating limits and focusing on solutions.

The building blocks of Positive Discipline include:

- **Mutual respect.** Parents model firmness by respecting themselves and the needs of the situation, and they model kindness by respecting the needs and humanity of the child.

- **Understanding the belief *behind* behavior.** All human behavior happens for a reason, and children start creating the beliefs that form their personality from the day they are born. You will be far more effective at changing your child's behavior when you understand the beliefs behind it. When your child is younger than three, you will also need to understand her developmental abilities and needs.

- **Understanding child development and age-appropriateness.** This is necessary so that we don't expect behavior of children that is beyond their ability and comprehension.

- **Effective communication.** Parents and children (even little ones) can learn to listen well and use respectful words to ask for what they need.

- **Discipline that teaches.** Effective discipline teaches valuable skills and attitudes, and is neither permissive nor punitive. We've found this to be the best method of instilling in your child the social and life skills he will need to navigate his way through life.

- **Focusing on solutions instead of punishment.** Blame never solves problems. At first, *you* will decide how to approach challenges and problems; as your little one grows and develops, you will work together to find respectful, helpful solutions to the challenges you face, from spilled Kool-Aid to bedtime woes.

- **Encouragement.** Encouragement celebrates effort and improvement, not just success, and builds long-term self-esteem and confidence.

- **Children *do* better when they *feel* better.** Where did we get the crazy idea that in order to "make" children behave, we should make them feel shame, humiliation, or even pain? Children are more motivated to cooperate, learn new skills, and offer affection and respect when they feel encouraged, connected, and loved.

We have included discipline tips in every chapter of this book (keeping in mind that discipline has nothing to do with punishment). In this chapter, we will look at why punishment should be avoided, and we will present suggestions for nonpunitive methods that will help your child develop into a capable and loving person.

DISCIPLINE METHODS TO AVOID

Most parents have done it at one time or another, but if you are screaming, yelling, or lecturing, stop. If you are spanking, stop. If you are trying to gain compliance through threats, warnings, and lectures, stop. All these methods are disrespectful and encourage doubt, shame, and guilt—now and in the future. Ultimately, punishment creates more misbehavior. (There are many studies that demonstrate the long-term negative effects of punishment, but these studies are usually buried in academic journals where parents don't see them.)

"Wait just one minute," you may be thinking. "These methods worked for my parents. You're taking away every tool I have to manage my child's behavior. What am I supposed to do, let my child do anything she wants?" No. We are not advocating permissiveness. Permissiveness is disrespectful and does not teach important life skills. True discipline guides, teaches, and invites healthy choices. As we've discovered, we can never really control anyone's behavior but our own, and our attempts to control our children usually create more problems, more power struggles, and more of what we've been trying to control! Later in this chapter, we offer several methods that invite cooperation (when applied with a kind and firm attitude) while encouraging your toddler to develop a healthy sense of autonomy and initiative.

Life with an active, challenging toddler becomes much easier when you accept that positive learning does not take place in a threatening atmosphere. Children don't listen when they are busy feeling scared, hurt, or angry. When children feel threatened, they go into a defensive mode. Defensive behavior may look like compliance, rebellion, or anything in between, because the child needs to regain his precious sense of belonging and significance—and will do almost anything to get it. Sadly, children often "misbehave" in situations where they have lost their sense of belonging or connection—and for very good reason. Misbehavior "works"—that is, it regains a parent's attention and involvement, even if that attention is negative.

She Wants What She Wants

Q. My sixteen-month-old daughter does whatever she wants even though my husband and I have tried various methods of punishment. We've tried saying no, putting her in time-out, slapping her hands, and yelling, but nothing seems to work on her. She throws some pretty bad temper tantrums too. I feel like we have tried everything. I am opposed to spanking and have given in to hand-slapping as a compromise, but it doesn't work either. My husband thinks we should spank so she knows she has done something wrong and will not repeat it. What do you suggest?

A. You are experiencing the frustration of so many parents who do not understand their child's development. Punishment—no matter what sort we use—is likely to produce what we call the Four Rs of Punishment:

1. Resentment
2. Rebellion
3. Revenge
4. Retreat, through
   a. Sneakiness ("I just won't get caught next time") or
   b. Low self-esteem ("I really am a bad person")

Has any young child you know responded in these ways? The latest brain research suggests that punishment hampers optimal brain development, so it should come as no surprise that the punishments you've tried are not working. Take heart: You have not yet "tried everything." The rest of this chapter will help you understand why punishment is not effective and will teach you what to do instead.

Your children are learning the right things when they know they belong and have significance, and that they can trust you, learn from you, and let you know what their world feels like. Punishment derails the learning process. Discipline that is kind and firm at the same time (you will learn more about this in the pages ahead) balances security and boundaries with the love and respect children need so much in their early years.

WHAT CHILDREN REALLY NEED

There is a difference between wants and needs, and your little one's needs are simpler than you might think. All genuine needs should be met. When you give in to all wants, however, you can create huge problems for your child and for yourself.

For example, your child needs food, shelter, and care. He needs warmth and security. He does not need a pint-sized computer, a television in his bedroom, a miniature monster truck to drive, or even the color-coordinated baby stroller with built-in DVD player and vibrating seat. He will love staring at a television screen when he is only three months old, but experts tell us that any kind of screen time at this age can hamper optimal brain development. (More about this later.) He may want to sleep in your bed, but if you let him learn to self-soothe in his own bed, he will feel a sense of self-reliance and capability. As soon as he is old enough for finger foods, he will love and want french fries. If you give in to these wants, you could be setting the stage for childhood (and adult) obesity. You get the idea.

From his earliest moments, your young child has four basic needs:

1. A sense of belonging and significance
2. Perceptions of capability
3. Personal power and autonomy
4. Social and life skills

If you can provide your child with these needs, he will be well on his way to life as a competent, resourceful, happy human being.

The Importance of Belonging and Significance

"Well, of course," you may be thinking. "Everyone knows a baby needs to belong." Most parents believe that what a child really needs is quite simple: He needs love. But love alone does not always create a sense of belonging or worth. In fact, love sometimes leads parents to pamper their children, to punish their children, or to make decisions that are not in their child's long-term best interest.

Everyone—adults and children alike—needs to belong somewhere. We need to know that we are accepted unconditionally for who we are, rather than just the way we behave or the abilities we might have. For very young children, this need to belong is even more crucial. After all, they're new here. They need to know they are loved and wanted even when they have a tantrum, spill their cereal, break Mom's favorite crystal dish, or throw up on Dad's best suit.

Children who don't believe they belong become discouraged, and discouraged children often misbehave. Notice the word "believe." You may "know" your child belongs and is significant, but if he doesn't believe it for some reason (the birth of another baby, being sent to his room without dinner, not spending enough time with a parent, etc.), he may try to get it back in mistaken ways. In fact, young children's misbehavior is a sort of "code" designed to let you know that they don't feel a sense of belonging and need your attention, connection, time, and teaching.

When you can create a sense of belonging and significance for every member of your family, your home becomes a place of peace, respect, and safety.

Perceptions of Capability

When a baby is born, she is all but helpless. It takes days, weeks, and months before she learns to control her own movements, reach and grasp, and walk on her own. In her early weeks and months, your job as her parent is to keep her safe, to tend to her needs, to comfort her when she cries, and to be patient—very patient. But as she grows into toddlerhood, you may be

11

surprised at how much she can do that will help her develop a sense of capability. On the other hand, if you do too much for her (in the name of love), she is likely to form the belief that she is not capable.

You will learn more in the chapters ahead about encouraging perceptions of capability in your little one, but for now, consider this: Words alone are not powerful enough to build a sense of competence and confidence in children. Capability comes from experiences of accomplishment and self-sufficiency, and from developing solid skills.

Personal Power and Autonomy

As you will see, developing autonomy and initiative are among the earliest developmental tasks your child will face. And while parents may not exactly like it, even the youngest child has personal power—and quickly learns how to use it. If you doubt this, think about the last time you saw a three-year-old jut out his jaw, fold his chubby arms, and say boldly, "No! You're not the boss of me!"

Over and over we hear complaints from parents about power struggles with *strong-willed* children (we always wonder, "Would they rather have weak-willed children?), children who won't mind, won't listen, have temper tantrums. Some of this behavior is developmentally appropriate and age-appropriate, as children explore and experiment to discover who they are and what they can do. Many of these power struggles are just that, however—power struggles because parents take power away from children instead of guiding them to develop their power in useful ways.

Part of your job as a parent will be to help your toddler learn to channel his power in positive directions—kind and firm distraction and redirection until he is old enough to help solve problems, to learn life skills, and to respect and cooperate with others. Punishment will not teach these vital lessons: effective and loving *discipline* will.

Social and Life Skills

Teaching your toddler skills—how to get along with other children and adults, how to fall asleep by herself, how to feed and dress herself—will occupy most of your parenting hours in these early years. But the need for social and practical life skills never goes away. In fact, true self-esteem does not come from being loved, praised, or showered with goodies; it comes from having *skills* that provide a sense of capability and resiliency to handle the ups and downs and disappointments of life.

When children are young, they love to imitate parents. Your toddler will want to push the vacuum cleaner, squirt the bottle of bathroom cleaner, and cook breakfast (with lots of supervision). As your little one grows more capable, you can use these everyday moments of life together to teach her how to become a competent, capable person. Working together to learn skills can occasionally be messy, but it's also an enjoyable and valuable part of raising your child.

METHODS THAT INVITE COOPERATION

So the stage is set. What tools and ideas will help your child learn all she needs to know? If punishment doesn't work, what does? Here are some suggestions. Remember, your child's individual development is critical in these early years; nothing works all the time for all children. As your own special little one grows and changes, you'll have to return to the drawing board many times, but these ideas will form the foundation for years of effective parenting.

Get Children Involved

During the first year of life, your child will depend on you for everything. But you may be surprised at how quickly he finds his voice and unique personality. Instead of telling children what to do, find ways to involve them in creating routines and to draw out what they think and perceive. "What" and "how" questions are one way to do this. Ask, "What do you think will happen if you push your tricycle over the curb?" or "How should we get ready for child care?"

Education comes from the Latin root *educare*, which means "to rear, educate," or "to draw out." This may explain why children "tune out"

Eight Methods for Implementing Positive Discipline

1. Get children involved:
   a. In the creation of routines.
   b. By giving them several acceptable choices.
   c. By providing opportunities to help.

2. Teach respect by being respectful.
3. Use your sense of humor.
4. Get into your child's world.
5. If you say it, mean it, and if you mean it, follow through with kind and firm action.
6. Be patient.
7. Provide lots of supervision, distraction, and redirection.
8. Accept your child's uniqueness.

when you try to "stuff in" by "telling" through constant demands and lectures.

For children who are not yet able to talk, say, "Next, we _____," while kindly and firmly showing them instead of telling them. Also remember to give children choices—although you must limit the choices to only those acceptable to you. Children given choices experience a healthy sense of personal power and autonomy.

Create Routines
Young children learn best by repetition and consistency. You can ease the transitions into autonomy by creating reliable routines for your little one. Routines can be created for every event that happens over and over: getting up, bedtime, dinner, shopping, and so on. Then you can say to your very young child, "Now it's time for us to _____." As soon as your child is old enough, get him involved in helping you create routine charts. Once he's older he will love telling you what's next on his routine chart. If he forgets, avoid telling. Instead ask, "What is next on your routine chart?" Be sure not to confuse these charts with sticker or reward charts—those take away from your child's inner sense of capability because the focus is on the reward. Routine charts simply list sequences of events and act as guidelines for common tasks.

Offer Choices
Having choices gives children a sense of power: They have the power to choose one possibility or another. Choices also invite a child to use his thinking skills as he contemplates what to do. And, of course, toddlers

often love it when choices include an opportunity to help. "What is the first thing we should put away when we get home—the ice cream or the orange juice? You decide." "Would you like to carry the blanket or the cracker box as we walk to the car? You decide." Adding "You decide" increases your child's sense of power. Be sure the choices are developmentally appropriate and are options with which you are comfortable. When your child wants to do something else, you can say, "That wasn't one of the choices. You can decide between this and this."

Provide Opportunities to Help

Toddlers often resist a command to get into the car but respond cheerfully to a request like "I need your help. Will you carry the keys to the car for me?" Activities that might easily have become power struggles and battles can become opportunities for laughter and closeness if you use your instincts and your creativity.

Teach Respect by Being Respectful

Parents usually believe children should show respect, not have it shown to them. But children learn respect by seeing what it looks like in action. Be respectful when you make requests. Don't expect a child to do something "right now" when you are interrupting something she is thoroughly engaged in. Give her some warning. "We need to leave the park in two minutes. Do you want to swing one more time or ride the teeter-totter?" Carry a small timer around with you. Teach her to set it to one or two minutes. Then let her put the timer in her pocket so she can be ready to go when the timer goes off.

Remember, too, that shame and humiliation are disrespectful and a child who is treated with disrespect is likely to return the favor. Kindness and firmness show respect for your child's dignity, your own dignity, and the needs of the situation.

Use Your Sense of Humor

No one ever said parenting had to be boring or unpleasant. Often, laughter is the best way to approach a situation. Try saying, "Here comes the tickle monster to get children who don't pick up their toys." Learn to laugh together and to create games to get unpleasant jobs done quickly. Humor is one of the best—and most enjoyable—parenting tools.

It is amazing how many children who resist a direct order will respond with enthusiasm when that order becomes an invitation to play. Try telling your toddler, "I bet you can't pick up all your little cars before I count to ten," or "I wonder if you can brush your teeth and get into your pajamas before Dad does."

Get into Your Child's World

Understanding your baby or toddler's developmental needs and limitations is critical to parenting in the first three years of life. Be empathetic when your child cries (or has a temper tantrum). He may just be frustrated with his lack of abilities. Empathy does not mean rescuing. It does mean understanding. If you want to leave the park and your child isn't ready to go, give her a hug and say, "You're really upset right now. I know you want to stay, but it's time to leave." Then hold your child and let her experience her feelings before you move on to the next activity. If you were instead to pamper your child by letting her stay at the park longer, she doesn't have the opportunity to learn from experience that she can survive disappointment.

Getting into your child's world also means seeing the world from her perspective and recognizing her abilities—and her limitations. Occasionally ask yourself how you might be feeling (and acting) if you were your child. It can be illuminating to view the world through a smaller person's eyes.

If You Say It, Mean It, and If You Mean It, Follow Through with Kind and Firm Action

Children usually sense when you mean what you say and when you don't. It's usually best not to say anything unless you mean it and can say it respectfully—and can follow through with dignity and respect. The fewer words you say, the better! This may mean redirecting your child or showing her what she *can* do instead of punishing her for what she *can't* do. It also might mean wordlessly removing a child from the slide when she's refusing to leave, rather than getting into an argument or a battle of wills. When this is done kindly, firmly, and without anger or words, it will be both respectful and effective.

Be Patient

Understand that you may need to teach your child many things over and over before she is developmentally ready to understand. For example, you can encourage a young child to share, but don't expect her to understand the concept and do it on her own when she doesn't feel like it. When she refuses to share, rest assured that this doesn't mean she will be forever selfish. It will help to understand that she is acting age-appropriately. (More on social skills in Chapter 10.) Don't take your child's behavior personally and think your child is mad at you, bad, or defiant. Act like the adult (sometimes easier said than done) and do what is necessary without guilt and shame. When two children are fighting over a toy, it may be necessary to take it away for a while and distract them by offering two other toys.

Provide Lots of Supervision, Distraction, and Redirection

Minimize your words and maximize your actions. As Rudolf Dreikurs once said, "Shut your mouth and act." Quietly take your child by the hand and lead her to where she needs to go. Show her what she *can* do instead of what she can't do. Instead of saying "Don't hit the dog," show her how to touch the dog nicely. When you understand that children don't really understand "no" the way you think they should, it makes more sense to use distraction, redirection, or any of the respectful Positive Discipline methods. (You'll learn more about all of these tools in the chapters ahead.)

Accept Your Child's Uniqueness

Remember that children develop differently and have different strengths. Expecting from a child what he cannot give will only frustrate both of you. Your sister's children may be able to sit quietly in a restaurant for hours, while yours get twitchy after just a few minutes, no matter how diligently you prepare. (Refer to Chapters 5 and 6 on temperament and developmentally appropriate behavior for more on this subject.) That being the case, you may decide to save that fancy meal out for a time when you can enjoy it in adult company—or for when your children have matured enough for all of you to enjoy it together.

It may help to think of yourself as a coach, helping your child succeed and learn how to do things. You're also an observer, learning who your child is as a unique human being. Never underestimate the ability of a young child. Watch carefully as you introduce new opportunities and activities; discover what your child is interested in, what your child can do by himself, and what he needs help learning from you.

RETHINK "TIME-OUT"

One common parenting tool deserves some special attention. If you've ever heard a parent say to a defiant toddler, "I've had it! Go to time-out and think about what you did," or "That's one . . . that's two . . . ," you may wonder where time-out fits into the Positive Discipline approach. Most parents use something called time-out, but few really understand what it is or how best to use it with young children.

Positive time-out can be an extremely effective way of helping a child (and a parent!) calm down enough to solve problems together when both are rational. In fact, when we are upset or angry, we actually lose access to the part of the brain that allows us to think clearly, so time-out is an effective and appropriate parenting tool—when it is positive and not punitive, and is used to teach, encourage, and soothe. But there are several points that need to be made regarding time-out for young children. (For extended information about time-outs, see *Positive Time-Out and Over 50 Ways to Avoid Power Struggles in the Home and the Classroom,* by Jane Nelsen, New York: Three Rivers Press, 1999.)

- Time-outs should not be used with children under the age of three and a half to four years of age. Until children reach the age of reason, which starts around age two and a half (and is an ongoing process that even some adults have not fully mastered), and logic (which is developed much later), supervision and distraction are the most effective parenting tools. Even when children reach the beginning stages of reason, they do not have the maturity and judgment to make logical decisions. This is why parents know they cannot allow their children to play near a busy street, unsupervised, even when they think their children "know" better than to run into the street. This is why young children need constant supervision and removal, kindly and firmly, from what they can't do and guidance to an activity they can do. Most parents have at one time or another found themselves in a heated debate with someone who only comes up to their kneecap—and most will admit that reason, lecturing, and argument just don't work. Young children often can read the energy of your feelings and understand that you want something; they may even be able to guess what that something is. But they do not understand the logic of your arguments in the way you think they do. It is usually wiser to remove them from the situation and distract them with something else than to expect words to resolve the situation. It breaks our hearts to see very young children sent to punitive time-outs when they are not developmentally able to understand what it is all about. A punitive time-out increases the probability that young children will develop a sense of doubt and shame instead of a healthy sense of autonomy. (See Chapter 7 for important information on the development of autonomy vs. doubt and shame.)

- Children do better when they feel better. Even younger children can benefit from an opportunity to "cool off," especially if you go with them. We know of one mother who used "positive time-out" successfully with her eighteen-month-old child. That it "worked" was undoubtedly due to her attitude. She would say to her child, "Would you like to lie on your comfy pillow for a while?" Sometimes he

would just toddle off to his pillow and lie down until he felt better. If he hesitated, she would ask, "Do you want me to go with you?" This mother understood the concept of positive time-out—to help children feel better, not to make them feel bad in the hope that feeling bad will inspire them to do better (it doesn't).

- Your attitude is the key. Time-out should not be used as a punishment but as a way to help children feel better. One of the silliest things parents say to children when using punitive time-out is, "You think about what you did and how bad you have been." This is a silly thing to say because of the assumption that adults can control what children will think about. It is especially silly to think that children from birth to age three have the kind of reasoning ability to think about what they did and know what they should do instead. And do you really want your children to start developing beliefs that they are bad?

  At this point in their young lives, children need lots of guidance without the expectation that they will be able to absorb and use what they are learning until their brains are more fully developed and until they gain a lot more maturity and judgment.

  The procedure for setting up "positive time-out" for children over age three and a half is explained thoroughly in *Positive Discipline for Preschoolers* (and in most of our other books as well). During the first three years, parents and teachers need to know that children cannot understand and master their feelings. Thus, in most cases, time-out should not be used at all—except by parents and teachers themselves. You can take time to calm down by counting to ten, take deep breaths, or let someone else take over (if possible) while you go for a short walk.

- Create a calming space. If you do decide to try positive time-outs with your little one, create a safe, comfortable area where you can go together. Remember, you're not punishing her; you're helping her to feel better so she can feel the sense of belonging and significance that leads to cooperation. This could be as simple as a favorite chair where your child can sit on your lap while you sing a calming song or read a book. No, this is not rewarding misbehavior. It is understanding that children do better when they feel better. Pillows, stuffed animals, or favorite soothing toys may help. Before the age of three and a half, you might find it helpful to say, "Let's take some time out to read a book or listen to music until we feel better." These words may not make much more sense than expecting your child to understand the purpose of time-out, but she will sense the "energy" behind your words and will respond accordingly.

- No parenting tool works all the time. Be sure to have more than just time-out in your toolbox. It is important to have many different parenting skills and tools. There is never one tool—or three, or even ten—that is effective for every situation and for every child. Filling your parenting toolbox with healthy, nonpunitive alternatives will help you avoid the temptation to punish when your child challenges you—and he undoubtedly will! The more you know, the more confident you will feel as you cope with the ups and downs of life with a young child.

Georgia sighed in exasperation—this was Amanda's third tantrum this afternoon. Two-year-old Amanda was having a rough day; Luke, her older brother, had invited a houseful of friends over to play for the afternoon, and Amanda hadn't been able to take her usual nap. Now, cranky and miserable, she had ripped half the pages from Georgia's new magazine, then swept it off the table. She gazed up at her mom with stubborn defiance—and a trembling chin.

Georgia was tired herself. She stifled the desire to lecture her small daughter and drew a deep breath. "Would you like to curl up in your special corner with your blankie?" she asked Amanda.

Amanda only shook her head and sat down in a heap amid the torn pages of the magazine.

"Well, how about playing with your dollhouse?" Georgia asked helpfully, reaching out to take Amanda's hand and lead her to her favorite toy.

Amanda yanked her hand away and let her little body go limp on the floor, shaking her head vehemently.

Georgia sighed again and sat down near her daughter. Let's see, she thought, what else did they suggest in that parenting class?

Finally she rose and gave Amanda a weary smile. "You know what, honey?" she said as kindly as she could. "I need to start dinner—and I sure could use some help. You can lie here and rest or you can join me in the kitchen and help me wash the lettuce—it's up to you." And with that, Georgia walked into the kitchen.

For a few moments, the sniffling and kicking from the family room floor continued. Soon, however, a small, tear-streaked face peered around the kitchen corner. Amanda looked uncertainly at her mom, but Georgia just smiled and gestured toward the sink.

Encouraged, Amanda went to get her little stool, dragged it over to the sink, and began dunking lettuce leaves in the water. By the time Amanda's dad arrived home, harmony had been restored, Georgia had helped Amanda clear away the ripped magazine, and Georgia, Luke, and Amanda were working companionably together to set the table. Georgia was glad that positive time-out wasn't the only tool in her parenting toolbox.

It is often true that what works with young children one day will not work the next. But if you've taken the time to know your child and to learn all the different ways there are to teach and encourage, chances are good that you will find *something* that works—just for today.

- Always remember your child's development and capabilities. Understanding what is (and is not) age-appropriate behavior will help you not to expect things that are beyond the ability of your child.

The Stantons took their eighteen-month-old twin boys to a band concert featuring their seven-year-old as a flute soloist. The twins were fascinated with the concert—for about ten minutes. Then they found other ways to entertain themselves. One twin started crawling under the seats, and the other soon joined the fun. Mr. Stanton took the twins outside and spanked them for not sitting still. The twins cried loudly and could not be taken back inside for the rest of the concert. Mr. Stanton was very disappointed that he missed his daughter's solo, his daughter was disappointed that her father didn't hear her, and Mrs. Stanton and the twins were upset about the spanking. Everyone was miserable.

It is a sad thing when children are punished for doing things that are developmentally appropriate, even though they are not situationally appropriate. It is unreasonable to expect young children to sit for long periods of time. But it is not okay to allow children to disturb others. Since the Stantons didn't choose to leave their twins with a caregiver, it would have been more effective for them to take turns taking their children outside so they could take turns hearing parts of the concert. It would not be appropriate to punish the children, but it would be appropriate to provide a distraction, such as providing picture books for them to look at. This kind of time-out removes children from inappropriate expectations without making everyone miserable.

LET THE MESSAGE OF LOVE GET THROUGH

We often ask parents in workshops why they want their children to "be good." After a few moments of head-scratching and blank stares, they tell us that they love their children and think that they will be happier people if they are "good." So they punish in the name of love. But do their children feel loved? Other parents share that they know their children won't be happy if they are spoiled brats—and they are right. As you will hear us say over and over again, the foundation for Positive Discipline is kindness and firmness at the same time.

Gaze down at your child's sleeping face or watch her grin at you through a mask of chocolate ice cream, and see if you can resist the urge to hug her. You know you love your child, but does your child know that you offer discipline, skills, and teaching because you love her?

Even the most effective nonpunitive parenting tools must be used in an atmosphere of love, of unconditional acceptance and belonging. Be sure you take time for hugs and cuddles, for smiles and loving touch. Your child will do better when he feels better, and he will feel better when he lives in a world of kindness and firmness that creates an atmosphere of love and belonging.

2

WELCOMING BABY

The birth of a baby is a momentous occasion, a landmark event never forgotten by those who have experienced it. A new parent may be shocked by the news that a baby is on the way or thrilled that the days of pregnancy tests and "trying" finally are finished. Either way, there is no ignoring this life-changing bit of news. Your life as an independent, spontaneous person will change: Baby is on the way.

Most adults find that adding an infant to the family, no matter how anticipated and dearly loved that infant may be, brings changes that take some getting used to. Adult relationships must flex and adapt, making room for the new addition. Schedules and priorities shift; even bodies change. And babies can be perplexing little people, operating by rules known only to them.

The first few months of your new baby's life will be exhausting, exhilarating, and challenging, all at once. It may be hard to believe, but one day you will look back at these exhausting times and sleepless nights with nostalgia and realize your child grew up far too fast. But for now, those days lie far in the future. No matter how you look at it, life once a baby arrives is forever changed.

SETTING THE STAGE FOR BABY

Close your eyes for just a moment and remember the first time you saw your child's face. That newborn infant may have been red, bald, and wrinkled, but chances are you felt you'd never seen anything more beautiful, or heard anything sweeter than your baby's first cries. Writers and painters have tried to capture the magic of those first moments of life, but words and pictures are rarely powerful enough to convey what happens between parent and child.

For most parents, the months leading up to that miraculous moment of birth are filled with plans, dreams, and a few worries. In reflective moments, you probably wondered whether you would be a good parent, whether you'd know what to do, whether the baby would be "all right." Expectant parents talk endlessly about the relative merits of cloth and paper diapers, about nursing or formula feeding. They discuss names for hours, saying them aloud to see how they fit.

New parents buy and are given impossibly tiny garments and mysterious articles with odd names like "receiving blanket." They wonder if they'll somehow know what to do with them when the time comes. They purchase and ponder over the fascinating gadgetry of babyhood: car seats, swings, carriers, cribs, pacifiers, bottles, breast pumps. The grandparents "tsk, tsk" as they point out that millions of children were raised without all these fancy gadgets. But in this age of consumerism, there are so many adorable clothes available that you probably just can't resist. Babies in the womb often have a larger wardrobe than their grandparents owned in an entire lifetime!

Your home probably overflows with stuffed animals, mobiles, and hand-knitted blankets and booties. It is a time for endless dreaming, a time for hope and wonder.

FANTASY VERSUS REALITY

Sometimes, though, when you carry that helpless little scrap of humanity home from the hospital, the dreams fade a bit in the harsh light of reality. The baby cries, sometimes for hours without ceasing, and it's up to you to figure out why. The little darling sleeps all day then gurgles happily all night, much to the dismay of his sleep-deprived parents. The baby spits up when you're dressed to go out, has twelve bowel movements in a single night, refuses all known varieties of food, and cries angrily when handed to eager relatives.

From those first moments, parenting young children can become an avalanche of questions, anxieties, and frustrations. The very real love and tenderness remain, but as that precious baby grows, develops, and changes, life becomes an apparently endless stream of new decisions to be made and new ideas to be tested. People look at your beloved child in public places, smile knowingly, and talk about the "terrible twos." Many a young parent feels hopelessly overwhelmed and completely at the mercy of the adorable little tyrant the baby has become.

HOW WILL I KNOW WHAT TO DO?

None of us is born knowing how to be a parent. We learn by watching our own parents and by trial and error. And we worry that those errors may cost more than we can afford. Many parents don't like the way they were raised and vow to be different from their own parents, or they see others raising children and disagree with their choices. But what should you do instead? You don't want to be too strict, but is permissiveness the only alternative? You don't want to be overly permissive—how do you create order and consistency? You have so many questions: Do I spank my child or not? If spanking is okay, how soon should I start? How do I get children to listen? How do I communicate with an infant who doesn't understand words? How do I handle a defiant toddler or a discouraged preschooler? How do I decide what's really important? How can I help my child develop a sense of self-esteem, and teach her responsibility and honesty and kindness? How do I get him to share and play nicely? How can I give her the tools to succeed on her own in a difficult and challenging world?

Advice is in plentiful supply—grandparents, uncles and aunts, and the lady behind you in line at the grocery store will have lots of it—but whose advice is right? Even the "experts" disagree. Some suggest punishment (even in the poorly disguised form of "logical consequences"), while others (including the authors) suggest that punishment is never effective. Some claim rewards are important. Others (including the authors) believe rewards teach manipulation instead of social and life skills. You will have to figure out for yourself which kind of parent you want to be, but it is our hope as authors—and as parents—that you will find some answers in this book that will make sense to you, as well as clues to help you use your own wisdom, creativity, and knowledge of your child to go beyond what can be written in words.

This book is designed to be of use to both parents and their frequent partners in child-rearing: child caregivers, nannies, and sitters. Examples of home, preschool, and childcare situations will be given throughout this book to show how the principles of Positive Discipline can be applied to all aspects of a young child's life. (If you have specific questions about childcare, find a copy of *Positive Discipline for Childcare Providers*.) Developmental information will be included wherever appropriate, along with recent discoveries about the way babies and young children grow and learn. Because it can be immensely helpful for all the adults who shape a child's life to have the same understanding about how to raise him, you may want to share this book with the people at your childcare center, your babysitter, or other members of your family.

YOUR FAMILY IS YOUR FAMILY

It can help to remind yourself that all families, like all children, are different. Not all babies are born into two-parent families with a home in the suburbs, two cars, and a family dog. Your family may indeed look like that, or it may take a different shape altogether. You may be a single parent, through divorce or death or because you never married; you and your partner may have brought children from previous relationships and added those you have together; you may have live-in grandparents or other relatives; or you may share a home with friends and their children.

A family, it has been said, is a circle of people who love one another. Whatever the form your family takes, it will be whatever you have the courage to make it. With wisdom, patience, and love, you can create a place where your children can feel safe, secure, and free to grow and learn and where they can become responsible, respectful, and resourceful people.

THE IMPORTANCE OF LONG-RANGE PARENTING

Life with an active toddler can make you feel as though you're aboard a runaway train if you let it. The days rush by, each one filled with new discoveries, new words, new crises. Parents often have to scurry to keep up with their young offspring and sometimes have little time available for thoughtful planning. But think for a moment: Wouldn't it be helpful, as you set out on the journey of parenting, to know your final destination?

Perhaps one of the wisest things you can do right now is to take a moment to ask yourself a very important question: What is it that I really want for my child? When your baby, your toddler, or your preschooler has grown into an adult (as impossible as that may seem now), what qualities and characteristics do you want that adult to have?

You may decide that you want your child to develop responsibility, honesty, compassion, self-reliance, courage, and gratitude—each parent's list will be a little different. What truly matters is this: From your child's earliest moments of life, the decisions you make as a parent will shape his or her future. Each and every action you take—whether or not you slap your child's hand as she reaches for a delicate object, how you deal with food thrown across the kitchen, or how you respond to bedtime demands—can nurture those qualities you want to encourage. Your child is constantly making decisions about himself and the world, and how to find belonging and significance in his world. These decisions create a "blueprint" for living. Your actions influence his decisions.

This thought feels overwhelming to most parents. You may be wondering, "What if I make mistakes? How will I know what to do?" Please, be reassured: *Mistakes are not insurmountable failures but valuable opportunities to learn.* Both you and your children will make many mistakes along the way, but they needn't cause irreparable damage if you're willing to learn from them together. The most valuable parenting tools are those you already possess: your love for your child and your own inner wisdom and common sense. Learning to trust these instincts will carry you far along the road to successful parenting.

Remember, too, that children, especially very young children, learn by watching and imitating those around them. Your little one not only will want to push the vacuum or wash the dishes the way Mom and Dad do, but also will imitate the values you live by, such as honesty, kindness, and justice. When you treat mistakes as opportunities to learn, your children will learn this valuable attitude. Remember, an action (with both positive and negative results) is a far more effective teacher than a thousand words. Let your actions as a parent teach your child that he or she is loved and respected, that choices have consequences, and that home is a safe and wonderful place to be.

A WORD ABOUT LOVE

Many things are done to children—or withheld from children—in the name of "love." "I spank my children because I love them," you might say. Or "I rescue and overprotect my children because I love them." "I love my children, so I don't help them much—they need to learn it's a tough world out there." "I push my children—in toilet training, or early reading, or sports activities, or academic excellence—because I love them." "I work long hours because I love my children and I want them to have everything money can buy." "I make decisions for my children because I love them too much to risk letting them make wrong choices." These actions may be done in the name of love, but they are not the best way to show love if you want your children to make decisions about themselves and their world that help them become responsible, respectful, and resourceful.

Actually, whether you love your children is not the question. The real issue is whether you can show that love in a way that nurtures accountability and self-esteem, a way that helps your children blossom into their full potential as happy, contributing members of society.

How much should you give your child? Is it harmful to let your child have her own way? Should you push your child or let her wander along at her own pace? You can never love your child too much, but you can show love in ways that are more harmful than helpful.

Parents often say that they feel overcome by the intensity of their love for their children, and it is tempting to demonstrate that love by allowing children to do, say, and have whatever they want. Your eighteen-month-old may be adorable *now* when he grabs the remote control and channel-surfs while you're watching your favorite television program. You may even giggle when he tries out the four-letter word he learned at the childcare center. Will it still be cute when he's twelve years old and does the same things?

Eventually, most parents realize that true love requires that they love their children enough to teach them, to set wise boundaries, to say no when they must, and to help them learn to live peacefully and respectfully in a world filled with other people. A primary goal of this book is an examination of techniques and tools for how to do this (and when to begin).

FIRM, FLEXIBLE, AND GENTLE

Imagine a tree, its roots anchoring it deep into the ground. Far above, at the tip of its slender branches, rests a bird's nest. In that nest are one or more tiny, fragile eggs. When the wind blows, the tree's branches sway in gentle arcs but its grip on that small nest remains firm.

This image of gentleness combined with flexibility and firmness translates well to the task of parenting young children and forms the foundation for many of the principles you will learn throughout this book. You can stand with your feet (or values) firmly rooted while still guiding your child with steady, gentle hands and a kind voice. This is not an easy task; it requires patience, energy, and boundless hope.

REDEFINING "WE" AND "ME"

Most people discover that the arrival of a new baby is a moment that transforms their lives forever. Some couples have been together only a short time when the baby arrives, while others have had years to get acquainted with each other and to build a comfortable life. And for many there is no partner to offer support of any kind. But no matter what the circumstances, becoming a parent does change everything.

Adding "parent" to your definition of who you are means adding all sorts of new roles and responsibilities. It also means rearranging some of the roles you already have. Most couples find it difficult to be spontaneous with an infant; after all, it's tough to jump up and do some-

---

Firm and Gentle in Practice

When Susan, who is two, doesn't want to leave the park, her mother, Fran, offers to hold hands with her while they walk to the car. Susan refuses. Fran bends down, lifting Susan and wrapping her arms around Susan's arched back, cradling the back of her head. She carries Susan to the car, all the while commiserating with her and validating her feelings: "You were having such a good time playing. You really wanted to play longer. We will come back again another day." Susan's body relaxes and the sobs get muffled as she snuggles into Mom's shoulder.

We can be firm and gentle at the same time.

---

thing on the spur of the moment when you're lugging diaper bags, infant seats, strollers, bottles, snacks—and a baby. Romantic evenings sometimes go the way of the dinosaur—and so does sex. Household chores that used to be a snap now linger for days, while job responsibilities are difficult to focus on. It certainly doesn't help that sleep and serenity may be in short supply.

Care for Parents

Parents who are contented, healthy, and relatively well rested (being tired seems an unavoidable part of raising young children) are, not surprisingly, best prepared to cope with the challenges of raising a young child. If you are a single parent who must handle it all, there is all the more reason to take special care of yourself. If you have a partner, remember that your relationship is the foundation of your family; invest the time and energy it takes to keep it strong.

It takes time to adjust when a child is added to a marriage, a relationship, or one's lifestyle. Tasks formerly allocated to one parent may need to be redistributed. A new mom caring for an infant, getting less sleep, and struggling with unfamiliar tasks and responsibilities might no longer have the energy to help her partner with mealtime cleanup. Household chores can seem overwhelming, and nursing an infant on demand seems to preclude even the simplest tasks being done. Sometimes it comes down to deciding whether to wash your hair or the clothes or simply take a nap when baby does. Your expectations (for yourself and for a partner) may need to change, at least temporarily.

Couples can easily lose sight of each other in their headlong rush to take care of the baby. Mom nurses the baby; Dad feels left out and a little jealous—and guilty for having those feelings. One parent wants a little snuggling, while the other is "too tired." One parent is dying for dinner and a movie out; the other doesn't trust the babysitter or spends the evening phoning home every fifteen minutes to make sure everything is okay. And sex? Baby seems to possess a sixth sense that tells him just when Mom and Dad are contemplating a little intimacy—and that's just when he feels hungry or damp and squalls to alert his frustrated parents!

Your decisions and actions teach your child from her earliest days about life, love, and relationships. If you do not have a partner, connecting with other adults will give you a valuable energy boost. Taking time to cherish a partner as well as your individual needs isn't selfishness or bad parenting—it's wisdom. Your child will learn to respect and value the needs and feelings of others by watching the choices you make. Be sure you leave time each week for activities you enjoy and that nurture your physical and emotional health, whether it's laughing with a neighbor over a rented movie while your child sleeps in the next room, a "date night" out with a partner, or a morning walk (perhaps with the baby along in a backpack or stroller).

Redefining "we" and "me" is an ongoing process rather than an intellectual activity. An older child who feels sad, a spouse who feels ignored, and a parent who feels lonely for adult companionship are all responding normally to this change in their family. Sometimes what is most needed is simply time to vent painful feelings in order to make room for feelings of love, joy, and compassion to be rekindled. Remember, too, that feelings can serve as useful reminders to take care of yourself and those you love. By honoring your own emotions or those of a partner, you may discover ways you can solve problems and enjoy life more fully, as you learn to cope with and care for this new family.

PARENTING PARTNERS

If you are a single mother or father, you can raise a happy, healthy child alone (pick up a copy of *Positive Discipline for Single Parents* to learn more), but if you're lucky enough to be part of a loving parenting team, make the most of it. Your child will benefit from what each of you has to give, and raising your young child can be more enjoyable and less frustrating when parents help each other, share ideas, and work together to solve the inevitable problems. But the idea of two parents working together is often more a fantasy than reality. It is common for parents to disagree on how to rear their children. One may favor firm-ness, while the other favors kindness—both to extremes. Ideally you will read this book or take parenting classes together so you will raise your children as a cooperative team. If your spouse does not have time to read a book, he or she may enjoy listening to "Positive Discipline Birth to Five"—a two-hour lecture by Jane Nelsen. (Available from www.positivediscipline.com.)

Resist the temptation to label caregiving tasks so that either parent feels like an assistant. Have you ever heard someone say, "My husband is watching the kids for me"? Aren't they his children too? How about "I don't know how to give him a bath (feed him, change his diaper, and so on). His mom's the expert on that!" Remember that practice makes bet-ter (not necessarily perfect)—and better is usually plenty good enough.

The world of babies and very young children often seems to be a very female place. But times are changing; it is often a child's father who can calm him down, coax a smile, or spoon in the strained peas. The world is a busy place, and these days both Mom and Dad are likely to be working—which is all the more reason for parents to share as much as possible in the joys and duties of parenting. Wise parents know that parenting is a partnership and that when parents treat it as such, the real winners will be their children. Sure, parents have differ-ent styles. The great news is that those differences can be a real plus for your child, who will learn skills for interacting with different kinds of people. This is particularly true for the different ways in which men and women tend to handle and interact with children.

Watch a mom greet her child. She may wrap her arms around little Annie or cuddle baby Megan against her chest, showering her soft head with kisses. Then watch Dad greet these same little ones. When Dad says "hi" to Annie, he swoops her into the air, holding her at arm's length as she squeals and giggles with delight. His greeting to Megan often begins with blowing raspberries on her round belly and laughing as she squirms with pleasure. These active or nurturing inter-actions each provide unique benefits. Physical stimulation is great for brain development and encourages healthy risk-taking. *(Warning:*

Never shake or toss a baby or leave a very young baby with her head unsupported!) Cuddling supports a child's sense of well-being, safety, and security. Also, recent research has demonstrated that a father's more active style of playing with his baby may actually help that baby learn self-awareness ("Is this fun?" "Am I getting tired?" "How do I let him know that I want to stop?") and begin communicating her feelings and needs to the adults around her.

GETTING THE HELP YOU NEED

All parents have questions and concerns. Fortunately, parent education and training is finally gaining wide acceptance and credibility. Society has never questioned the need for education and training in occupational fields, be it bricklaying or nursing, but somewhere along the line the notion got planted that parenting should come "naturally" and that attending a parenting class or reading a book on parenting was an admission of inadequacy.

These days, parents are reading books and attending parenting classes in droves, and they testify that what they learn helps them enjoy the important job of parenting as their children learn more self-discipline, responsibility, cooperation, and problem-solving skills.

We highly encourage you to seek out and get involved with a parenting group in your community or to start one yourself. Reading books and attending classes will not make you a perfect parent—there is no such thing. But you will have more awareness of what works and what doesn't work for the long-range benefit of your children. When you make mistakes, you will know how to correct them, and you will be able to teach your children that mistakes provide wonderful opportunities to learn. (We can't say it often enough!)

PARENTING FROM THE HEART

Parenting groups are great places to learn new skills and ideas and to get a little moral support along the way. But when all is said and done, parenting is essentially a matter of the heart and spirit as well as training and knowledge. Perhaps the greatest parenting skill of all is the ability to feel an unbreakable bond of love and warmth for your children and to be able to listen to the voice of love and wisdom even when your patience has been stretched to the breaking point.

No matter how often we say the words, it's all too easy to lose sight of love when we're confronted with the incredible variety of new misbehaviors our children can invent. The best parenting translates love from words into thoughtful, effective action. There is a popular children's book by Robert Munsch titled *Love You Forever*. In this little gem, a mother watches her infant sleep and croons to him, "I'll love you forever, I'll like you for always. As long as I'm living, my baby you'll be." As that child grows from baby to terrible toddler to awkward adolescent, the mother creeps into her son's room at night to watch him sleep and to croon that same little song. The day comes at last when the mother lies ill and dying, and the son sits by her bedside to sing the old song to her. When he returns home, he shares the song—and the bond of love—with his newborn baby daughter. That feeling—that indescribable tenderness and warmth that a parent feels for a sleeping child—is the heart of parenting.

The next time you tuck your little one in at night, let your gaze rest on that sleeping face; print it firmly in your memory. There are so many things in life that can shake a parent's confidence. You will make mistakes; your child will make mistakes too. We're all learning to be people as we go along, experimenting on each other, blundering occasionally, doing the best we can.

And when you're confronted with a hysterical infant, a defiant toddler, or an angry preschooler—and there will be many such times as the years roll by—close your eyes for just a moment and look in your memory for the face of a sleeping child. Then let that love and tenderness give you the wisdom to deal with the crisis at hand.

Parenting is rarely a simple matter, and no one can challenge or stretch a parent like a very young child who is learning and exploring his world one piece at a time. There will be ample room in the chapters ahead for information, tips, and techniques, but remember that it is always the relationship between parent and child that matters most. If that relationship is based on unconditional love and trust—if your children know from their earliest days that you love them no matter what—you'll probably do just fine. Taking the time now to build the proper foundation by entering your child's world and understanding how he or she feels and thinks, and by talking, laughing, playing, and just being together, may be the best investment you will ever make in the future of your family.

No one ever said it would be easy to be a parent; it is undoubtedly one of life's most demanding, time-consuming, and unappreciated jobs. But it isn't always easy to be a child these days, either. Have patience; work toward trust and closeness. A little love and understanding coupled with some solid skills and ideas will help you find your way to being the best parent you can be: one who parents from the heart.

3

GETTING TO KNOW YOUR YOUNG CHILD

Martha had a story to tell. She collapsed into a chair and waited impatiently for the other members of her parenting group to stop their friendly chatter and settle down.

The group's leader noticed Martha's exasperation and smiled. "Martha, it looks like you came prepared with something to share. Why don't you start us out?"

Martha sighed and shook her head. "I just don't know what to do," she moaned, the frustration in her voice obvious. "My two-year-old, Daniel, is driving me crazy. He insists on touching things in stores even though I must have told him a dozen times not to touch. He gets angry when I won't read to him or play with him right away—he just can't seem to wait patiently for even five minutes. He's always yanking his hand out of mine when we walk together, and I worry that he'll get away from me or run into the street."

The rest of the group smiled sympathetically and a few heads nodded as Martha told her tale of woe. Other parents had shared such experiences and understood this mom's feelings. "This morning was the last straw, though." Martha paused dramatically, then continued, her voice tight. "This morning Daniel deliberately lied to me. I've told him I won't tolerate lying, but he fibbed right to my face."

The leader met Martha's eyes and nodded. "I can see you're really upset. What did Daniel say?"

"Well," Martha said, "he told me he saw a lion in the backyard. Isn't that ridiculous? There couldn't possibly be a lion in our backyard! And if Daniel starts lying now, what will happen as he grows up?"

Another woman spoke up. "I worry too. Are the things my child does now signs of how she will turn out as an adult?" Other members of the group nodded.

The concern and confusion the parents in this story are feeling are easy to understand; most parents have similar moments of frustration and disappointment. But there's a good chance that young Daniel isn't intentionally driving his mother to distraction; it's very likely, as Martha's parenting group leader will undoubtedly explain, that Daniel is simply being his age-appropriate self: an active, curious two-year-old who is learning about his world in the only way he knows.

GETTING INTO YOUR CHILD'S WORLD

Your little one inhabits a vastly different world from yours. One of the first and most important challenges in parenting your baby or toddler is understanding what his world looks and feels like. Expecting your child to think, act, or feel the way you do will create all sorts of challenges.

One of the best ways of becoming an effective parent—or, for that matter, an effective human being—is to understand the perceptions of other people, to be able to "get into their world." This is especially true for parents of very young children—after all, their world is so different from yours!

A newborn infant arrives in this world from a place where he's been cradled in warmth and safety beside his mother's heart, his every need immediately met. Suddenly, after a convulsive and tiring journey out of his mother's body, he finds himself in a world of heat and cold, loud noises, moving objects, and bright lights. Faces come and go, voices come from all directions, and this new world runs on a schedule he doesn't yet understand. The instant nourishment and comfort are gone; now he must wail loudly for someone to satisfy his hunger or give him comfort. Sleeping, eating, simply functioning—a baby must adapt to the new world. It wouldn't be surprising if we somehow found scientific evidence that infants long to return to the womb!

From the moment of birth onward, a child's early months and years are a voyage of discovery, and one of the first things a child must discover is himself. An infant's control of himself moves from the center outward. In other words, he develops the large muscles at the center of his body before the small muscles in his extremities. At first he is helpless, doing for himself only the most basic bodily functions, unable even to lift his head or to turn over without help.

As time passes, his control increases. He learns to really see (*Is that Mom?*) and to track objects with his gaze. One day he realizes he can manipulate the hands that flap in front of his face; he can make them move, grab them, and even—oh, bliss!—stuff them into his mouth. Later, he learns that he can grab other things with them and stuff those into his mouth as well.

The other developmental milestones follow in due time. A baby learns to turn over, scoot, crawl, pull herself up on the furniture, and eventually walk. Running and getting into mischief come next. Toilet training happens eventually (more about that in Chapter 13). The last things to be mastered are the delicate ones, like balance and fine motor control, which explains why a five-year-old or even a six-year-old may have such a difficult time mastering the art of tying shoes. Part of becoming an effective and loving parent or teacher means understanding the world of the little ones you're working with and making every effort to get inside it.

UNDERSTANDING YOUR CHILD'S PERSONALITY

It's an old question: nature versus nurture, genes versus the environment. What shapes the personality of a human being? Why are children the people they are? Why is one two-year-old peaceful and compliant, eager to please and easy to get along with, while the two-year-old next door seems bent on challenging every rule, pushing every limit, and breaking everything in sight? We will spend more time discussing these questions in the chapters to follow, but there are a few ideas to keep in mind for now.

Children are a product of their parents' genes (nature), and they are undoubtedly influenced by the environment and ideas around them (nurture). We don't know the exact balance, although recent research  appears to indicate that genes and inborn temperament traits play a stronger role than we previously thought. Perhaps it is more important to realize that while children are shaped by both the raw material they inherit and the forces around them, they also bring to the world something uniquely their own: their own spirit and identity. These factors, combined with the individual decisions they make along the way about what they must do to survive or thrive, will form their personalities. Most people discuss nature and nurture, but fewer are aware of the impact of the individual decisions children make based on their life experiences. This factor is so important that we will come back to it often as we help you get into the world of your little one.

Have you ever noticed that despite having the same parents and the same home, children in the same family can be incredibly different?

That is because each child makes unique decisions based on his or her perceptions of the world. One child may decide, "I like the safety of boundaries." Another child may decide, "I feel thwarted by boundaries." Parents need to take time to get to know—and to accept—their children for exactly who they are.

Remember Martha and two-year-old Daniel? Let's take a look at some points that might explain the behavior this mom finds so frustrating. (We will examine these ideas in more detail in later chapters.)

A Child Learns About the World by Doing

A child who is "playing" is actually hard at work, trying on new roles and ideas, tasting, touching, smelling, and experimenting with life. Learning is a hands-on experience filled with the enthusiastic joy of discovery. It takes awhile (and some parental patience) before children learn where the boundaries lie. Some will accept those boundaries, while others will continuously push them. This doesn't make the "pusher" bad. He simply has a different temperament and will keep his parents busy using kind and firm discipline.

A Child's Birth Order Affects How She Sees the World

Each child born into your family experiences a different family configuration from that experienced by the children that came before and those who may follow. There are more people in the family, more siblings, plus the adult or adults have probably grown or changed in some way. They may be less experienced with a first child and gain a certain amount of perspective (and experience) by the time a new child joins the family.

Allison tells of the drama her daughter Monroe's tantrums would spark, and the way she and Monroe's aunts would try to reason with her, pick her up and beg her to calm down, or get exasperated and join in with their own wails of frustration. By the time Monroe's brother arrived two years later and began having his own tantrums, the rest of the family had calmed down. They knew that tantrums came with the territory, so to speak, of raising a toddler. Because they knew this phase would pass (and would pass more quickly if it wasn't given much attention), they found themselves regarding little Charlie's tantrums as endearing; they would smile and shake their heads while waiting them out. Charlie was born into a different, more relaxed household than was Monroe.

Another factor affecting birth order is the presence (or absence) of siblings. A hungry "only" or "firstborn" child usually has an adult available to get him a cracker when he wants it. When there are other children present, that cracker may have to wait until a younger brother gets his diaper changed or a baby sister finishes nursing. A firstborn child may also learn how to do things for himself at an earlier age, while his little sister will have older siblings around to hand out those crackers.

These differences are neither good nor bad, but they do affect children's behavior. The older child who suddenly begins misbehaving when her new baby brother is being fussed over is easy to understand. The little one who starts clinging to Mom when a sibling goes off to preschool may be less obvious. Whatever the behavior, taking into account the effect of a child's birth order can help you make sense of your child's "misbehavior."

A Child's Developmental Need to Explore and Experiment
May Be Labeled as Misbehavior
Children need secure, loving boundaries in order to feel safe, just as adults need a house with strong walls and a roof to feel protected from the weather. Still, any self-respecting child will feel obliged to cruise up to the boundaries you've set and test them occasionally, just to make sure they're firmly in place. He's not deliberately trying to drive you insane; he's either exploring at his age-appropriate level or learning about consistency and whether or not adults mean what they say (another version of trust).

Often adults fail to realize that they simply can't reason with a toddler and spend more time talking than acting. No matter how well you use them, words are sounds without real substance to young children.

Actions, like removing a child from a forbidden temptation by picking him up and carrying him to another location, provide a clear message. (Some actions, though, only make matters worse: slapping his hand, yelling "no-no," and engaging in a stare-down may invite a child to keep this entertaining adult involved with him—or to retaliate in kind!)

Is all of this testing annoying? Of course! Frustrating? Absolutely! But children are rarely as intentionally naughty as their parents think—they're just acting their age.

Young Children Rarely Misbehave Purposely

Adults mistakenly read motives—that is, intent—into children's behavior that reflect adult thinking rather than childish thinking. Some act as though their child lies awake at night plotting ways to drive them crazy. Martha's repeated warnings to her son not to touch things aren't terribly effective; kind, firm action would be more helpful. Toddlers are highly impulsive little people, and the warnings are simply overpowered by the desire to touch, hold, and explore. A toddler straining over the edge of his stroller to touch a shiny cup on the store shelf does not intend to disobey. The fact that this cup is at the bottom of a highly breakable pyramid of cups has no special meaning for him. The colors on the cup attract his attention; he reaches for it and wants to examine it. He is a mad scientist using his hands, mouth, and imperfect coordination to determine the properties of the marvelous world around him. Your real tasks as a parent are prevention, vigilance—and very quick reflexes.

A Child's Physical Size and Abilities Have a Strong Influence on Behavior

Take a moment sometime soon and put your face on the same level as your child's. What do you see? The world looks a lot different from down there! Seeing an adult's face requires tilting your head backward—an uncomfortable position if held too long. Most of the time, young children gaze out at a world of knees, shins, and feet, and the only reliable way to catch an adult's attention is to pull on his hands or legs! And just imagine how frightening a yelling, pointing parent would look from down there.

Crib mobiles took on a whole new look when someone had the good sense to look up at what a child was seeing. The cute little animals the adult saw swirling through the air looked like shapeless slivers of moving color when seen from below. Today's versions aim visual images downward.

A child's world shimmers with delightful, distracting images, sounds, and textures. The best way to be sure a tiny person realizes that you are talking to her is to make eye contact. Get down on her level, look into those curious eyes, and speak directly to her.

Are you still down near the floor? If another adult is handy, reach up and take his hand for a moment. Imagine going for a nice long walk through the nearest shopping mall in this position. What parents often believe is defiant yanking away may simply be a child trying to get some circulation back into her hand and arm! In addition, adults have much longer legs than their little ones; children almost always have to run to keep up. No wonder they lag behind us or run away to find their own pace.

It can be frustrating to be a small person whose hands won't quite do the tasks they're expected to do. Often children want very much to help, to dress themselves, and to do other tasks around the house, but the sheer mechanics are beyond them. The result is a frustrated, angry child—and a frustrated, angry parent. This does not create a positive atmosphere where learning can take place. How would adults feel if everything they tried was a little beyond their ability to succeed—and they were criticized for the efforts they made? Most would give up and possibly start misbehaving out of sheer frustration. Later we will talk more about expectations, encouragement, and celebrating small steps.

A Child's Concepts of Reality and Fantasy
Are Different from Those of an Adult
Did you know that when you walk out of your baby's line of sight, you have ceased to exist? That the toy accidentally dropped on the floor

has disappeared forever? No wonder babies cry when they are separated from people or things they want—the concept that objects are permanent hasn't developed yet.

In the same way, a young child experiments with his imagination to explore and learn. Our young friend Daniel may not have seen a lion in his backyard, but he may have seen the neighbor's cat. Or he may have watched a cartoon about lions in the jungle. Or his picture book may have included lions and their cubs. Daniel's lion wasn't a "lie" but the product of a vivid imagination and a great deal of curiosity. The line between fantasy and reality remains blurred throughout the first few years of a child's life.

Fantasy may also be a child's way of getting in touch with feelings for which he doesn't yet have words, a way of exploring his own inner being. The lion in the backyard may be another way of expressing a fear of being alone. Careful listening (more about that later) and acceptance by his parents will help him to understand his feelings, learn to sort them out, and find healthy ways of dealing with them.

Patience Is a Virtue Far Beyond the Reach of Most Young Children
Think back for a moment to when you were a child. Remember how long it took for your birthday to come? Have you noticed how quickly the entire process sped up as you grew older?

Time moves far more slowly for an eager child than it does for an adult. Adults need to learn that units of time simply don't have the same meaning for children. For young Daniel, five minutes may seem like an eternity, and his experience tells him Mom takes far too long to do everything. Yes, children need to learn patience eventually, but parents need to be patient long enough to let them learn. It's not realistic to expect toddlers to sit still for long periods of time—in church or even for storytelling time.

Jimmy was an extremely bright two-year-old. His parents took him to a drive-in theater one night. It didn't take long before Jimmy was fast asleep—just as his parents had planned. A week later the family drove past the drive-in, and Jimmy said excitedly, "Look, we went

> ### Understanding Your Child's World
>
> - A child learns about the world by doing.
> - A child's frustration due to a lack of abilities or skills may be labeled misbehavior.
> - A child's developmental need to explore and experiment may be labeled as misbehavior.
> - Young children rarely misbehave purposely.
> - A child's birth order affects how she sees the world.
> - A child's physical size and abilities have a strong influence on behavior.
> - A child's concepts of reality and fantasy are different from those of an adult.
> - Patience is a virtue far beyond the reach of most young children.

there last night!" His father spanked Jimmy for lying. But Jimmy wasn't lying; his father didn't understand child development and didn't realize that Jimmy simply hadn't mastered the concept of time yet. A week, an hour, or last night does not register as different time frames to Jimmy. With more understanding, his father would have been delighted at Jimmy's developing memory instead of concerned about his "untruthfulness."

BOYS AND GIRLS: DOES GENDER MATTER?

One of the first questions you're likely to be asked when you announce you have a new baby in the family is "What is it?" The curious folks aren't asking about the species; they're wondering about gender. Is it a boy or a girl? Did you have a preference? Why does gender matter so much? Well, gender involves much more than whether you dress your baby in blue or pink. There are some significant differences in male and female children (especially early in life); there also are often differences in the way parents talk, touch, and relate to boys and girls.

In most ways, girls and boys are more alike than different. Boys and girls both need love, belonging, and encouragement. They need to develop good character and social and life skills. Girls and boys need kind, firm discipline and connection with parents and caring adults. Cultural differences and beliefs play an important role in how boys and girls develop. Still, because a baby's brain is exposed to sex hormones during pregnancy, some gender differences appear to be part of the way children are wired.

The Truth About Boys and Girls
You may be surprised to learn that baby boys actually appear to be more fragile at birth than do baby girls. Yup, studies show that the rough, tough little guys made of "snakes and snails and puppy-dog tails" appear to be more easily stressed and more susceptible to health problems. They are often "fussier" than girls; they cry more easily and seem to have a harder time learning to calm themselves down (what is sometimes called "self-soothing"). Baby boys may be more sensitive to changes in routine, and to parental anger or depression.

Female infants, on the other hand, tend to make eye contact sooner than boys do. They often acquire language skills sooner than boys and have better social and emotional skills. They may also develop fine motor skills sooner than boys. As children grow into their toddler years, boys appear to be more impulsive; they learn self-control more slowly, are more physically active, and yes, they tend to be more aggressive and competitive than do little girls. Needless to say, parents and preschool teachers may prefer the more "obedient" behavior of little girls—which can teach little boys unintended lessons about their place in the world.

It's worth remembering that gender differences are generalizations, and that each child is special and unique; anyway, by the time your child goes off to school, these differences will have largely evened themselves out. Still, parents with a fussy, crying baby boy may be comforted to know that their son is neither weak nor oversensitive.

Parents and Gender

Parents have a strong influence on how young children develop gender identity. Research has shown that parents often speak to, touch, and cuddle female infants and toddlers more than boys. After all, if the culture insists that boys be "strong and silent" (and unfortunately, it still does), parents may instinctively and unconsciously try to "toughen up" their sons early in life. There is a direct connection between school readiness and the number of words infants and toddlers hear every day. Whether your child is a boy or a girl, it is important that you build a strong face-to-face connection, with lots of talking, laughing, and singing.

At some point during your child's early years, take time to explore what *you* believe about gender. What "should" little boys be like? Little girls? How can you best nurture the strengths and sensitivities of your own special little one? Getting into your child's world and understanding his development (including the influence of gender) will help you teach, encourage, and comfort your own unique child.

DEVELOPMENT? OR MISBEHAVIOR?

As you have learned, one of the challenges in parenting a young child is understanding the difference between normal development and intentional behavior. For instance, should you feed your baby whenever she's hungry (so-called on demand feeding) or should you set a strict schedule and teach your child self-control and respect for authority by sticking to it? Should you hold your infant over the toilet whenever she signals she might be urinating until she is toilet-trained ("infant elimination training") or should you wait until later, when your child can read her body's cues and learn for herself to use the toilet?

There is no one "right" answer for many everyday parenting dilemmas, especially during the first three years of life—except that non-punitive methods are more effective in the long term than punishment.

You and your child will benefit greatly if you learn all you can about growth and development. It is also important to know your own child well. And eventually, you must learn to trust your innate wisdom as a parent. No expert or book (including this one) can give you all the answers—although, as you will learn throughout this book, Positive Discipline tools and principles will help you guide and encourage your child during these first important years.

4

THE MIRACULOUS BRAIN: HELPING YOUR CHILD LEARN

Martin and Rosalie wanted only the best for their baby, Rachel. They spent at least half an hour every day speaking to Rachel while she was still in the womb; they held stereo head-phones against Rosalie's bulging abdomen so the baby could learn to appreciate music. When Rachel was born, her proud and ambitious parents brought her home to a nursery equipped with every possible device to speed the learning process. She had special mobiles dancing above her crib; music played con-stantly; and Martin and Rosalie invested a small fortune in flash cards, educational videos, music, and books. They were both intelligent, successful people, they reasoned, and certainly all this early stimulation would help their precious baby make the most of her opportunities in life.

Jeff and Carol were also eager to teach their son, but they chose a different approach. They spent hours talking, singing, and playing with ten-month-old Gregory. They gazed into his eyes, spoke to him frequently, responded to his cries and gestures, and encouraged him to explore his world. As Gregory crawled among his colorful toys, Jeff or Carol were often on the floor nearby, laughing when Gregory handed them toys and enjoying each new discovery. Gregory's parents focused on building a strong and loving connection with their young son—and in so doing, they helped set the stage for a lifetime of healthy learning and development.

There are many parents like Martin, Rosalie, Jeff, and Carol, loving people doing their best to get their children off to a good start and help them succeed in school, relationships, and life itself. Until quite recently, however, we had no way of knowing exactly what really worked. How do children learn? Are there ways to help them be more successful and to maximize their potential? Is it wrong to encourage early learning? What exactly is "success"? What's more important for young children—academic skills or social skills? Or are both equally important?

THE LIVING, GROWING BRAIN

We used to believe that babies were born with brains that were more or less "finished"; all that remained was to fill the waiting brain with the necessary information. Studies in the past few years have changed the way we understand the human brain and how babies and children learn about the world around them. Brain scans have allowed researchers to peer inside the living brain, to observe its structure, and to discover how it uses energy, blood flow, and special substances called neurotransmitters to think, to perceive, and to learn. What those researchers have discovered is extraordinary and makes it more important than ever for parents and caregivers to understand these critical early years of a child's life.

The human brain begins life as a small cluster of cells in the fetus. By the fourth week of pregnancy, these cells have begun to sort themselves out according to the function they will one day perform and, to the wonder of researchers, have begun to migrate to the part of the brain they are destined to occupy. Nature provides the fetus with more cells than it will need; some do not survive the migration, while others join together in a network of connections called synapses.

This network continues to grow even after the baby is born. By the time a child is two years old, his brain has the same number of synapses as an adult's; by the age of three, he has more than one thousand trillion connections—twice as many as his parents and caregivers! The human brain is "under construction" throughout childhood and adolescence; in fact, the prefrontal cortex—which is responsible for good judgment, reasoning, impulse control, and other admirable "adult" qualities—is not fully developed until after the age of twenty! Contrary to what you may have learned in school, the human brain never stops growing and never loses the ability to form new synapses and connections. Change may become more difficult as we age, but change—in attitudes, behavior, and relationships—is always possible.

The first three years, however, are especially important; what a child learns and decides about himself ("Am I good or bad, capable or not capable?"), and the world around him ("Is it safe or threatening, encouraging or discouraging?"), becomes part of the "wiring" of his brain. The outside world, which is experienced through a child's senses (hearing, seeing, smelling, and touching), enables the brain to create or change connections. By about the age of ten, a child's brain begins to prune away the excess synapses (those that haven't been used enough). By adolescence, half have been discarded.

While the brain is amazingly flexible and is able to adapt to change or injury, there are windows early in a child's life during which important learning (like vision and language development) takes place. If those windows are missed, it may become more difficult for a child to acquire those abilities. For some functions, brain development is a "use it or lose it" proposition; for others, such as social skills development, learning continues well into early adulthood. Parents and caregivers shape a child's world, and in so doing they also shape his growing brain.

NATURE OR NURTURE?

Books, magazines, and research journals are filled with new studies on human genes and their importance in how we live and who we become. Researchers now believe that genes may have an even stronger influence on temperament and personality than we previously thought. There is now evidence that genes influence such qualities as optimism, depression, aggression, and even whether or not a person is a thrill-seeker—which may be old news to parents who are forever plucking their daring toddlers from the tops of walls, jungle gyms, and trees! Parents may find themselves wondering just how much influence they have on their growing child. If genes are so powerful, does it really matter how you parent your children?

The answer is that it matters a great deal. While a child inherits certain traits and tendencies through her genes, the story of how those traits develop is written as your child interacts with the world around her. (Brain researchers call these early reactions and decisions "adaptations.") Your child may have arrived on the planet with her own unique temperament, but how you and her other caregivers interact with her will shape the person she becomes (more on temperament in Chapter 5). As educational psychologist Jane M. Healy puts it, "Brains shape behavior, and behavior shapes brains."

It is no longer a question of nature versus nurture: a child's inborn traits and abilities and her environment engage in an intimate, complicated dance, and both are part of who she will become. We parents, fragile and imperfect as we are, bear the responsibility for shaping a child's environment. Especially in the first years of life, connection with caring and responsive parents is critical for your child. You influence the very structure and wiring of your baby's brain; you influence the person she becomes and the future she will have.

"BETTER" BABIES

You may be wondering whether it is helpful to begin teaching children early in life, as Martin and Rosalie did with little Rachel. After all, if brains are still growing for the first few years, shouldn't you put in as much information as you can?

No one can say for certain how much teaching and stimulation is "enough" for young children. Some researchers believe that it may even be harmful to force children to learn too quickly or to absorb concepts that their brains are not yet mature enough to handle. If the brain isn't ready to learn abstract concepts (math, for instance), it may patch together a pathway of connections that is less effective than the one that would have been used later on—and the less effective pathway becomes wired in place.

Children are always making decisions about themselves and the world around them. When children have difficulty mastering a concept forced upon them by loving parents, they may make the decision "I'm not good enough." This decision can override optimal development when the brain is ready. (More about this when we discuss the controversy over pushing academics in preschools.)

There are few absolutes in brain development, however. Each human brain is unique and special and it is impossible to generalize about what is right or wrong for an individual child. Still, some scholars, like Jane Healy, believe that our fast-paced modern culture (and some of our "educational" television shows) may be adversely affecting children's ability to pay attention, to listen, and to learn later on in life.

It is also worth noting that experts such as Stanley I. Greenspan emphasize the importance of following your child's cues and signals and responding first and foremost to emotional information. The ability to link feelings with communication (for example, reaching for a desired object) emerges during a baby's first year of life; encouraging the growth of real relationship is certainly the most important task of early brain development. (You will learn more about emotional development in Chapter 9.)

"HARDWIRED TO CONNECT": WHAT YOUR CHILD REALLY NEEDS

Babies and young children learn best in the context of relationships. Recent research shows us that the human brain changes both its structure and its function in response to the nature and quality of the *relationships* each person experiences (rather than the facts, figures, or academic information she acquires). What your little one most needs to learn in the first three years of life isn't found on flash cards (or on television). Brain development is all about connection with other people, and your child's brain is wired to seek connection from the moment of birth. How you and your child's other caregivers relate to her—how you talk and play and nurture—is by far the most important factor in a baby's or toddler's development.

According to Ross A. Thompson, a professor of psychology at the University of California at Davis and a founding member of the National Scientific Council on the Developing Child (developingchild.net), young children learn best when they are unstressed and when they live in a reasonably stimulating environment. Thompson believes that special stimulation, such as videos and other academic learning tools, is unnecessary; in fact, what children really need to grow and develop is unhurried time with caring adults, people who will focus on the child and follow his cues without distraction or expectations. (Both parents and childcare providers can provide this sort of child-centered interaction.) It is important to note that this does not mean allowing children to rule the home.

A WORD ABOUT ATTACHMENT

When you connect well with your child—when you recognize and respond to his signals, offer love and belonging, and allow him to develop a sense of trust and security—you help him develop what is called a "secure attachment." Securely attached children can connect well with themselves and with others and have the best opportunity to develop healthy, balanced relationships. It is interesting to note that researchers such as Mary Main have discovered that the best predictor of a child's sense of attachment is her *parent's* level of attachment to his or her own family growing up. (Psychologist and developmental expert Erik Erikson also found that an infant's development of a sense of trust in the first year of life is directly related to a mother's sense of trust in herself.) How you understand and make sense of your own history and experiences has a direct effect on your growing child.

> ### Miraculous Mirror Neurons
>
> Have you ever wondered how your baby learns to clap his hands, wave bye-bye, or "gimme five"? Researchers recently discovered the presence in the human brain of "mirror neurons," which perceive physical action, facial expression, and emotion and prepare the brain to duplicate what it "sees." When you play peek-a-boo with your baby, his mirror neurons help him figure out how to imitate you. In the same way, when you are angry, excited, or anxious, his mirror neurons will "catch" your emotion and create that same feeling within him. Mirror neurons help explain why we weep, laugh, or get angry with each other so easily. It also explains why what you *do* (the behavior you model) as a parent is so much more powerful than your words in teaching your child.

The details of attachment are beyond the scope of this book, but it is wise to understand that you cannot give your child what you do not have yourself. Understanding and resolving your own struggles, challenges, and emotional issues may be one of the greatest gifts you give your child. To learn more about attachment, brain development, and parenting, see *Parenting from the Inside Out: How a Deeper Self-Understanding Can Help You Raise Children Who Thrive,* by Daniel J. Siegel and Mary Hartzell (New York: Tarcher Putnam, 2003).

HOW TO NURTURE A GROWING BRAIN—
AND THE CHILD WHO OWNS IT

A young child's flexible brain has the ability to adapt to many different environments and situations. What he learns in his first years determines which connections the brain will keep and which will be lost. Abuse or neglect in the early years of a child's life may damage her ability to trust and connect with others. On the other hand, children whose early experiences are happy and healthy will build into their growing brains qualities and perceptions that will help them thrive.

Many of the recommendations experts now make are steps wise parents have taken instinctively from the beginning of time. When you understand the true importance of these ways of nurturing a baby, however, you can do them consciously, with confidence that you are providing exactly what your little one most needs from you.

What should parents know? What can you do to give your child a healthy brain—and a healthy life?

Respond to Your Baby's Cues
Responding when a baby cries—providing food, a clean diaper, or a snuggle—is important in helping that baby learn trust, one of the most vital early lessons. Parents can respond to an infant's kicking legs and waving fists, smiling back or playing finger games when he is eager for stimulation, and they can learn to recognize when a baby needs quiet time to nap or just to be still. This sort of connection is called "contingent communication" by brain researchers and is one of the most important ingredients in early brain development. (It is also one of the few parenting skills that crosses all cultures.) Learning to hear, interpret, and respond appropriately to your baby's cues is one of your first and most important parenting tasks.

Your baby will let you know his preferences—what he needs and when—and the more time you spend with him the easier it will become to recognize his signals. There is simply no substitute for time and attention, and children who have the opportunity to bond well with parents find it easier to get along with others and to be comfortable in their world as they grow up. (Spending time with your baby, responding to his cues, and nurturing a healthy connection is not the same thing as pampering. Pampering, sometimes called "spoiling," makes your child dependent on you. As you will learn, it is important to meet all your child's needs for love and basic care, but it can be harmful to give in to all wants. As you gain information and knowledge, remember to access your heart and inner wisdom to find the balance of interaction that is respectful and healthy for you and your child.)

Touch, Speak, and Sing
Studies have shown that babies who are touched, massaged, and held often are less irritable and gain weight more quickly. Holding, rocking, and cuddling a child communicates love and acceptance perhaps better than anything else. Babies, toddlers, even parents need hugs, and a loving hug may be all the "help" your little one needs for many of life's small crises.

Many adults are not comfortable with physical touch. Many weren't hugged or touched themselves, or perhaps the touching happened in the wrong way. Fathers, especially, can feel uncomfortable touching or hugging their children and sometimes substitute roughhousing and wrestling (which can be lots of fun) for snuggling and affection. While touch should always happen in the right way and at the right time (even toddlers can be taught about "good touch" and "bad touch" in ways that won't frighten them), touch helps your little one attach to you and provides both comfort and stimulation. As children grow, a pat on the shoulder or a hug may communicate more than the most eloquent speech.

Speaking, too, is important. What grown-up can resist cooing gentle words to a newborn? Talking and reading to infants and young children who obviously can't yet understand your words may not seem important, but these "conversations" stimulate the parts of a child's brain responsible for speech and language development (more on language and feelings in Chapter 9).

While repetition may be boring to you, it isn't to your child. Babies and toddlers learn through repetition. You may think you cannot endure *Pat the Bunny* one more time, but your little one will remain delighted with the sounds and touchable textures of this old favorite for months. Knowing that you are shaping a healthy brain may give you the patience it takes to tell favorite stories over and over again. Incidentally, television does not have the same effect on babies and toddlers as real speech. Television is not conversation, and its frantic, flashy structure may negatively affect a child's attention span and ability to listen. There is no substitute for talking to your child and no better way for her to learn.

Music also appears to have a powerful influence on growing brains. While little Megan may not care whether it's Mozart or "Silly Songs" she hears, the melody and rhythm will affect her. Music seems to stimulate creativity; our hearts and brain waves tend to speed up and slow down to match the pace of the music we're listening to. In fact, gently bouncing your baby on your lap while you sing or listen to music actually helps wire his brain to "hear" rhythm. There can be few things as delightful as watching a dancing toddler, spinning and bouncing to the strains of a lively tune or one of Dad's old rock 'n' roll favorites. Don't rely only on recorded music, either: sing to your young child (yes, you can sing—your toddler isn't a critic!). At first, you will sing nursery rhymes and songs, lullabies, or a favorite from a child's recording alone, but before long your toddler will be yodeling along. It isn't noise: It's the sound of healthy brains growing!

Remember, music also soothes. Soft, gentle sounds are as relaxing to children as they are to adults. At rest time or before bedtime, try playing soothing music and watch how your busy baby will begin to slow down and become calm. (Music is a great way to ease into rest periods at childcare programs, too.)

Provide Opportunities to Play—and Play Along
In these days of busy parents and overburdened caregivers, confinement in infant seats and playpens and time spent in front of a video or

television show often substitute for play. But babies and toddlers are just discovering their bodies—and just forming the vital connections that link brain with action. They are developing their motor control and learning about textures and gravity. They need the opportunity to play actively.

Play truly is a child's work. It is how she experiences her world, learns about relationships, and tries on new roles and personalities. Parents are usually good at taking children places where they can play—they're endlessly on the road to gymnastics, "water babies," or playgroup—but many parents are less good at playing themselves.

Play is an important tool in building a loving and connected relationship with your young child. Parents often get so caught up in "getting things done" or "accomplishing something" that they forget to allow a child to play freely and spontaneously. The toys don't actually have to "do" anything; worthwhile play may mean handing the same brightly colored rattle back and forth and listening to the noise it makes (many, many times). You can offer your child toys, but allow him to "lead" and to experiment with objects and actions. It is usually much more fun to play with the paper in a magazine (it tears and crunches and crackles) than it is to hear the story on those pages—at least at this age. Be patient and recognize that simply using new muscles and brain connections is enough. There is no better way to understand your toddler's world than to play with him.

Your child will need lots of opportunities to exercise his imagination and creativity as he grows. (Sometimes that includes time to play alone.) Children can play with—and learn from—the box the toy comes in or the pots and pans under the sink. Who needs a battery-operated fire engine that makes siren noises when a child can—and should—do that for himself? The old-fashioned, interactive favorites still serve a valuable purpose; provide building blocks, dress-up clothes, a sandbox, and lumps of clay, then watch as your little one discovers the joy of building, touching, and shaping his world. Better yet, play with him. Get down on the floor and build a fort out of sofa cushions, or play a favorite board game (older toddlers love Chutes and

Ladders or Candy Land and can play well with only a little help from you); have a water fight or play in the mud. You'll be creating special memories and a bond with your child that both of you will treasure, and you will also be giving him opportunities to build vital connections in his growing brain.

Encourage Curiosity and Safe Exploration

Again, infant seats, baby swings, and playpens may be helpful when you need some free time, but your active toddler needs time and space to work on her sense of autonomy and initiative, and there's no better way than being allowed to roam and explore the house, the yard, or the neighborhood park—with your supervision, of course. (See Chapter 7 for more on autonomy—and childproofing.)

Research has shown that a child's brain grows best and is stimulated best when things that she is actively interested in are present. Whether your little one shows curiosity about colors and paints, animals, or big trucks, you'll be helping her brain develop by finding ways to explore what she most wants to learn about. You aren't pushing a three-year-old to read if she initiates the process—and a few do. On the other hand, pressuring a little one to read by placing flash cards on every item in the house is a waste of time at best; most children would prefer to explore every item instead of reading it. At worst, this sort of pressure can create feelings of inadequacy in a child who senses your disappointment in his failure to acquire scholarly accomplishments. Instead, take time to discover what makes your little one sparkle, then create opportunities to explore.

Allow Private Time for Your Baby

Please don't get the impression that your baby needs constant stimulation. Babies need private time to explore by themselves. When you see an infant staring at his fingers or playing with his toes, he is exploring. Many babies are very content to sit in their infant seats for short periods of time and follow you with their eyes as you occupy yourself in other tasks.

As usual, we come back to balance. It is good to provide stimulation—talking, cooing, and singing—but not all the time. Overstimulation can actually make a baby crabby, and too much stimulation can be counterproductive for optimal brain development. In his book *The Self-Calmed Baby,* William Sammons points out that "the ability to self-entertain is one of the most important skills children can develop." Babies can also learn to fall asleep by themselves (an issue discussed more thoroughly in Chapter 11). If your baby turns his face away from you while you're playing or talking, he may be letting you know that he needs some "quiet time" to rest and regroup.

Use Discipline to Teach—Never Shake or Hit

Growing brains are extremely fragile. Every day an infant dies or is permanently disabled by being shaken or hit by an angry, frustrated adult. "I would never hurt my baby," you may be saying, but it may come as a surprise to you to learn that harsh criticism, punishment, or shaming may also damage a child's brain. Remember, those connections that are used most will become permanent; those not used will be lost. All parents make mistakes, and all parents will experience the intense frustration and exhaustion that happen sometimes when you share your life with very young children. When you are aware of the long-range effect of the way you treat your child, you can make choices that will not only teach and provide the structure she needs but also allow her to learn that she does belong and have significance—lessons that will last a lifetime.

Take Care of Yourself

How, you may be wondering, do my health and state of mind affect my child's brain? Parents and caregivers are the most important people in a young child's life. The quality of what you have to offer is often affected by your own all-too-human moods and emotions. Stress, exhaustion, or worry affect the way you interact with your baby or toddler—and, consequently, the way she perceives you and herself.

You may have heard about (or even experienced) the so-called baby blues. Postpartum depression is common; some mothers even suffer severe clinical depression in the months after a child's birth. Unfortunately, a depressed caregiver cannot perceive or respond to a baby's cues and signals consistently, and the effect on an infant can be serious and can affect his development. It is essential that you receive help if you suffer from depression during your baby's first year. Treatment and support will help both of you recover and thrive.

In Chapter 17, we will take a closer look at the importance of care and nurturing for those essential people, the parents. For now, realize that your little one depends entirely on you. Taking care of yourself isn't selfishness; it is wisdom.

Select Childcare Carefully

A child's growing brain does not shut off when he is dropped off at the childcare center. Many parents must work outside the home these days, and many babies and toddlers spend the bulk of their waking hours in a childcare facility. Not surprisingly, the same skills that are essential for parents in nurturing developing brains are just as critical for childcare providers. Leaving your child in another's care may be difficult, but it helps to recognize that high-quality care can support a child's development. It also underscores how important it is to be sure that the care your child receives when he is away from you truly is *quality* care. (Chapter 16 will explain what constitutes quality care and how to find it.)

In the best of worlds, parents and caregivers work together to nurture developing brains, consistently providing the time, attention, conversation, and balance of freedom and structure that young children need. Time spent choosing a childcare provider is time invested in the long-range health and happiness of your child.

Love and Enjoy Your Child

Remember, what children (and all of us) need to know is that they belong, that they have a special place in life, and that they have value to those around them. No matter how busy your life and no matter how seriously you take your responsibilities as a parent, take time to simply love and enjoy your child. The quiet moments of wonder, the laughter and giggling, the delight you take in the special qualities, first words, and adorable actions of these new little people are not wasted time but precious investments in the future of your family. The housecleaning, yard work, and laundry will wait; slow down occasionally and just enjoy the time you have with your child. It speeds by all too quickly.

THE FIRST THREE YEARS LAST FOREVER

By now you may be feeling more than a little concerned. So much is happening in the first three years of a child's life; conscientious, loving parents frequently worry that they won't be able to meet their child's needs, that they will leave some task undone or fail to provide the care and environment that their child's growing brain requires. Just remember that no one is perfect—and you don't need to be. Your baby or toddler doesn't require perfection; he only needs you to be warm, loving, and aware of his needs.

The Positive Discipline approach to raising young children fits well with our new knowledge of how the human brain develops, and doing your best will almost certainly be "good enough." Awareness is always the first step to action, and knowledge will help you make choices and decisions that are in the best interest of your baby or toddler. (For more information on brain development and your child's first three years, visit www.parentsaction.org or www.zerotothree.org.)

Raising a young child is indeed a serious responsibility. In many ways, a child's first three years last for the rest of his life.

> **Encourage Your Baby's Brain Development**
>
> - Respond to your baby's cues.
> - Touch, speak, and sing.
> - Provide opportunities to play—and play along.
> - Encourage curiosity and safe exploration.
> - Allow private time for your baby.
> - Use discipline to teach—never shake or hit.
> - Take care of yourself.
> - Select childcare carefully.
> - Love and enjoy your child.

5

TEMPERAMENT: WHAT MAKES YOUR CHILD UNIQUE?

Most parents cherish a fantasy about having "the perfect baby" or "the perfect child." The conventional description of this ideal baby is one who doesn't cry or fuss very often, who sleeps peacefully through the night, takes long naps, eats her food without spitting it out (or up), and who can happily entertain herself, gurgling and cooing angelically at her crib mobile. "Oh," we say when confronted with one of these enviable specimens, "what a good baby." Does this mean that all babies who don't fit this description are "bad"?

THE MYTH OF THE PERFECT CHILD

Of course, there is no such thing as a "bad" baby or child, even though most don't fit the fantasy description. Babies are born with different, unique personalities, as any parent with more than one child knows. In fact, we worry about the "fantasy child." As she grows up, this child may not feel secure enough to test power boundaries and find out who she is apart from her parents and teachers; she may be afraid to make mistakes or risk disapproval. Still, some babies do fit the fantasy description and still feel secure and aren't afraid to make mistakes. They are called "easy" children.

Each child is born with a unique style of processing sensory information and responding to the world around her. Stella Chess and Alexander Thomas investigated the miracle of personality in their longitudinal study of the nine major temperaments found in children. These temperaments—the qualities and characteristics that contribute to individual personalities—describe a child's "personal style." As discussed in Chapter 4, brain researchers believe that many temperament traits are inborn, part of each child's "wiring." How babies and toddlers interact with their parents and other caregivers appears to have a strong effect on how these inborn tendencies actually develop. It's a complex process, one that we don't yet fully understand. (For more information, we highly recommend *Know Your Child* and other related works by Chess and Thomas.)

While attitudes, behavior, and decisions may change with time and experience, our temperament appears to be part of us for life. Although some temperaments are "easier" than others, none are good or bad, right or wrong; they are just different. Understanding your child's unique temperament will help you work *with* her to learn, to grow, and to thrive.

THE BERKELEY STUDIES

Scientific investigation of temperament theory began in the late sixties and seventies with the Berkeley studies, a longitudinal study of two basic temperaments, active and passive. This study revealed that these temperaments were lifelong characteristics; in other words, passive infants grew up to be passive adults, while active infants grew up to be active adults. (Activity levels can even be measured in the womb.)

Chess and Thomas expanded the temperament theory significantly, even though their nine temperaments all fit under the general headings of active and passive. A major benefit of understanding temperament is that parents and caregivers can truly know their children, learn to respond to them in ways that encourage development and growth, and appreciate and accept them as they are. With understanding and acceptance, parents are equipped to help children reach their full potential rather than trying to mold them into fantasy children. Knowing your child's unique temperament (and, perhaps, your own) will enable you to teach and connect with her more effectively.

THE NINE TEMPERAMENTS

The nine temperaments are activity level, rhythmicity, initial response (approach or withdrawal), adaptability, sensory threshold, quality of mood, intensity of reactions, distractibility, and persistence and attention span. All children possess varying degrees of each characteristic. The following sections will describe what they look like in real life. (You may want to think about children you know as we examine these aspects of temperament.)

Activity Level

Activity level refers to the level of motor activity and the proportion of active and inactive periods. For instance, an infant with high activity might kick and splash so much in his bath that the floor needs a good mopping afterward, while a low-activity infant can turn over but doesn't often choose to do so. Activity level will influence a parent's interactions with a child—parents of active children will often have to be more active and alert themselves.

> *Barry's mom lay next to her six-month-old on a beach blanket, pleading for his cooperation. "Could you just stay still for a*

few minutes?" she asked, as more sand from a vigorously kicking foot sprayed her face.

Two years later, Barry's mom found herself tiptoeing into the nursery at regular intervals. She would place her finger next to Baby Jeremy's nose to reassure herself that he was still breathing. After raising Barry, she could not quite believe that a baby could sleep for such long stretches of time.

If your little one has a high activity level, you will want to provide lots of opportunities for safe exploration and play. (Be sure to childproof your home first!) He may need some active play before settling down to focus on a task. A less active infant or toddler may need to be invited to go exploring; you can use bright toys, interesting noises, and smiles to gently encourage him to interact with his world.

When making plans, taking activity level into account will help you prevent problems and provide appropriate movement for your child's needs.

Rhythmicity

Rhythmicity refers to the predictability (or unpredictability) of biological functions, such as hunger, sleeping, and bowel movements. One infant might have one bowel movement daily, immediately after breakfast, while another infant's schedule seems different each day. One child might eat her biggest meal at lunch, while another child prefers dinner—or a different meal each day!

Carla was so proud: She thought her little Jackie was toilet-trained by the time he was two years old. She put him on his toilet chair several times a day, and he obligingly produced a bowel movement each morning and urinated on each succeeding visit. But Jackie wasn't toilet-trained—his mom was trained. Jackie was so regular that when his mom remembered to put him on his chair, he performed. Whenever they were in a different setting and Carla forgot to put him on his chair,

Jackie would have an "accident." Jackie stopped having accidents when he was three—and was really toilet-trained.

Carla's other children were not so regular, and she reproached herself for having "failed" to train them. Learning about temperament helped her to realize that she hadn't succeeded or failed; her children simply had different temperaments of regularity, as well as other differences.

Understanding the degree of rhythmicity of your own child will help you build effective routines for your everyday life together and will allow you to see these differences as part of her personality rather than as misbehavior or lack of cooperation.

Approach or Withdrawal
This temperament describes the way a child reacts to a new situation or stimulus, such as a new food, toy, person, or place. Approach responses are often displayed by mood expression (smiling, speech, facial expression) or motor activity (swallowing a new food, reaching for a new toy). Withdrawal responses look more negative and are expressed by mood (crying, fussing, speech, facial expression) or motor activity (moving away, spitting food out, pushing a new toy away). Learning to parent your unique child means recognizing these cues and responding in encouraging, nurturing ways.

Some babies are open to just about any new experience—new foods, new people—while others are more reluctant.

Ted traveled several weeks each month as part of his job. When he returned home and attempted to pick up Isabelle, his new daughter, she would stiffen, resist, and begin crying. Ted felt devastated. He adored his baby girl. When he learned about temperament, he began to understand that his daughter simply reacted to changes of any kind with initial alarm. He began to take a gentler, more gradual approach after his prolonged absences. While his wife held Isabelle, he tickled the baby's feet, stroked her arms, and talked softly to her. Though Isabelle still was slow to warm up, this method allowed her more time to adjust. In the meantime, Ted no longer felt rejected but could be sympathetic to his daughter's needs.

Your child's ability to feel comfortable with the world around him is part of his inborn personality. If your child welcomes new experiences, celebrate: It will undoubtedly make life together easier. If your little one takes longer to adjust, however, you can look for small steps to help him adjust to change and new situations without taking his reactions personally.

Adaptability

Adaptability describes how a child reacts to a new situation over time—her ability to adjust and change. Some children initially spit out a new food but accept it after a few trial tastes. Others accept a new food, a new article of clothing, or a new preschool far more slowly, if at all.

When Jenna's new baby son arrived, his older sister and brother were already in grade school and involved in a whirl of sports, music lessons, and other activities. Because of their busy schedule, the baby was rarely at home for a regular nap time. But that posed no problem: This baby was a highly adaptable child, perfectly content to curl up and sleep wherever he happened to be at the time, whether at a basketball game or in the grocery cart.

Meanwhile, Kate often found herself looking for rides for her eight-year-old son when his activities occurred during the baby's nap time. If they weren't home at the proper time, the baby fell apart, crying, whining, and fussing. She wouldn't fall asleep anywhere except in her own bed. She would stay awake well past midnight if her family happened to be away from home. This baby had low adaptability, and all the family members suffered when they didn't take her temperament into account.

It is tempting to try to force your child to adapt to your busy schedule—after all, most parents have far more to do than there are hours in the day. But wise parents learn to adjust their schedules to their child's adaptability. It's true that you may not get all your errands done on any given day, but isn't it more important (and far more pleasant) to have a cheerful, calm child?

Sensory Threshold

Some children wake up from a nap every time a door opens, no matter how softly, while others can sleep through a carnival. The level of sensitivity to sensory input (touch, taste, vision, smell, and hearing) varies from one child to the next and affects how they behave and view the world.

> When Marjorie was eight months old, her grandmother took her outside to play. The day was warm and the yard sported a soft, new lawn. The moment Marjorie's knees touched the grass, her bottom popped into the air. She balanced herself with her hands and feet clutching the ground, avoiding contact between her bare knees and the tickly grass.
>
> The same afternoon, Marjorie's cousin, Nellie, arrived for a visit. Nellie's mother plopped her down on the grass, and Nellie crawled off, not even slowing down when she crossed a gravel pathway. Nellie's high sensory threshold allowed her to be an intrepid explorer, while Marjorie became cautious in response to new textures and experiences.

Time and experience will teach you about your own child's sensitivity to physical sensation and stimulation. Does your child like noise and music or does he become fussy? Does he gaze at bright or flashing lights or does he turn his face away? Will he eat new foods or does he spit out unusual tastes or textures? Does he like to be touched and hugged or does he wriggle away from too much contact?

If your child is more sensitive to stimulation, you will need to go slowly when introducing new toys, new experiences, and new people.

Sensory Integration Dysfunction

Some children are deeply influenced by sensory input; in fact, in some cases, a child's brain may have difficulty integrating sensory information. A child may find his socks "painful" or his shirt "too tight"; he may insist on the same foods and routines, because others are uncomfortable or "bad." Other children do not respond strongly to any stimulation; they may rock, spin, or bang their heads in an effort to generate sensory input, which they find comforting. Such children may have "sensory integration dysfunction" and can benefit from a variety of therapies that will help them make sense of sensory information and feel more comfortable.

If you suspect that your child's reaction to sensory input is different from that of other children the same age, it may be wise to ask your pediatrician for an evaluation. (For more information, see Carol Stock Kranowitz's excellent book *The Out-of-Sync Child* [New York: Perigree, rev. ed., 2006].)

Soft light and quiet will help him calm down, and he may become nervous or irritable in noisy, crowded places (such as birthday parties, amusement parks, or busy malls). A less sensitive child may be more willing to try new experiences. Discover what engages his attention; then create opportunities for him to explore and experiment.

Quality of Mood

Have you ever noticed how some children (and adults) react to life with pleasure and acceptance, while others can find fault with everything and everybody? One baby might favor her family with smiles and coos, while another feels compelled to cry a bit, just "because."

Baby Brent smiled happily when his mom tickled his toes. When he was a toddler, his grin would melt her heart—and he grinned in response to just about every interaction, even gentle scolding. Then baby Cris was born. Instead of smiling when she tickled his toes, Cris would cry. He didn't seem to think anything was funny, and appeared to be in a sour mood most of the time. As an adult Cris still smiles rarely, yet he is a loving father and son. Brent, as an adult, is also a loving father, and he still loves to laugh.

Parents of less sunny little ones can take heart. Those tiny scowls are not in response to you or your parenting skills. Be sensitive to his mood, but take time to stroke your sober little fellow, massage his chubby cheeks, and share your own sunshine with him. As he grows, help him to see the world for the lovely place it is.

If your baby beams a happy face to the world, enjoy the gift her temperament brings to your life. Don't rain on her parade. Take a moment to savor the day through her rosy outlook.

Intensity of Reactions

Children often respond to events around them in different ways. Some smile quietly or merely take a look, then go back to what they were doing; others react with action and emotion. Some children wear their hearts on their little sleeves; they giggle and shriek with laughter when happy and throw impressive tantrums when angry. Some children barely react to outside events and may need your encouragement to get involved in play or other interaction.

At play group, Maya had her hair pulled by an inquisitive classmate. The teacher panicked, sure from the way Maya hollered that she required a trip to the emergency room. When the same miscreant pulled Juan's hair, Juan hardly looked up from his blocks, swatting the other child's hand away as though it was no more worrisome than a gnat alighting nearby.

Maya's mom has learned to sit quietly, waiting until Maya's initial reaction subsides before she evaluates the seriousness of the situation. Juan's mother becomes truly alarmed when he cries loudly, knowing how much it takes to elicit such a response. Both children and parents have learned to interact differently based on the intensity of each child's reactions.

As you get to know your child's unique temperament, you will be able to shape his environment in a way that allows him to feel safe, connected, and curious.

Distractibility

"If I sit my toddler down with a box of blocks, he won't notice anything else in the room," says one father. "Well," says a mother, "if someone walks by while my baby is nursing, she not only looks but stops sucking until the person is gone." Another mom adds, "I've noticed that my daughter simply can't concentrate on eating when the whole family is at the table. I have to feed her ahead of the rest of us." They may not realize it, but these parents are actually talking about their children's distractibility, the way in which an outside stimulus interferes with a child's present behavior and his willingness (or unwillingness) to be diverted.

> *Joe heads for the stereo every time he comes into the living room. His sitter picks him up, carries him to his toy box, and sometimes even succeeds in distracting him for a moment or two. But minutes later, he sets his course for the stereo with an accuracy any pilot would admire. Joe's ability to remain single-minded and focused may be a great strength someday; for now, his weary sitter must make yet another trip to remove his fingers from the delicate stereo knobs.*
>
> *Ben picks up his dad's beeper, bringing it to his open mouth for a taste. Dad intercepts, tickling Ben and substituting a piece of toast. Ben gurgles, hardly noticing that the object clutched in his hand has changed. Ben's distractibility makes him an easy child to watch, while Joe's sitter is working up the courage to ask for an increase in pay.*

Distraction and redirection are two of the most common and effective methods for managing the behavior of young children. At least, they are effective if your child is easily distracted and redirected. Your child's ability to focus on an object or task will influence his behavior—and your response. Rather than becoming frustrated and angry about your child's distractibility (or lack thereof), look for ways to make her environment safe and easy to explore, focus on solutions to the problems you encounter, and recognize and accept her inherent temperament.

Persistence and Attention Span

Persistence refers to a child's willingness to pursue an activity in the face of obstacles or difficulties; attention span describes the length of time he will pursue an activity without interruption. The two characteristics are usually related. A toddler who is content to tear up an old magazine for half an hour at a time has a fairly long attention span, while another who plays with ten different toys in ten minutes or less has a short one. Again, no combination is necessarily better than another; they're simply different, and present different challenges in parenting and teaching.

Baby Edith has spent the past half hour sitting in her high chair, lining up rows of Cheerios. Sometimes she finds one big enough to fit onto her finger. Her twin sister, Emma, did not even make it through breakfast before her cereal, bowl, and cup hit the floor. Emma dismantled the pot-and-pan cupboard, explored the heating vent, and had to be retrieved from a foray into the bathroom—all while Edith patiently arranged her Cheerios. Edith might have a future as an accountant, while Emma might make a brilliant sportscaster. Edith's attention span extends for long periods, while Emma rarely stays with one thing for more than a few minutes—a talent that may someday help her keep up with rapidly changing game configurations and split-second moves. It is important to understand that both girls' temperaments can be strengths in the right situation. Wise parents and caregivers will help Emma and Edith maximize the potential of their inborn temperaments by providing teaching, nurturing—and lots of supervision.

Q. My son is three years old. He is incredibly active; he won't take a nap, hates to sit and look at a book, and is always in motion. I try to keep him occupied but he goes through every toy in his toy box in about ten minutes. My sister says he probably has attention deficit disorder because he's "hyper" and has such a short attention span; she says I should put him on medication. What should I do?

A. At this age, your son's behavior is more likely to be due to his inborn temperament and development than it is to a disorder like ADD or ADHD. Your son seems to have a high activity level, less persistence, and a short attention span. While this certainly creates challenges for you as his parent, you will help him best by accepting his temperament and finding ways to create structure and routine; to use kind, firm teaching; and to keep him active and engaged. ADHD cannot be diagnosed reliably until a child is of school age (around five or six). Most of the Positive Discipline tools help your active child cope with home and classroom responsibilities whether he has ADHD or not.

If your child is less patient and persistent, there are ways you can help her get along in a sometimes frustrating world. Be sure she has something to engage her attention if you must wait quietly at a doctor's office. Break challenging tasks into small, achievable steps; you can coach, but don't rush to rescue your child. When she gets frustrated, let her know that you understand her feelings and don't give up on her. You can use humor and playfulness to defuse a frustrating situation, and walk away for a calming positive time-out if tempers flare.

"GOODNESS OF FIT"

Chess and Thomas emphasize the importance of "goodness of fit," the depth of understanding parents and teachers have of a child's temperament and their willingness to work with that child to encourage healthy development. Children experience enough stress in life as they struggle for competency and belonging. It does not help to compound that stress by expecting a child to be someone he is not.

Understanding a child's temperament doesn't mean shrugging your shoulders and saying, "Oh well, that's just the way this child is." It is an invitation to help a child develop acceptable behavior and skills through patience, encouragement, and kind, firm teaching. For instance, a child with a short attention span will still need to learn to accept some structure. Offering limited choices is one way to be respectful of the child's needs and of the "needs of the situation" (behavior appropriate for the present environment).

Unfortunately, no matter how much you love your child, your own temperament and hers may not mesh easily. Working out a match between your tempera-  ment and needs and your child's is critical to good- ness of fit. If your child has an irregular sleep pattern and you can hardly keep your eyes open after being up night after night with your little owl, you have a poor fit. An understanding of temperament can help you adjust and create a better fit. The key is to find *balance*. Your baby might not sleep through the night because of her temperament, but she can learn to entertain herself when she wakes up. You may need to learn to stagger over and offer a gentle stroke or pat on the back, whisper a few loving words, then allow her to get back to sleep on her own.

The first step is to determine what will work for all family members, with no one's needs being ignored. (This includes your needs. It is not in a child's best interest to have an exhausted, crabby parent.) Yelling at, threatening, or totally ignoring a wakeful child also is not helpful. Finding the balance between your needs and those of your child can take some time and practice, but learning to accept and work with the individual, special temperament of your child will benefit you both as the years go by.

POSITIVE DISCIPLINE SKILLS FOR PARENTS AND CAREGIVERS

Many of the skills we suggest are appropriate for children of all temperaments, because they invite children to learn cooperation, responsibility, and life skills. But an understanding of temperament helps us understand why different methods may be more or less effective, depending on the temperament and needs of an individual child.

A child with a low sensory threshold may need a few moments alone to cry and release the tensions built up during a busy afternoon before settling down to fall asleep. It is respectful to provide this child with a quiet environment with books, stuffed animals, or soft music. It would not be appropriate to continue cooing to, cuddling, and generally overstimulating this little one. His sister, with her different sensory threshold, may thrive on lullabies, tickling games, and noisy family members careening through the halls.

A child with low distractibility will need patient preparation to switch from one activity to another. Planning ahead becomes a vital tool to smooth the way for transitions. A low-regularity parent living with a high-regularity toddler must learn to plan meals at predictable intervals, develop routines for daily activities, and establish a more defined rhythm to her day. Her child must learn to cope with occasional revised plans, survive on a cracker or two when a meal is delayed, and develop personal flexibility. The good news is that parents and children can adapt to each other. Our brains are designed to respond to the world around us, and patience, sensitivity, and love can help all of us learn to live peacefully together.

INDIVIDUALITY AND CREATIVITY

Parents and caregivers may not be aware of how they squelch individuality and creativity when they (often subconsciously) buy in to the myth of the perfect child. It is tempting for adults to prefer the "easy" child, or to want children to conform to the norms of society. Egos often get involved; you may worry about what others think and fear that your competency may be questioned if your children aren't "good" in the eyes of others.

One of the primary motivators for the studies of Chess and Thomas was their desire to stop society's tendency to blame mothers for the characteristics of their children. Chess and Thomas state, "A child's temperament can actively influence the attitudes and behavior of her parents, other family members, playmates, and teachers, and in turn help to shape their effect on her behavioral development." In this way, the relationship between child and parents is a two-way street, each continuously influencing the other.

What if the mother whose twins behaved so differently had been two different mothers? It would have been easy to decide that quiet, focused Edith's mother was very effective, while active, busy Emma's mother "just couldn't control that child!" It may be wise to ask yourself occasionally, "Are you looking for blame or are you looking for solutions?" It is not reasonable or respectful (nor is it effective) to blame your child for behavior caused by her temperament. The more you know about temperament and effective parenting skills, the better you will be at finding solutions that help your child develop into a capable individual, despite her differences and uniqueness.

WORK FOR IMPROVEMENT, NOT PERFECTION

Even with understanding and the best intentions, most parents struggle occasionally with their children's temperaments and behavior. You may lack patience at

Know Your Child

Temperament is inborn and has a powerful effect on the way your young child reacts to his environment—and to you. Take a moment to consider your child and each of the nine temperaments:

1. Activity level
2. Rhythmicity
3. Initial response (approach or withdrawal)
4. Adaptability
5. Sensory threshold
6. Quality of mood
7. Intensity of reactions
8. Distractibility
9. Persistence and attention span

times, or get hooked into *reacting* to behavior instead of *acting* thoughtfully. Awareness and understanding do not mean we become perfect; mistakes are inevitable. However, once you have had time to cool off after a mistake, you need to resolve it with your children. They're usually more than willing to hug and offer forgiveness, especially when they know you'll do the same for them. It is important to help children work for improvement, not perfection; you can give this gift to yourself as well.

KINDNESS AND FIRMNESS

Rudolf Dreikurs continually made a plea for parents and caregivers to use kindness *and* firmness with children. An understanding of temperament shows just how important this is. Kindness shows respect for the child and his uniqueness; firmness shows respect for the needs of the situation, including a child's developing need to learn social skills. By understanding and respecting your child's temperament, you will be able to help him reach his full potential as a capable, confident, contented person. And there's a bonus: You will probably get a lot more rest, laugh more, and learn a great deal about yourself and your child in the process.

6

TRUST VERSUS MISTRUST: "CAN I COUNT ON YOU?"

In his pioneering work on emotional development, Erik Erikson identified critical tasks that all humans must master. The mastery of the first of these—and perhaps the most important—happens during an infant's first year of life: All infants must develop a sense of trust. To develop a sense of trust, a baby must learn that he can rely on the affections and support of others, so he needs to have his basic needs met consistently and lovingly. These needs include proper nutrition, a comfortable temperature, dry diapers, adequate sleep, and lots and lots of love: touching, holding, and cuddling. In fact, the same "contingent communication" that you learned about in Chapter 4 nurtures and supports the development of trust and a secure attachment. Many parents feel confused about the difference between meeting their babies' needs and spoiling—and they're sure to hear many points of view (some welcome, some not).

Opinions range from "put your baby on a strict schedule (after all, he or she has come to live in your house and there is no reason to change your life too much)" to "forget about your life; hover around your baby and try to anticipate every need and whimper." Understanding the importance of your child developing trust instead of mistrust is a key factor in deciding what is right for you and your baby.

A neglected baby (one whose basic needs for food, comfort, and loving touch are not met) will develop a sense of mistrust in life. Perhaps surprisingly, an extremely pampered baby may also develop a sense of mistrust, because he has never had to learn patience and self-reliance. Many new parents are plagued with guilt if they don't devote twenty-four hours a day to their new baby, but as with so many aspects of parenting, the best solution is creating a healthy balance.

DEVELOPMENTAL APPROPRIATENESS IN THE FIRST YEAR OF LIFE

Part of dealing with young children's behavior to achieve positive outcomes involves knowing what is "developmentally appropriate," a term we use to describe the characteristics and behaviors that are expected for children at certain ages. The more we know about the psychological, intellectual, and physical development of the child, the more we know what is developmentally appropriate and the better our ability to get into our child's world and shape his early decisions and behavior. An understanding of developmental appropriateness helps us know that it is almost impossible to spoil an infant.

SPOILING

Don't worry about spoiling your baby during the first three months of life. It can happen, but it is very rare. As your baby grows, however, you will need to pay attention to what he is learning and deciding about you, about himself, and about what "works" to achieve a sense of belonging and connection.

Babies need to have their cries responded to, at least initially (this teaches trust more effectively than anything else), but considering your baby's needs, your own needs, and the needs of other members of your family will help you introduce routines and begin to find a good balance. Sometimes crying may be a child's way of saying, "I don't like this." That doesn't mean he can't deal with it, however. This is an important concept to master, and you will learn more about it in the chapters ahead. (Allowing your baby to self-soothe when learning to go to sleep by herself—even when crying is involved—is covered in Chapter 11.)

For instance, if your six-month-old baby cries to be held, pick him up and cuddle for a few minutes; then put him in a safe infant seat where he can watch you and be close to you. A baby should not be left in an infant seat or playpen too long, and a parent should not feel like a slave to his or her child. As he grows older, your child will learn trust when you follow through and do what you have promised. Loving, respectful teaching and follow-through are the best ways to teach your child trust.

Learning the difference between what an infant truly *needs* and what he simply *wants* causes considerable anxiety for parents, but as your understanding increases so will your confidence. As we have said before, it is important to meet all your child's needs but not all her wants. You will need to use your head *and* your heart to be an effective parent. The more information you have, the more you can trust your head. The more you know how important it is to enjoy your children, the more you can trust your heart. When in doubt, always trust your heart.

UNIQUENESS, SELF-TRUST, AND PARENT CONFIDENCE

To say that people are different and unique isn't new or profound, but it doesn't hurt to be reminded. With time, you will discover parenting tools that feel

Trust Versus Mistrust

During the first year of life, a child begins to learn the fundamental concept of a sense of trust, the first important stage of emotional development. If she cries, does someone come? If she's hungry, cold, or wet, will someone help? Do the routines and rituals of daily life happen predictably? It is by these simple experiences that she will learn to trust and rely on her parents.

Without this basic sense of trust, life becomes far more difficult. Children who have been shuttled in and out of foster homes during their early years or who have been denied affection and consistent care often refuse to make eye contact or to respond to even the most loving attempts later on. It can take a great deal of patience and determination to build in these children the sense of trust that was stunted during their early years.

Most of us know people who have a hard time trusting themselves or others and who seem to have little faith in their ability to influence what happens to them. Will your child go through life with a sense of trust or mistrust, faith or doubt? It depends on how he is treated in the first year of life (and the subconscious decisions he makes about his experiences). This critical first year of life is also the first stage of emotional development. The development of a sense of trust begins in the first year of life and will continue as your child grows.

comfortable and effective for you; you will also learn that nothing works all the time for all children. What does this have to do with the development of trust or mistrust? Erikson found that a primary factor in the development of a child's trust is her sense that her primary caretaker—usually her mother—has confidence in herself.

Because self-confidence is so important, we want to repeat that most mothers find they can trust themselves more when they have a basic understanding of child development and parenting skills—and faith in their own instincts. This is one reason that parent education can be so important. When you have learned all you can about child development, age-appropriate behavior, and nonpunitive methods to help your child thrive, you will feel more confident about your ability to understand and care for your child.

Children develop a sense of trust when someone comes when they cry, but do not misinterpret this to mean that your child will be traumatized if you don't respond to every whimper. If you pamper and coddle your children, you fail to help them develop courage and self-confidence. For example, after a child has been fed, changed, and cuddled, she might whimper (or even cry) for a few minutes after being put into her crib. She hasn't yet had the opportunity to learn that she is capable of falling asleep by herself.

Sometimes a baby will cry to release excess energy; allowing her to cry until she settles may actually help her learn to self-soothe. When parents think they have to help their children get to sleep by rocking them, nursing them or giving them a bottle, or even lying down with them, their children may be learning manipulation skills instead of trust (in themselves and in their parents).

It takes knowledge and confidence (and faith in your child) to know when it is okay to allow your child to experience a little discomfort in order to develop a sense of trust and confidence in herself. Remember that no parent is born knowing where this balance lies—and mistakes are opportunities to learn. Pay attention not only to your baby but also to your own feelings and wisdom, and chances are good that you'll soon know what works for your child.

FOUR PILLARS OF SECURITY

In their book *What Happened to the World?: Helping Children Cope in Turbulent Times* (New South Wales, Australia: Pademelon Press, 2002), Jim Greenman and Anne Stonehouse list what they call the "four pillars of security": people, place, routine, and ritual. When these four things are stable, children feel the most secure. When we consider the early foundation of trust we can see that these four pillars affect even very young children.

Colic

Some babies seem to fuss, cry, or scream for no apparent reason for long periods of time. If your baby cries or screams excessively, check with your doctor to be sure there is no medical reason. Many times, however, the doctor will say, "There is nothing seriously wrong. It is just colic." You will find it reassuring to know that your child is not in physical danger, but you may find it extremely frustrating when you seem unable to comfort your child.

What is colic, anyway? No one seems to know. It is a catchall description for long periods of crying in babies when they appear inconsolable and often draw their tiny legs up as though in terrible pain. What can you do? First, remember that it doesn't last forever. Also, don't look for blame. Try to remain calm and connected as you rock, burp, walk the floor with, and offer a pacifier to your little one (unless you are nursing), holding your arms tightly (but not too tightly) around her tummy. Nursing more frequently can be the most soothing thing you can do. Go to www.lalecheleague.com for more information. Unfortunately, none of these methods may work for long. It is nice if you have the luxury of a spouse or relative who will take turns trying to help your baby through this miserable time. Don't worry about household chores that can wait awhile; your family can survive on soup and sandwiches.

Caring adults are the "people" part of a child's early years; at times, they may also be the "place" part, as well. Being in Mommy's arms or feeling the motion of a rocking chair while lying on Grandma's lap constitute "place" for a baby as much as a crib, bedroom, or apartment does.

The other two pillars—"routine" and "ritual"—are more elusive. These early months and years represent a time of constant change. Any mom with a newborn can testify that her daily routines change drastically from day to day, because everything is new—for infants and their parents! For a child to develop trust, life must become predictable, and that is the role of routines. Establishing routines forms an important part of a parent and child's first months and years together. By the age of three months, most babies have settled into a routine. If a mother is nursing, three months seems to be the time when growth spurts that cause fussiness cease. Milk supply now meets the child's needs. But routines will be tested along the way as a child grows and develops—for example, when she is ready to give up naps but you aren't ready to give up that quiet time for yourself.

Routine and Ritual

Babies understand the world through the ways in which their most basic needs (hunger, fatigue, warmth, clothing, and shelter) are met: "When I cry, I am fed; when I am cold or wet or tired, I am warmed, changed, or given a chance to rest." These daily activities, when done in ways that can be counted upon, form the backdrop of predictability and connection that becomes a child's life experience.

When we see things in this context, it makes sense that whenever there is disruption in our lives—from a move, to a divorce, to the chaos caused by natural or man-made disasters—our sense of safety is reestablished by following routines, allowing us to resume our trust in living and the world around us. The early activities of caregiving may not seem critical, but these simple everyday acts constitute our lifelong ability to trust.

Rituals, the fourth pillar of security, though not very elaborate in these early years, do contribute important elements to the strengthening and development of trust. Mom blowing kisses on baby's tummy before bath time, Dad making smacking sounds with his lips to coax a smile before offering baby's bottle, or an older sister singing "Twinkle, Twinkle, Little Star" at bedtime—all are rituals that add texture to a young child's life and begin to define it. They confirm his experience of the world as a predictable and

> ## The Comfort of Routines
>
> Bath time comes midway through the morning or each afternoon; rooms darken and become quiet at night; there is music and talking early each morning. By their rhythm and repetition, these events form patterns, helping little ones make sense of their days and nights. When a child can count on having her needs met and having life progress in predictable ways, she feels secure and learns to trust others and the world around her.

trustworthy place and tell him that he is secure and safe. As he grows, the rituals of family celebrations and traditions will continue to add joy and a sense of connection to his life.

ENJOY YOUR CHILDREN AND YOURSELF

Life throws plenty of curveballs to all new parents, from ear infections to big unpaid bills, and if you forget to enjoy special moments, learning new skills and adjusting to life with a developing child can seem like a heavy burden. Do we really need to mention the importance of enjoying your children? We think so.

Sharing your life with a child, especially during his first year of life, can be an overwhelming experience. Everything is new; the baby is demanding, and you may have moments when you worry whether you're doing it "right." Your baby will sense your worry and doubt, and his growing sense of trust may be hindered. Use this opportunity to increase your trust in yourself, remembering that it is not helpful to take mistakes too seriously. It is helpful to learn from them with gratitude. When this learning is built upon the foundation of enjoyment, awareness, and education, confidence will filter through your heart and you will know what to do. (Yes, you really will!)

MAKE ENJOYMENT A PRIORITY

We suggest you forget about being a perfect housekeeper, running the PTA, or taking on anything that makes you feel overly stressed or robs you of time to enjoy your children. Discuss priorities with your partner (or conduct a personal monologue if you are a single parent) and decide to put first things first—each other, your children, and yourself. Make peace with menus of soup and sandwiches for a while instead of feeling inadequate for not producing elaborate meals.

Why is this important? Isn't it possible to "do it all"? It may be, but keep in mind that thanks to their mirror neurons, infants can sense the energy of others. They often become fussy when their parents are upset. They also sense when we enjoy them—and know when we don't. How can infants develop a sense of trust if they don't feel the energy of enjoyment from their parents or caregivers, knowing that they are loved, wanted, and appreciated? Toni Morrison said it all on an Oprah show: "Do your eyes light up when your children walk into the room?" When your child is an infant, make sure your eyes light up when you walk into her presence—and continue this practice for the rest of her life.

Ask yourself this question when circumstances get in the way of simply enjoying your children: "What difference will this make ten years from now?" Whether or not the house is clean, the lawn is mowed, or the furniture is waxed won't make any difference; on the other hand, time you spend with your partner and your children will make all the difference in the world!

Help Your Infant Develop a Sense of Trust

- Meet all your baby's needs in the first three months of her life.
- Learn the difference between needs and wants.
- Avoid pampering (have faith in children to handle not receiving all wants).
- Learn about developmental needs (social, intellectual, and physical).
- Learn parenting skills (including long-range results of what you do).
- Have confidence and trust in yourself.
- Enjoy your child.

7

AUTONOMY VERSUS DOUBT AND SHAME: "I CAN STAND ON MY OWN TWO FEET (BUT DON'T ABANDON ME!)"

What do toddlers want to do? Just about everything: explore, touch, examine, put their fingers in sockets, play with the television knobs, empty cupboards of every pot and pan, play in the toilet, unravel the toilet paper, eat lipstick, spill perfume, and investigate everything they can get their hands on.

What happens when parents don't allow toddlers to explore, or slap their children's hands when they touch something they are not supposed to touch? They may develop a sense of shame.

Well-meaning parents who have not learned about this important developmental phase may not know that too much confinement and punishment can instill doubt and shame instead of a sense of autonomy. Notice that we said a *sense of* autonomy—not autonomy itself. Erik Erikson used the words "sense of" to describe a tendency in one direction or the other. Erikson believed that between the ages of one and three, children have the opportunity, with the help of their parents, to begin their quest for a sense of autonomy that is stronger and healthier than feelings of doubt and shame.

A healthy sense of autonomy is critical in healthy development; it is autonomy that gives a child confidence and the ability to pursue his own ideas and plans. Not surprisingly, a young child's desire for autonomy presents some challenges for parents (as anyone who has shared a home with a toddler can testify), but children could not thrive without it. Your child's search for a sense of autonomy will continue throughout his childhood, but the foundation is established in the second and third years. A strong sense of trust developed in the first year and a strong sense of autonomy developed in the second and third years also build the foundation for healthy self-worth.

WHAT IS AUTONOMY?

Since a strong sense of autonomy is so important, we need to know what it is and how to help toddlers develop it. The dictionary defines "autonomy" as independence or freedom, having the will of one's actions. "What?" you might ask. "My toddler is still a baby who needs to be dependent on me!" The truth is that your toddler needs both autonomy *and* healthy dependence on you. He needs a balance between the security provided by parents and home and the freedom to discover his own capabilities.

This is illustrated beautifully by the research of Harry F. Harlow using monkeys and their young. In his study, the mother monkeys took their babies into a room full of toys. The baby monkeys clung to their mothers while they surveyed the interesting toys in the room. Eventually, their need to explore took over, and they left their mothers to play with the toys. Periodically, they would return and jump into their mothers' arms for another dose of security before going back to their play. Children, too, need this gentle blending of safety and freedom. Too much freedom could feel dangerous and threatening for a toddler.

ENCOURAGING AUTONOMY WITHOUT BEING PERMISSIVE

It is easy to misunderstand what autonomy means for a toddler. Possessing a sense of autonomy does not mean that children no longer need guidance and safe boundaries. They do. It does not mean that they should rule the house and do whatever they want. They shouldn't. The development of autonomy requires a lot of freedom within safe boundaries so they can begin that important journey toward independence.

Autonomy does not mean that children are prepared to make decisions about life situations. Asking a child whether he wants to hold the keys or your purse gives him a healthy opportunity to experience his own power. Asking him whether he would prefer this preschool or that one, whether the family should visit Grandma's at Thanksgiving, or whether he would mind if Mommy and Daddy go to a movie tonight may lead him to believe he is (or should be) in charge. Such decisions are adult responsibilities. Burdening children with too many choices— or the wrong sort of choices—creates demanding, anxious tyrants. This is ineffective—and possibly harmful—parenting.

HOW TO SAFELY PROMOTE AUTONOMY

As autonomy is such an important step in healthy development, you may wonder just what your role should be in promoting your little one's self-confidence without exposing her to undue risk.

We want to emphasize again that autonomy does not mean children should be allowed to do anything they want. One of the more persistent debates about parenting in early childhood concerns childproofing a home: removing poisons, plugging electrical sockets, latching kitchen cabinets, putting valuable or fragile items out of reach of young hands, and otherwise making the home environment safe for a child to explore. The importance of developing a child's autonomy is an excellent argument in favor of childproofing your home. Some adults fret that childproofing fails to teach children about restraint. Just remember that this is the age for supervision. Self-restraint will come later. Young children are developmentally programmed to explore and lack impulse control. If you ignore developmental needs and limitations, stress is the most likely result. The accompanying conflict and power struggles will not create a sense of healthy autonomy.

Once the home is childproofed, there will still be many things children should not be allowed to do, such as throw crackers or jump on the sofa. Many adults believe the best way to teach toddlers not to touch things or do what they shouldn't is to slap their hands. Not so. One childcare director who was leading a parenting class was asked how he kept children away from things they should not touch. Without any hesitation he said, "If they shouldn't touch it, it is not within their reach." Pretty simple, really. If your little one does throw crackers or jump on the sofa, removing the crackers or setting her on the floor while giving her a toy are solutions that allow the needs of both the child and the situation to be met with respect. (We'll learn more about distraction and other Positive Discipline tools later on.)

Of course, homes are not as easy to rearrange, but there is still much we can do to provide a safe and exploration-friendly environment. If those tempting television knobs or a computer keyboard cannot be placed out of reach, try covering them with a small cloth or towel. You can block access to wires and other forbidden objects by placing tempting "toys" on shelves or placing drawers between the wires and your curious toddler. Put boundaries on what your toddler can reach and offer something appropriate to explore instead.

Think for just a moment. Toddlers would not be normal if they didn't want to explore and touch. They're doing their developmental job, and it is an important ingredient in their sense of autonomy. Does it make sense to slap or spank them for doing something that is normal and important for healthy development? Slapping and spanking, especially for something that is a part of normal development, is far more likely to create a sense of doubt and shame than healthy autonomy. Effective parenting can help children learn limits without creating doubt and shame. The key is kindness and firmness at the same time.

AUTONOMY AS A LIFE SKILL

Imagine awaking from a deep sleep and discovering that you are in an unfamiliar new world and must learn not only how your own brand-new body and emotions work, but how the people around you live— and what they expect from you. Learning to survive and thrive would require a great deal of courage.

Just being a toddler takes courage. A young child's budding sense of autonomy gives him the courage and energy to set about exploring how this world works. It's a task fraught with perils—for toddlers and for parents. Healthy autonomy is a balance between protecting children and allowing them to explore and test the world they will inhabit. How much is too much? How will you know when you (and your child) have the balance right?

THE NEED TO EXPLORE
IN A SAFE ENVIRONMENT

An important part of the development of autonomy during the second year of life lies in the maturation of the muscle system. Providing a safe environment for exploration is one of the best ways to help toddlers develop autonomy as well as healthy muscles. As they explore, they exercise their muscles and enhance muscle maturation by experimenting with such activities as holding on and letting go. (Yes, dropping that spoon over and over is helping them develop both their sense of autonomy and their muscles.) Children who are confined too much will not have the opportunity to develop a strong sense of autonomy. They need the opportunity to explore and test what they can and cannot do.

> *Jenny did not know about the importance of helping her toddler develop a strong sense of autonomy. She was an artist who loved to paint during the day when the light was good. Her daughter, Dani, seemed content to sit in a high chair eating crackers for long periods of time. When Dani would tire of the high chair, Jenny would move her to a playpen or windup swing. Dani was rarely let out to roam around the house.*

Jenny was not a "bad" parent. She felt lucky that Dani seemed so content with her confinement and that she could get so much painting done. Jenny didn't understand that she was hindering Dani's sense of autonomy and muscle development by not giving her more opportunities to explore. As we discussed in Chapter 4, lack of physical and intellectual stimulation can also hamper optimal brain development.

Positive Discipline methods help children develop a sense of autonomy as well as the characteristics and the life skills they need when they no longer depend on adults. Children, from birth through the preschool years, always need adults around. They also need opportunities to learn the attitudes and skills they will need to make decisions and solve problems when parents are not around.

PUNISHMENT EQUALS DOUBT AND SHAME

Punishment does not foster a healthy sense of autonomy and it does not teach life skills, but *not* punishing seems to require a real shift in attitude for many parents. Punishment (spanking and shaming children for doing things that are developmentally appropriate) fosters doubt and shame. Children will experience enough self-imposed doubt and shame as they encounter the real limits of their abilities. An understanding of this important developmental stage will help parents avoid adding to the frustration children experience as they progress in their desire for more independence.

Do not slap hands, spank, or use shaming words, such as "bad girl." A young child often does not understand the connection between what she did (reach for an electrical cord) and the response (a quick slap). Too many parents have had the unsettling experience of reaching for their child in love and having that child cringe away in fear, as if a slap is on the way—this is certainly not the sort of relationship that fosters trust and closeness and certainly not what most parents would choose.

You may be thinking, "But I have to spank my children when it is a matter of life or death. I have to spank my child to teach her not to run into the street." But does spanking really teach your child what you intend? Even after you have spanked her, would you let her play near a busy street unsupervised?

Most parents are quick to realize that spanking is neither teaching nor training—it is a reaction usually born out of fear, worry, and frustration. A parent might spank a child a hundred times, but even so, it would be unwise to allow that child to play unsupervised by a busy street.

Children may experience frustration at not being allowed to play with the stereo or to run into the street. This is what Erikson called the real "crisis" of this stage of development. But adding punishment to the natural crisis is like pouring salt on a wound. The frustration is greatly eased when parents remember to be kind when they are being firm. Children feel the difference.

USE TRAINING, NOT PUNISHMENT

How, then, might you effectively deal with a child who is fond of running into the middle of the road? Take time for training every time you have the occasion to cross a busy street by asking your child to look both ways and tell you when no cars are coming. Ask your child to tell you when it is safe to cross the street. If you don't agree with his assessment, ask, "What about the big truck that's coming? What do

To Spank or Not to Spank

Q. When my son was three years old, he was very good. The few times he was bad, I used to take him to his room and put him on the time-out chair, and it worked. Now my daughter is three. She is a horror. She is always bad. I've done everything I can think of. The time-out chair didn't work, so I tried telling her no, taking away toys, talking about why she was bad, and even hugging her a lot, saying what she did was bad and she should try not to do it again. The only thing left to do is spank. I never spanked my son, and my mother never spanked me. I don't know if I should. If I do spank, which way is best? Should I use my hand or a belt? Should she be standing or over my knee? I want to do what is best for my daughter.

A. Parents need to understand that their children are never "bad." It is so important that parents understand developmental appropriateness, Erikson's social and emotional stages of development, and temperament. Your daughter is not "bad" any more than your son is perfect—they have different temperaments. (And even though your son's temperament is easier to deal with, we worry that he might become an approval junkie or develop low self-esteem. Children are not developing appropriate autonomy and initiative if they do not go through lots of exploring, experimenting, and testing of the rules.) Your daughter sounds very normal, not "bad." The problem is that when punitive methods are used with normal children (who can have any of a wide range of different temperament types), it is the *punishment* that creates defiance, rebellion, and power struggles. All the methods you have been using are punitive. (You are even turning hugs into punishment by telling her she is bad while hugging her.) We're glad you have avoided spanking. Many research studies have shown that over time, spanking creates even worse behavior.

So what should you do? Learn to see every problem as an opportunity for helping your child develop a sense of healthy self-worth and important life skills. Learn to take good care of your own physical and emotional health so that you have the patience and energy to be kind and firm with your challenging toddler.

you think will happen if that truck hits us?" Throughout this process, your child needs to be holding your hand. Remember, he is just learning this skill. Training and skill mastery are not synonymous. At least your child will not be learning that you are scarier than the street!

Children need to be supervised when they are near any kind of danger that requires mature judgment and skills. Your supervision, guidance, and warm, reassuring hand are essential. As you have learned, the best discipline is always kind, firm *teaching*. Focus on connection and relationship, and use respectful actions to teach about skills and limits when dealing with age-appropriate behavior.

TEACHING TODDLERS?

You absolutely can teach a toddler. Encourage autonomy by asking questions, and encourage your toddler to ask questions too. (The importance of asking curiosity questions is discussed in more detail in Chapter 8.) Skip the lectures. They invite avoidance or resistance, while questions invite thinking and participation. Questions draw forth. Lectures attempt to stuff in—a method that usually fails.

Toddlers can understand more than they can verbalize. Asking questions such as "What might happen if we cross the street without looking first?" helps with their language development, their thinking skills, and their sense of autonomy.

SHOW THEM WHAT TO DO
INSTEAD OF WHAT NOT TO DO

Many toddlers go through a hitting stage. Believe it or not, when they do this they are not misbehaving. It could be that they are frustrated and don't have the skills to accomplish their goals. Many are just exploring possibilities by hitting (such as what happens when they hit the water in the tub). An amazing phenomenon is to watch parents hit their children while telling them not to hit. More common is for parents to scold and say, "We don't hit!" We watch the twinkle in the child's eye and can just imagine her saying, "Yes we do. We just did."

Instead of hitting back or scolding, it is more effective to show her what to do instead of what not to do. Increase your supervision during the *hitting pattern of behavior*. Quickly catch her hand that is poised to hit and say, "Touch nicely," while showing her what this looks like.

Eighteen-month-old Cecelia was going through a hitting phase. She would hit her mother in the face "for no reason at all." Mom was just holding her. She would also hit the dog. Mom became more vigilant at supervision and started catching her in the act. She would gently guide Cecelia's hand to stroke her face while saying, "Touch nicely." Mom would "catch" Cecelia's hand as she started to hit the dog and would guide her hand to gently stroke the dog while saying, "Touch nicely."

After this scene was repeated four or five times, Cecelia would raise her hand to hit and then look at her mom with an impish grin. Mom would say, "Touch nicely," and Cecelia would.

DEVELOPMENTALLY APPROPRIATE BEHAVIOR

Patsy had her arms full. The diaper bag was slung over one shoulder, two overdue library books were gripped in one hand, and the car keys dangled from one finger. Patsy's other arm cradled her two-month-old baby son. "Come on, Marissa," she called to her two-and-a-half-year-old. "It's time to go to the library. Let's get in the car."

But Marissa wasn't having anything to do with the idea. She stood miserably at the top of the porch steps with her arms stretched out toward her mother. "Up!" she insisted.

Patsy sighed with exasperation. "You can walk," she said encouragingly. "Come on, sweetie—Mommy's arms are full."

Marissa's small face crumpled. "Can't walk," she wailed, collapsing in a pitiful little heap. "Uuuuppp!"

Patsy sighed and her overloaded shoulders sagged. Was it wrong to ask Marissa to use her own two legs? Would she feel unloved if Patsy didn't pick her up?

Marissa wants to be carried but she does not *need* to be carried unless she is exhausted or ill. It is developmentally appropriate to carry an infant but less appropriate to carry a toddler. Understanding Marissa's need for healthy autonomy will help her mother decide when to carry her and when to allow her to struggle on her own.

Suppose you have a toddler who wants to be carried to the car. Instead of carrying her, you may stoop down, give her a hug (you may need to put a few things down first), and tell her you are sure she can walk to the car by herself. If she still whines to be carried, you might say, "I'll hold your hand and walk slowly, but I know you can do it." You might even add, "I really need your help. Will you carry my book?" Yes, it would be easier to just pick her up and carry her to the car. Helping children develop the confidence and life skills they need is not always easy or convenient. But who said parenting would be easy? It need not be so difficult, either. Successful parenting is often a matter of knowing what is effective and what is not. (For more on developmentally appropriate behavior, see Chapter 8.)

DISTRACTION AND CHOICES

Since it is normal and developmentally appropriate for toddlers to explore and want to touch, it is wise to provide them with areas where they can do so safely. In the kitchen, you might have a cupboard full of plastic containers, wooden spoons, lightweight pots and pans, and other items that can't hurt or be hurt by your child. In the living room, you can provide a box of special toys.

When your child wants to touch something that shouldn't be touched, such as a stereo, kindly and firmly pick her up and remove

The Triple A's of Autonomy

Attitude

1. Change your perception. Recognize your child's developmental abilities, then calm yourself before responding.
2. Recognize your child's limited understanding. "No" is an abstract concept and one that toddlers do not fully understand.
3. Accept that developmental timetables differ. Each child will develop in his own unique way.
4. Value the *process*, not only the *product*. Make time to enjoy getting there or doing something, instead of focusing only on the destination or outcome.

Atmosphere

1. Provide practice. Accept that skill practice can be messy. Support mastery by making tasks child-friendly with scaled-down implements and small, easy steps. Remember, your child is growing brain connections.
2. Encourage thinking. Involve your child in planning by asking "what" and "how" questions.
3. Allow appropriate power. Provide choices and reasonable chances to say no.
4. Avoid power struggles. Give a hug instead of engaging in "yes" and "no" shouting matches.

Action

1. Be kind *and* firm. Follow through by doing what you say you will do.
2. Teach by doing. Talk less, avoid lectures—act instead.
3. Show children what to do instead of what not to do. Again, avoid lectures and teach by modeling appropriate behavior.
4. Offer limited choices (all of which are acceptable). Avoid open-ended choices, such as "Do you want to go to bed?" with its potential answer, the unacceptable "no."
5. Use redirection and distraction—as many times as it takes.

her from that item and place her by the toy box. Don't slap or say "No!" Instead, tell her what she can do. "You can play with your toys. Look at the big truck. I'll bet you can make it move." This is called distraction, and you may have to do it over and over and over. Does this take time? Yes. Too many parents don't realize how much time they spend when they spank over and over, or say no over and over, or wrestle over the same table ornament daily. It is easier to put the expensive table ornament out of little Jamie's reach. When adults continue to repeat the same ineffective responses and then say that this child "never learns," they may need to wonder who the slow learner is. (Distraction, much more peaceful for both parent and child, will be discussed in more detail in Chapter 8.)

It is also important to realize that words alone will not be effective in managing your child's behavior—or keeping her safe. Rather than saying "No!" or "Don't touch that!" from across the room, get up and go to your child. Make eye contact, then use kind, firm *action* to move her away from forbidden or dangerous objects. Relying on words alone often teaches children that they can safely ignore you. After all, there's not much you can do from across the room.

Toddlers are interested in exploring so many things that it is not difficult to use distraction at this age. When a toddler wants to touch something that isn't appropriate, offer a substitute—or a choice of substitutes. "You can't jump on the couch. Would you like to play with your truck or help me wash the dishes?" "It is time for bed. Which story do you want me to read when you've put on your pajamas?" (Yes, toddlers can learn to put on their pajamas, with or without your help, depending on their age.) "I need to talk on the phone now. You can play in the junk drawer (prepared in advance with age-appropriate items) or the pan cupboard while I'm on the phone." One mom kept several activity baskets on top of her refrigerator. When she wanted to talk on the phone, she brought out a basket. Her daughter eagerly looked forward to a chance to play with her special toys. The baskets came down only during phone calls. With simple additions—such as a new ball, a different-sized block, or a puzzle—the baskets remained intriguing. Offering choices and using distraction are simple and respectful responses to a toddler's need for guidance.

UNCONSCIOUS LIFE DECISIONS

One thing children do not consciously understand and cannot verbalize is the unconscious decisions they are constantly making about themselves, about the world, about others, and about how they need to behave in the world to survive and thrive. They are making these decisions based on their interpretation of their life experiences, and these early decisions or "adaptations" become part of the wiring of each child's brain.

When you distract your child by removing her from what she can't touch and guide her to what she can touch, what will she decide? That it is okay to explore, to try new things, to learn about the world around her. Which lesson do you want to teach? Distraction does not damage her self-esteem or self-confidence the way spanking and shaming can. It does let her know that some things are acceptable to touch and some are unacceptable. Self-esteem begins here. The seeds are planted early.

I BLEW IT!

Sometimes parents feel guilty when they discover new information, especially when it seems to point out mistakes they may have made. You may be saying, "Oh my goodness! That's what I did! Have I ruined my children forever?" Absolutely not. As we say over and over, mistakes are wonderful opportunities to learn—for adults and for children.

Sometimes you will need to tell your child about your mistakes and start over. "Honey, I thought the best way to show you how much I love you was to do everything for you. Now I know that is not the best thing for you. It may be hard for both of us when I stop being a super-mom and help you learn how capable you are, but I have faith in both of us. We can do it!" And it's true. Don't waste any time on guilt. You will continue to make mistakes; so will your child. Isn't that exciting? If your child isn't talking yet, you can convey the same message through the energy of your attitude and confidence.

Understanding the importance of this developmental age can help parents learn the skills and provide the atmosphere (at least, most of the time) that encourage children to acquire important competency skills that will serve them all their lives. Parents can also interact with their children (most of the time) in ways that invite them to make healthy decisions about themselves, others, and the world. Notice we said "invite." We can never be sure how individuals will interpret their own life experiences and what they will decide about them. Notice, too, that we say "most of the time." None of us—parents or children—gets it right all the time. Teaching, loving, and acting respectfully most of the time really is enough.

A child may still feel frustrated and upset about not being allowed to touch whatever she wants. She may even have a temper tantrum. When supervised with firmness and kindness, however, she will

> ### Tools for Developing Healthy Autonomy
>
> - Provide security *and* opportunities to explore.
> - Remove dangerous objects and create safe boundaries, then let go and allow your child to investigate his world.
> - Use distraction, redirection, and kind, firm action to guide your toddler's behavior rather than slapping, spanking, or words alone.
> - Allow your toddler to run, climb, and develop healthy muscles in a safe space.
> - Recognize the difference between your child's *wants* and *needs*; you should always respond to his needs, but wants provide opportunities for him to learn character and life skills.
> - Teach skills *and* provide careful supervision.
> - Focus on connection, love, and relationship.

be left with a much different feeling from the feelings she would have when she is forced or punished.

Children who are encouraged to develop a sense of autonomy usually make healthier decisions later in life. Children who are not allowed to develop a sense of autonomy will more often make decisions based on doubt and shame.

LOVE AND ENJOYMENT

It always comes back to love and enjoyment, connection and relationship. Nothing is more important to the emotional development of your child. Understanding how important it is for a child to develop autonomy can help parents know that overprotection is not the best way to show love. Instead, they can have fun showing love by watching freedom and independence develop in their children and by enjoying the promise of confidence and courage in years to come.

8

UNDERSTANDING AGE-APPROPRIATE BEHAVIOR — AND HOW TO MANAGE IT

"Me do it!" This is the cry of the eager two-year-old who is trying to tell us, "I'm ready for big-time autonomy." A sense of autonomy is an important step on the developmental path toward confidence and capability—but it certainly creates challenges for parents.

Jeremy is almost three years old, and while his parents often laugh that he is a "handful," they delight in their son's curiosity and willingness to experiment with and experience the world around him. Jeremy's mother discovered him one bright morning making a cake in the kitchen; he had stirred milk, raisins, two eggs (with shells), cereal, and lots of flour in the largest bowl he could find. Jeremy's dad found him a few days later with a screwdriver and pliers, investigating the inner workings of the vacuum cleaner. Jeremy, his parents have decided, needs invitations to help in the kitchen, a set of his own small tools (and nonelectrical objects to experiment with)—and lots of supervision. Despite the occasional messes, they're happy to know that their son finds his world a fascinating and welcoming place.

Matthew is also nearly three years of age, but Matthew's world is a different sort of place from Jeremy's. Matthew is most comfortable in front of the television. New people and places frighten him, and he rarely speaks, although his parents often encourage him not to be "so shy." Matthew loves the computer and tried to help his dad with his work, but something happened to Dad's files and Dad got mad. Matthew would like to work in the garden with his mom, too, but after he dug a whole row of small holes for her to put plants in, she sighed the big sigh that Matthew hates and told him to go play in the house. It feels safer to Matthew not to have too many ideas, and when people raise their voices he hunches into a small ball. It will take some time and a lot of encouragement for Matthew to show his curiosity again.

AUTONOMY AND "DEVELOPMENTAL APPROPRIATENESS"

You may wonder why we talk so much about autonomy in a book on discipline. One of the most important concepts in parenting your young child is understanding "developmental appropriateness"—in other words, knowing the difference between intentional misbehavior and a child's inborn need to explore and grow. Two-year-olds like Jeremy and Matthew see the world as an exciting and fascinating place, especially as they develop more autonomy and a greater physical and intellectual capacity to explore. At the same time, however, they are often frustrated when adults get in their way or when they find they do not have the skills or abilities to accomplish what they want. Children may respond to these frustrations by withdrawing and adopting a sense of doubt about their ability to "conquer the world." Adults can help develop toddlers' confidence (and guide behavior) by providing a range of opportunities, time for training, and encouragement for the many things children *can* do so they have the opportunity to gain a sense of healthy autonomy.

IS THIS REALLY MISBEHAVIOR?

Parenting a toddler will be much less frustrating when parents respond to the intention *behind* the behavior. This is often more easily said than done, especially when you're face-to-face with a two-year-old in a temper. Still, the following concepts may help you work effectively with your child's development:

- "Defiance" looks (and feels) much different when you understand that a child is struggling to develop a sense of autonomy. Her perception of a situation is almost certainly very different from yours. Does this mean that it's okay for your two-year-old to shout "No!" in your face? No, but it may mean that you should calm yourself down and think before responding. (Such encounters usually go more smoothly when only one of you is having a tantrum.)

- It makes sense that a child doesn't listen to you when you understand that his developmental urges have a "louder voice." He doesn't intend to disobey or to forget what you've asked; your requests and instructions are simply overwhelmed by his own needs and developmental process.

- It makes sense to use kindness and firmness instead of punishment or useless lectures ("How many times do I have to tell you?") when you understand developmental appropriateness. The kindness shows love and respect for your child's needs and limitations and an understanding of brain development; the firmness provides structure, teaching, and safety.

Adults also may need a slight attitude adjustment. Parents are often disappointed or angry when their young children don't live up to their expectations. Two-year-olds are too little to do things perfectly. It is simpler and faster for you to do things for your child instead of taking the time and having the patience to help him do things (such as dressing) himself. But which is more important—ease and speed and perfection, or helping children develop confidence, perceptions of capability, and strong life skills?

Who ever said parenting was easy? Quick and efficient? Tidy? The truth about toddlers is that they are inconvenient and often messy. Too many parents want confident, courageous, cooperative, respectful, resourceful, responsible children, but they don't understand what children need in order to develop these characteristics. Discipline means

teaching—with lots and lots of patience until the brain develops and matures enough for your child to absorb what you are teaching.

With training, two-year-olds can dress themselves, pour their own cereal and milk, and help set the table. They can learn to help out at the grocery store, join in activities at church, or behave in other public places. Learning these kinds of skills is an important part of developing a sense of autonomy, but it takes time.

SKILLS ARE LEARNED, NOT INBORN

No one is born with the ability to eat with a spoon. There are no genetic codes that enable a child to ease her arms into narrow coat sleeves. Even child prodigies cannot carry a full cup of juice without losing a drop or two. Skills are learned, not inborn. When you understand that *all* skills require training and lots and lots of practice, you can begin to see your child as a competent learner with unlimited potential, instead of a clumsy little burden.

One of the most exciting insights of brain research tells us that brain connections strengthen with repetition. This applies directly to skill development. Young Isobel might not perfect the art of fitting her feet into her shoes on the first try. It requires regular repetition of this act to achieve proficiency. Her brain is mastering the skill by linking up new connections while she works persistently with her chubby fingers and squirmy toes. Research has taught us that knowledge and experience are inseparably entwined; each increases the other. When you teach your child to master tasks step-by-step and provide lots of opportunities to practice, you create a competent, confident child.

SKILLS VERSUS SPILLS

Life with two-year-olds gets messy. The process of learning skills means there are lots of opportunities to spill, drip, and dump. Think of a typical activity: pouring morning cereal and milk. Teaching a skill is easiest when you modify the task to help your little one experience success.

The cereal box is big and unwieldy; so is the milk container. But you can adjust both so that your child can practice autonomy and learn

Understanding Developmental Appropriateness

The following are parenting fantasies that thrive when parents lack understanding about developmental appropriateness. Do you recognize any of them?

1. Believing that your child should listen to you and do what you say.
2. Believing that your toddler understands when you say no and can learn to be obedient.
3. Hoping your child will be "good" because you are tired and don't want to be bothered.

The truth is . . .

1. Toddlers are too busy following their developmental blueprint to do what you say—most of the time.
2. "No" is an abstract concept that cannot be understood by toddlers in the way parents think they can understand.
3. Children are always "good," but they are not always obedient—especially during the development of autonomy.

new skills. Serve milk in a little pitcher or measuring cup, repackage cereal in small plastic containers, and place everything at a convenient height. Demonstrate pouring the cereal, then add the milk. At first, let your child hold her hands on yours (to get a feel for the task), then rest yours lightly on top of hers as she repeats the movements. Finally, stay nearby and encourage her efforts.

If there are spills (and there will be!), then you can anticipate the need for another skill: wiping up puddles. Teach your child how to use a sponge, or provide a rag or a mop nearby, one with a cutoff handle to make it child-sized. Celebrate as your child gradually masters these new skills.

GOING OUT IN PUBLIC

With time for training, children can learn to behave in those famous child-development observation laboratories: public places. Taking time for training can involve many strategies. Consider the following tools to help your child learn to behave in public places.

Plan Ahead—or Expect Resistance Ahead
Young children live in the present moment. And like many adults, they often find transitions and change difficult to deal with. A shift from playing with blocks in the living room to rolling along in a grocery basket takes considerable adjustment, and as we've learned, some children find it easier than others do.

When moving from one activity or location to another, planning ahead is critical. Remember that your young explorer may want to climb under the clothing racks, sneak a peek at the world from the top of the chair, and

Five Ways to Provide Skill Training for Your Child

1. Plan ahead—or expect resistance ahead.
2. Involve children in the planning process.
3. Offer limited choices.
4. Ask curiosity questions to encourage thinking.
5. Follow through with dignity and respect.

mount an expedition to discover what lies beyond the corner—any corner. Be sure you have taught the necessary skills *before* taking your toddler out in public—and carry along small toys and snacks to provide entertainment and nourishment.

Involve Children in the Planning Process
You might set the stage with something like this: "We are going to eat with Aunt Annie and Cousin Jamie at the restaurant. Before we get there, what will you do in the car?" (If a child is preverbal, use simple language to describe the event. If she is verbal, allow her to supply the answers as the planning proceeds.) Mention the car seat, buckling in, and playing with toys en route. You can explore the coming occasion with your child using simple questions and descriptions.

Invite your child to picture the setting or describe it for her: sitting in the chair, drawing with special crayons, and eating her lunch. What will she be allowed to order? Must she eat things she doesn't like? Bit by bit, the picture grows. Be sure to clarify expectations—and keep them realistic.

"Is it okay to throw your food? What about running around the restaurant? Should you grab the sugar container?" Do not get carried away with *don'ts:* focus more on *do's* and/or *choices.* "Food is for eating." "Do you want to sit at the table, or go sit in the car with me for a while?" Inconvenient? Yes. Good training? Yes. Kindness and firmness at the same time help children understand that you mean what you say and will follow through with action. Remember, "let's pretend" is often a painless, enjoyable way to establish limits and expectations.

Be sure your plans account for your child's individual temperament as well as the social situation. How long can she sit still during a meal? What activities are available? Will there be time to play with her cousins? Perhaps this outing would be better held at a fast-food joint than at an elegant restaurant. Remember, plan for success, and realize that your little one will need more than one practice session before she masters these skills.

Offer Limited Choices

You may have heard that "choices" are a great parenting tool for young children. And so they are—as long as you understand the ground rules. Choices can support a child's growing sense of autonomy, but they must be appropriate and clearly defined, and all the choices must be choices *you* can live with. For example, the following choices might cause problems:

- "Would you like to go to childcare today?" (This is the adult's responsibility and often isn't a choice but a necessity.)

- "What would you like to do today?" (The child needs some hints here. Are we talking coloring, baking cookies, watching television all day, or a trip to Disneyland?)

- "You may pick out any toy you want; you get to choose." (Does this include the $200 motorized kiddie car or a toy machine gun? Be sure you can keep the promises you make. It is usually wise to think carefully before speaking.)

Ask Curiosity Questions to Encourage Thinking

Children do not develop a strong sense of autonomy when parents and teachers spend too much time talking—telling children what happened, what caused it to happen, how they should feel about it, and what they should do about it. "Telling" may keep children from seeing mistakes as opportunities to learn, or send the discouraging message that children aren't living up to adult expectations. Lecturing often goes over children's heads, because they're not ready to understand the concepts adults are trying to establish—and they usually discover they can simply tune adults out (unintentional training in the art of not listening). Last but not least, telling children what, how, and why teaches them *what* to think, not *how* to think. Parents are often disappointed when their child doesn't develop more self-control, but they may not realize they are not using the kind of parenting skills that encourage self-control.

A powerful way to help children develop thinking skills, judgment skills, problem-solving skills, and autonomy is to ask them, "What happened? What were you trying to do? Why do you think this happened? How do you feel about it? How could you fix it? What else could you do if you don't want this to happen again?" (These skills depend on language—and language takes time to learn. You can and should talk with your child about these ideas, but her response will be limited for a while.)

When children are younger, they need more clues as part of the curiosity questions. For example, if a two-year-old gets stuck on her tricycle, she will be invited to think if you ask, "What do you think would happen if you got off and backed up?" This is very different from *telling* her to get off and back up. Even a question that contains clues invites thought and a decision.

Follow Through with Dignity and Respect

Again, we want to stress that permissiveness is not the way to help children develop autonomy. The best alternative to permissiveness is kind and firm follow-through.

What might follow-through look like in the restaurant meal described earlier? Mom might have explained in advance that if her daughter had trouble remembering how to behave in the restaurant, they would have to leave. Kind and firm follow-through means that if she misbehaves, Mom will take her out to wait in the car together while the others in the group finish their meal. It is not respectful (or helpful) to scold or spank while removing her. A parent can either say nothing or say firmly (but kindly), "I'm sorry you didn't feel like behaving in the restaurant today. You can try again next time."

Giving a child a chance to try again is reasonable and encouraging. It is not reasonable to say, "I'm never taking you out to eat again—or anywhere else, for that matter!" Not only is this statement unreasonable, most parents do not follow through on such threats. This does not demonstrate kindness or firmness, nor does it inspire trust.

Yes, it is inconvenient for you to miss your meal at the restaurant while using kind and firm follow-through. But you also have a choice. Which is more important, a restaurant meal or the self-esteem and confidence your child will develop by learning appropriate social skills? Action is far more effective than words with young children. When you follow through with kindness and firmness, your child will

Out of Control

Q. My two-and-a-half-year-old son is out of control! He doesn't respond to the words "Wait, please!" If I don't jump at his every command, he throws a fit or goes on like a broken record, repeating over and over again what he wants. Lately he has been totally out of control when we go out in public. He will kick, hit me, and scream at the top of his lungs to get what he wants. Last time it was because I told him we had to leave the jungle gym at the park. He didn't want to leave and made such a scene that everyone was watching. What do I do in this situation? I don't believe in hitting him, yet I don't appreciate being hit and humiliated like this, either.

A. Some people would call your toddler "spirited"; others might label him "strong-willed." Whatever you call him (and it is best to avoid labels), trying to control him will never work. There are three ways you can increase cooperation:

1. Your child does not understand "Wait, please!" in the way you think he does. This is an abstract concept that is in direct opposition to his developmental need to explore his world and his growing sense of autonomy. He should not be allowed to do anything he wants, however. Attempt to gain his cooperation in a kind and firm way instead of being controlling and/or punitive.

learn that you say what you mean and that you will do what you say, important elements of trust and respect.

SUPERVISION

Safety is an important consideration during the first years of life, and your job is to keep your child safe without letting your fears discourage her. For this reason, supervision is an important parenting tool for little ones, along with kindness and firmness while guiding and teach-

2. Instead of telling him what to do, find ways to involve him in the decision so he gets a sense of *appropriate* personal power and autonomy. For example:

   - Give him some warning. "We need to leave in a minute. What is the last thing you want to do on the jungle gym?"

   - Carry a small timer around with you. Let him help you set it to one or two minutes and keep it in his pocket so he can be ready to go when the timer goes off.

   - Give him a choice that requires his help. "Do you want to carry my purse to the car, or do you want to carry the keys? You decide."

   - Help him visualize the next activity. "What is the first thing we should do when we get home?"

3. If these don't work, you may need to take him by the hand and lead him to the car. Every time he resists, stop pulling and let your hand go in his direction until he stops resisting. Then pull toward the car again, giving slack every time he resists. This may look like a see-saw. When he catches on that you are going to be both kind and firm, he will eventually go with you. If not, you may need to pick him up and carry him to the car while ignoring his kicks and screams. The key is to avoid the "emotional hook" (that feeling parents get that they have to "win" or enforce their will)—it invites a power struggle every time.

ing your child. Even if you tell your child one hundred times not to go near the fireplace, you cannot expect him to have the maturity and judgment to stay away from the fireplace if you leave him alone in the room with a fire. This is just one example of the hundreds of things parents expect their children to "learn" from nagging and lectures. Children just don't understand cause and effect the way adults do. Save your breath and supervise.

Adults must be alert to danger, provide consistent and firm guidance, and be able to move very quickly. There is no substitute for alert supervision when you have a young child in your home, no matter how much teaching you've done.

DISTRACTION AND REDIRECTION

Redirection and distraction are among the most useful parenting tools for living with toddlers.

> *Thirteen-month-old Ellen was crawling rapidly toward the dog's dish—one of her favorite "toys"—when her dad spotted her. He called out her name firmly. Ellen paused and looked back over her shoulder. Her dad gathered her up and carried her across the room to where her barnyard set was waiting. "Here, sweetie," he said with a tickle, "see what the pigs and cows are up to."*
>
> *If Ellen chooses to head for the dog's dish again, her dad can intercept her and direct her toward a more acceptable object. Acting without lecturing or shaming avoids a power struggle and lets Ellen learn by experience that Dad won't let her play with the dish.*

What if Ellen keeps returning to the forbidden dish? How many times must a parent redirect a child's attention? Well, as many times as it takes. As we've mentioned before, it takes patience and perseverance to train a young child. If Ellen's dad yelled at her or spanked her, would she still want to play with the dish? Probably so—unless she absorbs doubt and shame earlier than most. Kindly but firmly directing Ellen toward acceptable objects, and continuing to do so until she gets the message, guides her behavior without punishing or shaming and without inviting a battle of wills.

After her parenting class on developmental appropriateness, Lisa reported to her classmates, "I sure do have a happier home since I stopped yelling at Melissa. The things she does that used to make me angry are now fascinating to me. I think she'll get an A in autonomy. I will also get an A in kind and firm distraction because I'm getting lots of practice!"

9

UNDERSTANDING THE LEARNING PROCESS FOR NURTURING SELF-RELIANCE AND CONFIDENCE

Rudolf Dreikers said, "Never do anything for a child that the child can do for himself." The reason: to help children develop a healthy sense of self-confidence and a belief in their capability through experience. It is developmentally appropriate to meet the needs of a crying infant by comforting and soothing him, but a crying toddler (or older child) will develop strong skills only if you help him learn to help himself instead of doing too much for him.

Glenda gives Casey a glass of milk with his lunch. He looks at the glass and scowls. "Don't want this glass," he announces.

Glenda sighs in exasperation; then she recognizes an opportunity to teach her small son. "If you want another glass," she says gently, "what do you need to do to get it?"

Casey isn't particularly interested in learning at the moment. "Can't reach it," he whines.

Glenda asks, "What would happen if you pushed the chair over to the cupboard? Then what could you do?"

This new prospect captures Casey's imagination. He stops whining and thinks about it. "Climb and reach it?" he says.

Glenda offers a choice. "Do you need my help pushing the chair over to the cupboard, or can you do it by yourself?"

With enthusiasm, Casey says, "I can do it!"

He pushes the chair over to the cupboard, gets the glass, climbs down, and takes the glass over to the table, looking very proud of himself. Casey pours his milk from the old glass into the new one, creating several puddles in the process.

Instead of becoming annoyed, Glenda recognizes more opportunities to teach. "What do you need to do now to clean up the milk you spilled?"

By now, Casey is feeling very capable. He jumps from the table, gets a sponge from under the sink, and cleans up the spilled milk. He leaves the sponge on the table.

Glenda continues, "Do you know what happens to milk when it is left in a sponge?"

Casey looks closely at the sponge but doesn't see anything happening. He is curious. "What?" he says.

Glenda explains, "It turns sour and smells very bad. You'll need to rinse out the sponge in the sink really well before you put it back under the sink."

Casey never turns down an opportunity to play with water. He happily moves the chair over to the sink, climbs up, and rinses out the sponge. His mother teaches him how to squeeze it thoroughly to get all the milk out.

After the sponge is rinsed, Casey moves the chair back to

the table and proudly sits down to drink his milk out of his special glass.

Time-consuming? Yes! Is it worth it? Absolutely. Through curiosity questions and choices, Casey has learned that his needs and desires are valid and that he is capable of taking care of them himself. It takes more than kind words to build self-esteem; it takes "competency experiences," moments when you and your child accept a challenge—and succeed. Casey's mother took the time to teach him the skills he needed to feel capable rather than encouraging whining or manipulation. This is kind and firm, developmentally appropriate discipline in action.

LIVING WITH—AND LEARNING FROM—MISTAKES

Parents and children are alike in one important respect: They never stop making mistakes. It doesn't matter how much we learn or how much we know. As human beings, we sometimes forget what we know and get hooked into emotional reactions. (You'll learn more about emotions and calming yourself and your toddler in Chapter 10.) Sometimes we just goof up. Once we accept this, we can see mistakes as the important life processes they are: interesting opportunities to learn.

Wouldn't it be wonderful if we could instill this attitude in our children so they wouldn't be burdened with all the baggage we carry about mistakes? Many children (and adults) short-circuit the lifelong process of developing a healthy sense of autonomy (and fail to develop the courage it requires to take risks and try new things) because they are afraid to make mistakes. Mistakes aren't the same as failures, although we often behave as though they are. Asking curiosity questions to help children learn from their mistakes will make a tremendous difference as they work their way through the learning process.

MAINTAINING DIGNITY AND RESPECT

There are two beliefs that most parents share—beliefs that must be changed before you can work effectively with young children. Do you recognize either of these beliefs?

- The belief that you can control toddlers and make them "mind."

- The belief that children are intentionally trying to defeat you.

Because infants and toddlers are small and adults can easily pick them up and move them around, you may be seduced into believing that you can control their behavior. Think about this for a moment, though: Can any of us truly control another person's behavior?

Feelings? Beliefs? It is often difficult enough for us to control our own! Instead of expecting to control young children, consider learning methods that invite cooperation. Abandoning the mistaken notion of control and working toward cooperation may save your dignity and sanity—and those of your child.

The cooperative child you envision living with five years from now is being shaped and encouraged each moment of every day. The toddler you swat and scold when she pulls books out of the bookcase is likely to become the six-year-old who refuses to do anything you ask—or the teenager who slips out the bedroom window after you've grounded her for a month. The toddler who is gently redirected to the pot-and-pan cupboard without punishment is learning to cooperate.

You will know that children aren't trying to defeat you when you understand developmental stages and age-appropriate behavior. An eighteen-month-old who heads for your new laptop computer has no intention of defying you. He sees something new, colorful, and interesting. He wants to touch and explore it. Previous experience may have taught him to glance at you as he reaches for it, but his wired-in need to explore is much stronger than your warnings. His behavior isn't defiance—it's curiosity. Once you realize this, it becomes far easier to respond without anger or punishment. Let's take another look at this as we explore every toddler's favorite word: "No!"

WHAT DOES YOUR TODDLER REALLY "KNOW" ABOUT "NO"?

Children under the age of three do not understand "no" in the way most parents think they do (and a full understanding of "no" doesn't occur magically when the child turns three or four; it is a developmental process). "No" is an abstract concept that is in direct opposition to the developmental need of young children to explore their world and to develop their sense of autonomy and initiative.

Oh, your child may "know" you don't want her to do something. She may even know she will get an angry reaction from you if she does it. But her behavior is not yet truly intentional. Knowing things as a toddler means something far different from knowing things as an adult. Her version of knowing lacks the internal controls necessary to halt her roving fingers. Researchers including Jean Piaget discovered long ago that toddlers lack the ability to understand cause and effect in the same way adults do (an excellent reason not to try to lecture and argue a toddler into doing what you want). In fact, higher-order thinking like understanding consequences and ethics may not develop until children are as old as ten.

AT ANOTHER LEVEL: THE "CHILD POWER" OF "NO"

Toddlers are learning to see themselves as separate, independent beings. They are finding out who they are separate from adults. (This "individuation process" escalates when they become teenagers.) It's a natural and healthy process, but one that is frequently trying for parents and teachers. It doesn't take long for a young child to learn the

Cognitive Development—and Why Children Don't Understand "No" the Way You Think They Should

· Take two balls of clay that are exactly the same size. Ask a three-year-old if they are the same. Then, right in front of her, smash one ball of clay. Then ask her if they are still the same. She will say no and will tell you which one she thinks is bigger. A five-year-old will tell you they are the same and can tell you why.

· Find four glasses: two glasses that are of the same size, one glass that is tall and thin, and one glass that is short and fat. Fill the two identical glasses with water and ask a three-year-old if they have the same amount. Then, right in front of her, pour the water from one into the short, fat glass, and the other one into the tall, thin glass. Then ask her if these still hold the same amount of water. Again, she will say no and will tell you which glass she thinks contains the most water. A five-year-old will tell you they contain the same amount and can tell you why.

Both of these examples demonstrate thinking abilities identified by Piaget. When you understand that perceiving, interpreting, and comprehending an event are different for young children, your expectations will change.

power of the word "no" or that by using it he can provoke all sorts of interesting reactions. Adults can't always avoid these confrontations, but changing your own behavior and expectations can lessen their impact. There are actually three types of "no": the ones you can avoid saying, the ones you can avoid hearing, and the ones that you just learn to live with.

HOW NOT TO SAY NO

"Sometimes I listen to myself talking to my two-year-old," one mom confided to a group of friends, "and all I hear myself saying is 'no' and 'don't.' I sound so negative, but I don't know what else to do." There are actually a number of ways adults can avoid saying "no" themselves.

- Say what you *do* want. Emma, who is three years old, is delightedly throwing blocks across the room. Her teacher walks in and immediately says, "No throwing blocks!" Now Emma hears what not to do, but she may have a hard time figuring out what she *can* do. It might be more effective if her teacher says, "Blocks are for using on the floor" or "You look as though you want to do some throwing. Would you like me to help you find a toy you can throw?" The next time you start to tell your child no, ask yourself what you want to have happen. Then tell your child what you want.

- Say "yes" instead. Many parents are programmed to respond with an automatic no. When you are about to say no, try asking yourself, "Why not?" Take a look at eighteen-month-old Cindy. She is playing in the kitchen sink, splashing water everywhere, and having a wonderful time. When Mom enters the room, her first response is to grab Cindy and say, "Stop that!"

  But why? Cindy's eyes are sparkling; she is absorbed in the feel of the water and the magic of the droplets flying around. Her clothes can be changed, and she'll probably think it's a terrific game to help Mom mop the floor afterward. In other words, there may be no reason to say no this time. Mom and Cindy may be better off if they forget the "no" and simply enjoy themselves.

- Try distraction and redirection. Act firmly, and calmly remove a child from the forbidden item. Refocus attention: "Let's see how many birds are at the bird feeder this morning."

- Offer limited choices. When your toddler demands a different cup for his juice, hold up the cup you gave him or offer to put the juice away until later. (Remember, toddlers may use their whole bodies to object, as in a tantrum. Just because little Jessica throws a tantrum doesn't mean that your handling of the situation was inappropriate. Tantrums happen.) Next time, try offering a choice of two cups before pouring the juice.

WHEN YOU MUST SAY "NO"

Where do children learn the word "no"? Obviously, from hearing their parents and caregivers say it so often. It is important to say no to children only when necessary during the first three years of their lives. If you say no too frequently, you may be hampering normal development.

We do not mean to imply that a parent should never say no, but you must always *teach* before comprehension occurs. That is part of the learning process. For example, we talk to children before they comprehend words, we remove them from things they can't do before they comprehend why, we hug and cuddle before they are able to hug back.

Real understanding—the ability to use a skill without consciously thinking about it—takes time. Providing kind and firm discipline and teaching developmentally appropriate boundaries is the goal, but we will make many mistakes along the way. Because infants and toddlers do not always comprehend, saying no is effective only when used with other methods.

TEACH WITH YOUR ACTIONS

With children from birth to age three, it is best to say no with actions instead of words. As Rudolf Dreikurs used to say, "Shut your mouth and act."

> *Little Nina was curious and very social. When Nina was only nine months old, her mother, Cynthia, often got frustrated while nursing her because Nina would insist on turning toward music on television and always wanted to watch the cat saunter past, seldom remembering to let go of Mom when she did so. Ouch! Instead of bawling Nina out, which would have been upsetting and counterproductive, Cynthia took action. She wanted to support Nina's curiosity but for her own safety she made sure to always nurse Nina in a quiet corner where interruptions could be kept to a minimum.*

When two-and-a-half-year-old Michael started a temper tantrum in the supermarket, his mother picked him up and took him to the car. She calmly held him on her lap until he stopped screaming and writhing. They then went into the store and tried again. They made three trips to the car that day. The next time they went to the supermarket, they made only one trip to the car. The third time, Michael stopped crying as soon as his mother picked him up and headed for the car.

Tanya and her dad went for a walk. Every time two-year-old Tanya started for the street, her father would quickly clasp her hand in his own. She would squirm, resist, and try to pull away. Dad held on. After a moment, she would continue, holding hands with Dad. He would let go after a few moments, only to repeat his action if she again headed for the street. Tanya soon stopped running into the street. One reason Dad's strategy was effective was that he did not say a word. (We don't know why words seem to invite a power struggle from toddlers—but they do!) Actions speak louder than words, and are much more effective when applied kindly and firmly.

It was easier for these parents to act kindly and firmly because they understood developmental and age appropriateness. Were they embarrassed when the other shoppers stared at them or suggested that their child "needed a good spanking"? Perhaps. They also knew that it is a parent's

A Hugging No

We saw a delightful cartoon that depicted a mother shouting "No!" to her toddler. The child shouted back, "Yes!" The mother shouted louder, "No!" The child screamed, "Yes!" Then the mother remembered the importance of being kind and firm at the same time. She knelt down, gave her child a hug and softly said, "No." The little boy said, "Okay." In the last frame the little boy is sitting on a curb saying, "A hugging no isn't fair." Actually, it is both fair and effective.

Saying no is fine when you are aware of what your child does and does not understand. The frustration occurs when parents think the word "no" by itself is enough to create obedience.

job to provide constant supervision at this age and to redirect misbehavior through kind and firm action. Parenting requires both patience and courage, and raising active, curious, energetic toddlers merits a medal of special honor. It is an awesome task.

Instead of expecting your child to comprehend and "mind" when you say no, follow through with action. You might say "No biting" while gently cupping your hand over the child's mouth and removing her from biting range. You might say "No hitting" while removing him and showing him what he can do, "Touch nicely." The "no" may be more for your benefit than the child's—it helps you create the energy you need for kind and firm action.

THE "NO" YOU WANT CHILDREN TO SAY

Believe it or not, children need to learn to say no. Saying no is a valuable life skill. Toddlers will one day grow into teenagers who will be faced with offers of drugs, alcohol, and other dangerous options. When these choices loom, you undoubtedly want your young adult to say no. Right now, when his entire vocabulary seems to consist of only that word, you may not be so thrilled.

Give children chances to say no in appropriate ways. "Do you want some juice?" A "no" response to juice is perfectly acceptable. Or you might ask, "May Auntie give you a hug before she leaves?" Because children need to have some control over their bodies, the answer of "no" ought to be an option, one that hopefully Auntie can accept without offense.

DEVELOPMENTAL CLOCKS MAY VARY

Each human being is a work of art. Look at the variety we see in appearance alone: skin color, hair color and texture, shape of the nose, color of the eyes, height, weight, shape—each one of us is unique. And physical characteristics are only the beginning of our uniqueness. Temperament, as we have discovered, is as individual as a fingerprint. So is the rate at which we develop and grow.

Very few things in the world of parenting come in only black or white. This book is all about choices and possibilities. Understanding your child's individual progress—her development of trust, autonomy, and initiative, her temperament, her physical development—will help you make the best choices for her and for you. Let's take a look at one way developmental stages influence your child's perceptions and behavior.

PROCESS VERSUS PRODUCT

It's a busy Friday evening, and you're off on a quick trip to the grocery store with your toddler. You have a definite goal in mind, namely to grab the necessary ingredients for dinner in time to get home, prepare and eat it, and still be on time for your older son's soccer game. For you, going to the store means obtaining the desired product. For your toddler, however, the product just isn't the point. Children are firmly rooted in the here and now; they think and experience life differently from the way adults do. A trip to the store is all about the process— the smells, the colors, the feelings, the experience. Being sandwiched into a busy schedule just doesn't allow time to enjoy the process!

Children do not share our goal-oriented expectations. It isn't always possible to go along with a child's relaxed approach, either. Sometimes you really will need to run in, grab the chicken, and run home again. But being aware of your child's tendency to focus on process rather than product can help you provide a balance. There may be times when you can take a leisurely browse through the store, enjoying the flowers in the floral department and the magazines in the rack or smelling the fragrant peaches and naming colors together. Children are miniature Zen masters, able to focus on the moment and enjoy it—an ability many adults would do well to remember.

When you must hurry, take time to explain to your child why you have to shop quickly this time. You can explain that you want him to hold your hand and that you will have to walk past the toys and other interesting things. You can offer to let him help you find the chicken and carry it to the checkout stand. Then you will walk back to the car and drive home. Helping a child understand clearly what is expected and what will happen makes it more likely he will cooperate with you.

LEARNING THROUGH EXPERIENCE

Remember that the world is a brand-new place for young children. At one preschool, a two-year-old pulled his mittens off to scoop up handfuls of snow. After a minute or two, he came to his teacher in tears. His hands hurt! He had no idea that his hands hurt because they were cold, or that the sensation had anything to do with the exciting white stuff covering the playground. Snow was rare in this child's town and he had never seen it before. The teacher warmed his hands, replaced his mittens, and showed him how much better his hands felt when they weren't touching the snow directly. He gained new information, added another life experience to his small portion, and was careful to keep his mittens in place the rest of the morning.

THE JOY OF UNDERSTANDING YOUR CHILD

Parents often say in their more frazzled moments, "I can hardly wait until my child is two—or three, or ten, or twenty-one." Remaining patient, kind, and firm requires effort and energy that may be in short supply sometimes. But you cannot turn the clock ahead, and when you take time to enjoy your child, you won't want to. You and your young child are in the here and now of his personal developmental timeline. There are important lessons to be learned and tasks to be accomplished—and there are no shortcuts.

Parenting can bring more joy than frustration when you understand developmental and age-appropriate behavior and know effective parenting skills.

10

THE DEVELOPMENT OF EMOTIONAL SKILLS AND LANGUAGE

Have you ever watched a parent cradle an infant, gaze down into his face, and coo words of love? What does it all mean to the baby? He can't understand the words; how does he learn to recognize the feelings? How do feelings and vague impressions grow into words, thoughts, and real communication?

EMOTIONS AND CONNECTION

Babies generally do not begin to understand the meanings of words until they are six or seven months of age. Long before that time, however, a baby will turn toward a familiar voice, smile into a parent's face, or reach with delight for favorite people. A bond of love and trust obviously exists, but how has an infant learned to respond to connection and familiar faces with pleasure?

Babies and very young children read nonverbal cues, facial expressions, and emotional energy to learn about the world of relationships. An infant does not understand all the complex meanings and concepts contained in the word "love," but she does learn to interpret the world around her. Sadly, in some families there is little connection, security, or trust. In most, however, a baby experiences contingent communication, adults who hear and respond to her cries and other signals for attention. She senses that the hands that touch her are gentle and caressing and the voice that speaks to her is warm and soft. Mom or Dad looks into her eyes and holds her attention (until she looks away as part of her innate ability to "self-soothe" from all the excitement). She feels the gentle rain of kisses that tickle her feathery hair. She recognizes familiar smells that communicate the approach of special people, and she senses the environment of caring that supports her in her new life. These sensations convey a feeling of "love" to a young child, and she responds with similar feelings and behavior.

The early weeks and months of life represent a critical period in which a child bonds with the adults who love her; as we learned in Chapter 4, her brain is growing (and discarding) connections throughout the first years of life, and the interactions this infant has with the world around her are shaping the way she will grow and develop. Isn't it wonderful that the things we instinctively long to do with babies—touch, tickle, smile, love—are the very things that nurture health and happiness?

CHILDREN ABSORB THE ENERGY OF FEELINGS

The nonverbal signals you send your child are far more powerful than your words. Young children are acutely sensitive to nonverbal communication. Infants "tune in" to human faces and seek connection with the adults around them. When Mom sits down to nurse feeling annoyed, tired, or cranky, her baby squirms, fusses, and won't settle into nursing. A baby as young as a few weeks of age can sense the tension in her mother's body, feel the rigid muscles in her arms, and hear the thumping of her heart as she lies close to her mother's chest.

Marta enjoyed quiet mornings and afternoons with her three-week-old baby, Julian. Her husband was at work, and the older children were in school. Julian slept much of the time. During his waking moments, after being fed and diapered, he seemed content in his infant seat, watching his mother move about the kitchen. Marta was certain those brief smiles were not gas.

Every day, however, around four o'clock in the afternoon, Julian would start to fuss. Holding and cuddling did not seem to comfort him. Could it be that the baby sensed the stress his mother was feeling about getting dinner on the table and taking care of the older children when they came home from school? This seemed to be a reasonable explanation, because the baby would calm down as soon as the busy evening had passed and Marta was able to relax.

CREATE A CALM ATMOSPHERE

It is both wonderful and a bit unsettling to have an infant or very young child around the house. Because little ones are so directly attuned to the emotional state of their parents, it is helpful (if not always possible) when you can relax, stay calm, and find ways to build a loving, trusting connection with your child. Your family won't suffer if you have simple dinners while adjusting to a new baby (and helping him adjust to you). A calm atmosphere is much more pleasant—and much healthier—for everyone. You can be more sensitive to your baby's moods and needs when you slow down and take time to read the energy of all the members of your family.

After a tiring day at work, Sucheta made her daily trek to the childcare center to pick up her infant son, Rafael. She hurriedly

Is My Child Okay?

Pediatricians have learned that parents are often the best judge of a child's development. Because early intervention is essential in the treatment of many developmental delays and disorders, your instincts—and concerns—about your child are always worth paying attention to. The incidence of autism and autism-related disorders has risen dramatically in recent years, now occurring in approximately one out of every 500 births. While only a trained specialist can diagnose autism, the following questions may help you decide if your child needs help:

- Does your child recognize and respond to familiar faces?
- Does he use his finger to point or show you something?
- Does your child turn his head toward you when you say his name?
- Does he imitate your actions, gestures, and facial expressions?
- Does he make eye contact with you?
- Is your child interested in other children, people, or objects?
- Does he respond to your smiles, cuddles, and gestures?
- Does your child try to attract your attention to his own activities?

If you've answered yes to a good number of the above questions, you probably have nothing to worry about. If you answered no to many of them, if your child rocks, bounces, spends long periods of time staring into space, or if he is unusually insistent on routines, predictability, or specific objects, you might think about talking to a doctor. Only a specialist can accurately diagnose autism or other developmental delays, and "symptoms" do not necessarily indicate a problem. Early intervention is critical, however; if you suspect that your child is not developing on schedule, do not hesitate to talk to your pediatrician.

gathered up the baby and his various belongings, rushed through traffic, and, once home, settled Rafael into his high chair with a snack. She immediately set about fixing dinner. This was the worst hour of the day for mother and son. Rafael fussed, squirmed, and pushed his crackers onto the floor. Sucheta cut herself as she tried to slice the vegetables, spilled too much spice into the recipe, and was not even hungry by the time her husband walked through the door. All she felt was exhaustion and frustration.

Sucheta's husband, Carlos, felt pretty miserable himself, coming home to a squalling baby, undercooked or overcooked meals, and a wife who spent the evening complaining. Watching her husband crush the crackers into the floor when he went over to hug Rafael didn't help Sucheta's mood.

One evening, Carlos pushed aside his plate of overseasoned vegetables. He gazed across the table at his weary wife and began to discuss their miserable evening routine. An understanding smile on his face, he assured Sucheta that he would be glad to make sandwiches for both of them if he could come home to a more relaxed wife and child.

Sucheta felt very relieved. She admitted that she felt overwhelmed preparing the elaborate meals they both had enjoyed before Rafael's birth. The next evening, when Sucheta entered the house with Rafael in tow, she put down all the bags, papers, and toys she had carried in with her. She gave Rafael a big hug and snuggled with him in the rocking chair, where they spent the next half hour playing tickling games, cooing and smiling at each other. When Carlos walked through the door, he found Rafael giggling as Sucheta nibbled his toes. Rafael shrieked with laughter as his dad joined in the fun. A short while later, a relaxed family enjoyed sandwiches washed down with hot cups of canned soup. Food hadn't tasted this good in far too long.

Rafael and Sucheta needed time to reconnect each day far more than anyone in the family needed gourmet cooking. By slowing down and allowing time to make the transition from the hectic daily routine to their family time at home, Sucheta was able to tune in to Rafael's needs—and to her husband's. The entire family thrived as the energy in their home improved.

TANTRUMS: EMOTIONAL MELTDOWNS

Everyone has feelings. In fact, researchers tell us that emotion (not logic or reason) is the energy that runs the human brain. Still, emotions are not mysterious forces that take over and cause difficult or embarrassing behavior. Emotions are simply information and are intended to help each of us make decisions about what we need to stay healthy and safe. There's no denying, however, that strong emotions can be challenging—especially when children are around. Like it or not, all young children have tantrums from time to time. Understanding why tantrums happen—and knowing how to deal with them—can help you remain calm and composed in the midst of even the most severe emotional storm.

The Kitagawa family walked through the shopping mall together. Two-year-old Nicholas was holding the last bite of his cookie in one hand and a new box of crayons in the other when he spied a display of stuffed Easter bunnies in a store window. He darted off, pointing to the display and dropping the crayons in his haste. Mom and Dad followed him to the store window, retrieving the spilled crayons. They admired the bunnies together. Not surprisingly, Nicholas wanted one. "Nicky's bunny!" he said, pointing to a particularly jolly blue specimen. His parents agreed that the bunnies looked lovely and suggested that perhaps another day he might get one. Nicholas wasn't satisfied with this answer and fell to the floor, a writhing mass of pumping legs and pounding fists, wailing with a noisy sincerity that would have impressed any passing Hollywood producers. Mom glanced around in embarrassment while her husband stood over young Nick, telling him to get up right now! Nick landed a random kick on Dad's knee. Dad's voice got louder than Nick's. Mom, meanwhile, wished she had a bag to put over her head. Surely, everyone was watching and thinking what horrible parents they were.

In fact, Nick's parents aren't horrible at all—and neither is Nick. They were sailing along pretty smoothly until the bunnies intervened. Nick's parents tried to respond to him in ways that did not invite a power struggle; they had given him one special treat already, and they responded to his demands calmly. So why did Nick throw a tantrum? Is he a spoiled brat? Does he "just need a good spanking"? No. The most likely answer is that Nick threw a tantrum "just because"—he wants what he wants and he wants it now. He has no concept of *reasonable, practical,* or *delayed gratification.* "Delayed what?" he might ask, if he could even conceive of such a question.

Tantrums are loud, highly visible, and embarrassing (at least, to adults). They are also quite normal. Young children have all the feelings adults have. They feel sad, happy, and frustrated, but they lack both the words for those feelings and the skills (and impulse control) to cope with them. In fact, the part of the brain that is responsible for emotional regulation and self-calming (the prefrontal cortex) is not completely grown until a person is twenty to twenty-five years old. Until that time, a child's ability to recognize and manage his emotions is sketchy at best. If you think about how hard it can be to control your own feelings, you may not be surprised that your toddler will rarely be successful at it.

Once adults understand why children's overloaded senses sometimes flash into tantrums, they can quit feeling responsible for them. Sometimes, no matter what you say or do, your child will get overwhelmed and throw tantrums. Adults can learn not to add to the chaos. It is unfortunate (but all too human) that Nick's dad got into the act by throwing a tantrum of his own. Nick's tantrum will pass quickly but it may take his parents—now carrying their howling son to the car—longer to recover their equilibrium.

Giving In Is Not the Answer
You may be wondering, "Okay, then what am I supposed to do when confronted with a temper tantrum—especially in public?" Giving in

may stop the temper tantrum for the moment, but it has some negative long-term effects.

What do you think your child is learning and deciding when he has a temper tantrum and you give in? Our guess is that he has just learned a negative life skill: do whatever it takes to get people to let you have your way. He may be deciding, "I'm loved when people give me whatever I want."

Instead, follow Dreikurs's advice to "shut your mouth and act," remembering that what you do isn't as important as the attitude *behind* what you do. You might pick up your screaming child and carry him to the car. Do this with a calm, kind, and firm manner. Allow him to have his feelings. He will learn (eventually) that he can survive disappointment—a very good life skill. There are three reasons to avoid words:

1. He can't hear them anyway.
2. Often, words are like throwing fuel on the flames.
3. Silence reminds you to stay calm.

If he does calm down enough to be able to hear your words, avoid scolding. Simply validate his feelings. We know we have said this before, and will say it again. Validating feelings softens the disappointment blow. It is soothing to feel the energy of words such as "I can see that you are really angry." This may be a step toward self-calming.

THE IMPORTANCE OF SELF-CALMING

Brain researchers tell us that when we "lose it" (and all parents do from time to time), the prefrontal cortex effectively "disconnects," leaving us with input from only the parts of the brain responsible for emotion and physical sensation. And because all humans have mirror neurons, when one person becomes highly emotional, those nearby are likely to do the same. Anger and tantrums are contagious—and no parent does his or her best work when angry.

The first step in dealing with a tantrum (either your own or your child's) is to calm down. A quick solution is to breathe deeply and count to ten. Researchers tell us that focused, calm breathing helps the brain "integrate"—that is, the brain reconnects, and the ability to think clearly and look for real solutions is restored. The most important step in dealing with tantrums and emotional meltdowns is to take time to cool off, and to help your child do the same. And he *does* need your help: Emotional regulation is a skill that will take him years to master. Allowing him to have his feelings without trying to talk him out of them or rescuing him is a good beginning.

WEATHERING THE STORM: WHAT TO DO DURING (AND AFTER) A TANTRUM

What can parents and caregivers do to help a child through a tantrum? Here are some suggestions:

- Calm yourself down first. You will respond to your child's intense emotions more effectively when you are calm. Take a moment to breathe deeply. If necessary, be sure your child is safe and then walk away for a few seconds to gather your own resources. Do your best to remain kind and firm.

- Provide safety and damage control. While tantrums may be part of living with young children, damage and injury need not be. It may be wise to move a child to a safer location or, if you are in a public place, to a more private corner. Without yelling or lecturing, calmly move out of your child's reach any objects that may be thrown or damaged.

- Do not try to "fix" a tantrum or coax a child with rewards. Offering to give a child a disputed item teaches him that tantrums are a good tool for getting his way. Remember that tantrums are

Positive Time-Out for Young Children

Positive time-out was discussed in Chapter 1. Since this is a popular parenting method that is usually misused, we will review effective uses of positive time-out. Young children lack the ability to recognize and manage their emotions, and punishing them for this inability isn't fair or helpful. But sometimes children need time to cool off; if your child is older than three and a half, you can use *positive* time-out as one way to teach her to calm down when she is angry or unhappy.

Here's what to do:

- Recognize that positive time-out is *not* punishment. (Punishment is not an effective teaching tool.) Positive time-out is intended to provide a place for your child to calm down so that, eventually, she can respond with more appropriate behavior.

- Involve your child in creating a safe place for positive time-out. (If your child isn't old enough to help create a positive time-out area, she is too young to benefit from it.) Ask your child what kinds of things help her feel better. She might want stuffed animals, books, a blanket, or quiet toys. Then let your child give the spot a name, such as the "feel-good place," the "happy place," or the "cool-off spot." (One three-year-old decided to call her positive time-out place "Bob." Her parents have no idea why, but it was fun for them to ask, "Would it help you to go see Bob?")

- When your child loses control, recognize her feelings ("You're really angry at me right now.") and ask if it would help her to visit her "cool-off spot." (If she isn't old enough to choose it,

normal but giving in to demands for toys or special service will only earn you more tantrums. Remain kind, calm, and firm, and let the storm blow over.

- Don't get hooked by your child's behavior. Tantrums are rarely as personal as they seem. Remember that your child is not being malicious or "bad" and lacks the ability to fully control his emotions. If you are at home and your child is safe, you may want to go into the next room or pick up a book to look at. This sends the message that you aren't angry but neither will you let yourself be manipulated by kicking and screaming.

don't force her to use it.) If your child is too upset to think rationally and says "no," ask if she would like for you to go with her. (Why not? You probably need it just as much.) If she still says "no," say, "Okay. I think I'll go."

- Offer two choices. Ask, "What would help you the most? To sit on my lap, or to go to your 'special place'?" If she refuses to choose, say, "Okay. I'll be in my bedroom. Come get me when you are ready to make a choice." If she follows you into the bedroom, still crying, get into the shower and let her have her feelings until she calms down.

- When she is calm, repair any damage and talk together about ways to solve the problem. Real problem-solving and learning can happen only when everyone is calm and feels safe.

- Teach valuable life skills. When positive time-out is used in this way, it teaches children to participate in creating a plan for dealing with future upsets, and that they have a choice regarding what is most helpful for them during times of upset. Eventually they will learn the value of calming down before acting and that mistakes are opportunities to learn.

If your child is younger than three and a half, focus on soothing her before dealing with problems. Gentle touch, rhythmic breathing, or soft music may help her regain control. It is also okay to simply allow her to have her feelings until they dissipate without trying to change them or fix them. You can sit nearby and send out loving energy without interfering. Remember, the goal is to help her calm down, not to punish her or make her "think about what she did."

After the Tantrum, Try the Following:

- Allow emotions to settle. Allow your child a quiet moment to cool down and catch his breath. Talk quietly about what happened and reassure your child that while his behavior may have been inappropriate, you love him very much.

- Offer support. Children may need a hug after such a powerful emotional storm. Tears and sniffles often follow tantrums as the child clears out the overload of emotions. A wordless, comforting hug may help both of you feel better.

- Help your child make amends. When everyone has calmed down, any damage should be addressed. Thrown items can be picked up, torn papers gathered and discarded, or pillows stacked back on the bed or sofa. Adults may offer to help a child with these tasks. It may also be appropriate to help your child repair additional damage, such as a broken toy. Recognize your child's abilities and development and don't expect things she can't do, but allowing her to squeeze some glue, run the DustBuster, or put tape on a torn book may help her feel a sense of self-control again and give her a very real way to learn about making things right.

- Forgive and forget—and plan ahead. Once the tantrum is over and the mess has been cleaned up, let it go. Concentrate on building relationship and trust and, if you can, on recognizing what led up to the tantrum. Prevention is often the best way of dealing with children's emotional outbursts. Tantrums may happen when children have missed naps or meals, are in unfamiliar surroundings, or are coping with stressed-out adults. Understanding your child's temperament and daily rhythms will help you both avoid many of these outbursts.

BABY-SIZED OVERLOAD

Q. I know this sounds unbelievable (at least it does to me), but my eleven-month-old daughter screams and kicks like she's having a tantrum. I walk away and let her scream because I don't want to reinforce the negative behavior. She only screams a little while, mostly when she's going to bed. Is there anything else I should be doing to discourage this behavior? Is this normal behavior for an eleven-month-old?

A. What you describe sounds like a child who is just feeling overwhelmed. Young children do not have the ability to regulate their emotions. Crying is a way for them to release tension, which is a normal part of everyday life. A tired baby actually might just want to be left alone to calm down.

Raul and Carlota's attempts to soothe their youngest daughter with walking, singing, and stroking only made her cry harder. When they would finally lay her down, she seemed relieved. She would cry a minute or two, then relax and fall asleep. Their well-meaning stimulation actually prolonged her distress; what she really wanted was alone time.

Remember, crying is communication for infants, *not* misbehavior. Each parent must learn to interpret the message her child is sending. Crying does not always mean the same thing; it is not reinforcing negative behavior to respond to a baby's cries. In fact, parents must respond so they can learn what the crying means.

WHAT ABOUT HEAD BANGING?

Q. I have three girls, ages five, three, and two. I am wondering how I can stop my two-year-old from having temper tantrums. I've already tried ignoring them. If she doesn't get what she wants, she falls to the floor and begins to bang her head, sometimes very hard. I don't know what to do. Please help.

A. Tantrums, head banging, holding one's breath—all are common in young children who aren't getting their way. All are very upsetting to concerned parents. Sometimes these behaviors are the means by which a child vents her frustration. Your two-year-old may also have discovered that these behaviors "work"—in other words, they get her something she believes she needs: the object of her demands, or your attention and involvement. Two-year-olds usually want autonomy and the right to make their own choices, even when they lack the skills to do so appropriately.

If you're worried that your daughter may bruise herself by banging her head on something hard, pick her up and without saying anything move her to a softer spot (the carpet, her bed, a pillow). You might try saying, "I'd like to work on this with you, but we can't talk when you're so upset." Then let her know you are available when she's calmed down. Make sure she's in a safe place and take some deep breaths to calm yourself. It will take time, but if you're kind and firm, she'll get the message that you can't be manipulated by tantrums, tears, and threats.

ACTIVE LISTENING: GIVING NAMES TO FEELINGS

Children constantly send nonverbal messages. Their facial expressions, gestures, and behavior provide clues to perceptive adults about what they're feeling. An eighteen-month-old child cannot tell you, "I'm feeling tired, confused, and a bit frustrated because I can't reach the cookie jar"; he doesn't have the words to express such a complicated sequence of thoughts and feelings. What you might hear are wails and shrieks accompanied by a toy thrown to the ground, a crumpled-up face, and a small body collapsing on the floor.

A parent may feel understandable frustration of her own and may express that frustration with harsh words. Or she can choose to help her child understand his feelings, give them a label that will help him to identify them in the future, and open the door to a way of dealing with the situation at hand.

Mom might respond like this: "I can see that you feel frustrated because you can't reach the cookie jar. I feel frustrated when I can't do something, too. I'll bet we can figure out a way to solve this problem. What do you think?"

Once a child's feelings are named, validated, and understood, he usually feels better and is more willing to work on solutions. In this instance, Mom helped her son figure out that he could push a chair over to the counter so he could reach the cookie jar. They also decided to fill the cookie jar with healthy snacks, such as crackers or raisins, so he could help himself anytime.

Remember, your child was not born with an emotional vocabulary. He cannot identify feelings with words and may not understand exactly what they are. Active listening—the art of noticing a child's feelings and identifying them calmly and clearly with words—is an important step in teaching your child to manage both his emotions and, eventually, his behavior. Even when your child is too young to understand the words themselves, you will be offering clues to the often confusing world of feelings. The day will come when he begins to connect his own emotions with the words you offer and no longer needs to "act out"—at least, not as often.

GENDER AND EMOTIONAL LITERACY

There are a number of significant differences between boys and girls during the first few years of life, especially where emotions are concerned. Girls often acquire social, language, and emotional skills sooner than boys do; boys often are more easily upset (and harder to soothe) than girls. In addition, our culture sends boys messages about emotional expression that may make it more difficult for them to identify and manage their own feelings.

Numerous researchers—such as William Pollack, Dan Kindlon, and Michael Thompson—have noted that while little girls are expected to cry, giggle, and express their feelings, adults and peers (intentionally or unintentionally) may give little boys the message that openly expressing emotions such as sadness, fear, or loneliness is "weak." In addition, research has shown that parents talk more often to daughters than to sons about feelings (in fact, parents talk more to girls overall, using more words per day than they speak to boys). It shouldn't be surprising that little boys sometimes develop the belief that having feelings is "wrong."

Interestingly, while there are indeed gender-based differences in the human brain, emotional sensitivity is not among them. Boys have exactly the same feelings that girls do, and the same need to learn emotional awareness and regulation skills. Kindlon and Thompson call this "emotional literacy" and believe that an inability to identify and express emotions may be one reason why boys are at greater risk during adolescence for depression, drug and alcohol abuse, dropping out of school,

and suicide, and for the frequency of anger in both adolescent boys and adult men.

Cuddling, touching, and talking about feelings will not make your son "weak"—it *will* help your son become a healthy young man. Practice active listening with both boys and girls; use lots of "feeling words" in conversation. As your child grows up, you will find ways to teach him to understand what he feels—and to choose behavior that is respectful and appropriate. For more information, see *Raising Cain: Protecting the Emotional Life of Boys,* by Dan Kindlon and Michael Thompson (New York: Ballantine, 2000).

DEALING WITH ANGER AND DEFIANCE

There is, perhaps, no emotion that causes more parental concern than a child's anger. Young children express anger in ways their parents find alarming: temper tantrums, throwing objects, yelling, hitting, kicking, even biting. (Biting is a common way for children who aren't yet verbally skilled to express anger or frustration.) All human beings have feelings—lots of them—and all of us, adults and children, need ways to express and understand our feelings.

Does this mean parents should tolerate hitting, yelling, or kicking as acceptable expressions of anger? Of course not. Actions that harm others (or oneself) are not appropriate ways of expressing feelings. Parents and teachers can make an effort to get into the young child's world and understand it. They can practice active listening to validate and clarify feelings, and they can then teach children to express their anger (which may be completely justified) in acceptable ways.

Children learn by watching adults. Parents model how to deal with strong feelings when they stand quietly and take some deep breaths instead of reacting immediately to upsets, when they respond to a child who tries to hit without hitting back, or when they walk over to a child, get down on his eye level, and distract, redirect, or show her what she can do rather than hollering from across the room.

Children learn about anger by:

- Watching how adults behave when angry

- Experiencing how others treat them when angry

- Learning to identify feelings of anger within themselves

It is tempting to respond to anger with anger—to join in the yelling, send kids off to a punitive time-out, or otherwise try to fix the situation at hand. These responses usually escalate the conflict and destroy any opportunity there might have been to teach, to understand, or to find a workable solution to the problem.

Remember, your little one does not have the same understanding of anger that you do. He needs your help both to identify this feeling and to learn to manage and express it in appropriate ways. How can parents and caregivers help an angry child?

Use Words to Label the Feelings
Using a calm voice, "reflect" the feeling to your child. You might say, "Boy, you look angry! I see that your chin is sticking out, your eyebrows are all scrunched up, and your fists are clenched." Giving these clues helps a child make the connection between how he feels and what he is doing. Obviously, real understanding takes time, but it's never too soon to start.

Validate the Feelings
Emotions are generated by the brain's limbic system. Your child does not "choose" his emotions, and there really is no such thing as a "wrong" feeling—something

> **How Should You React When Your Child Shows Anger?**
>
> - Use words to label the feelings.
> - Validate your child's feelings.
> - Provide appropriate ways for your child to express his feelings.

many adults have yet to learn. Your child has reasons for his feelings, even when he does not consciously know what those reasons are. Begin teaching your child that his feelings are always okay but some actions are not.

Provide Appropriate Ways for Your Child to Express His Feelings
What might an angry toddler do? Well, it might help to roar like a dinosaur, scribble on paper with markers, run around the backyard, or knead a ball of clay. These provide physical outlets for emotional energy. Parents usually discover that anger expressed in healthy ways dissipates much more quickly; in fact, they often find themselves giggling with the same toddler who was so furious only moments before. Try saying, "It's okay to be mad—I'd feel pretty mad, too, if I were you. It's not okay to hit me or hurt yourself. What would help you feel better?" Remember, we usually *do* better when we *feel* better. Lessons learned now about recognizing and managing feelings will benefit your child his entire life.

A WORD ABOUT "BLANKIES" AND OTHER SECURITY OBJECTS

Closely tied to a child's feelings of trust and security is one accessory of young childhood that has passed into folklore: the security blanket. Linus, in the cartoon strip *Peanuts,* carries his everywhere, even using it to zap his obnoxious older sister. Children the world over rely on scraps of blanket, favorite stuffed animals, or imaginary friends to help them feel secure—and parents the world over often wonder if it's healthy to allow them to do so.

With a little thought, it's easy to understand how intimidating a place this world of ours can be to a very young child. A child's attachment to his blankie can be very strong; it often has its own feel and taste, and a child can usually tell if an attempt is made to replace or switch the favorite object. Many parents have had the alarming experience of leaving a teddy or blankie at the grocery store or in a motel, then having to make an emergency return trip with an hysterical child.

Feelings of insecurity and fear, while they can be upsetting for parents, are like all other emotions: They are just feelings and can be handled with active listening, warmth, and understanding. If sleeping with a special blanket or a stuffed animal helps a child relax and feel cozy, is there truly any harm in it?

Some children never adopt a blankie or stuffed animal, preferring instead to suck on their thumbs or on a pacifier. Monica believed that her children would not suck their thumbs if they had plenty of opportunity to suck at the breast. But the one child she had nursed on demand sucked her thumb until she was six. Monica had to admit, "So much for that theory!"

Pacifiers provide a helpful way to allow an infant to satisfy her need to suck, and they can provide security (and peace) during times of upset or stress. In fact, children who appear to have given up their thumb or pacifier often resume the habit if the family moves, if they change childcare settings or caregivers, or if there is some other upheaval in their lives. Most parents eventually wonder if thumb sucking or using a pacifier is wise, especially as a child grows older, but the problem is more the adult's attitude than the child's well-being.

If you have concerns about sucking needs, especially where teeth and orthodontia are concerned, you may be able to put your fears at rest by talking to a pediatric dentist. As a general rule, the less fuss adults make, the sooner the issue tends to be resolved. As they grow older, children often are willing to restrict use of their security objects to bedtime or naptime, especially if they have experienced understanding and acceptance from their parents. Most children, left to themselves, give up their blankies or pacifiers of their own free will, usually by the age of six.

"Maria's blankie sort of fell apart," said Carol. "It literally disintegrated until she was down to a few shredded pieces. It became a bother for her to find these fragments and so the blankie passed quietly into history. Actually, I gathered up a couple of these pieces and tucked them into my jewelry box. I couldn't part with them. I plan on adding them to a quilt for my grandchild someday." It is amazing how many parents who lamented their child's attachment to a blanket keep a small scrap as a memento long after their child has abandoned it.

LANGUAGE SKILLS AND COMMUNICATION

It can be frustrating to try to communicate with and understand a young child who can't yet express his feelings and ideas—and it is frustrating for the child as well. Like most other developmental skills, the acquisition of language takes place at different rates for different children, and how comfortable your child is with using words will affect the way he behaves and expresses his feelings.

Most parents eagerly await their children's first words, sharing them with friends and family and recording them for posterity in baby books and journals. Parents smile over the innocent mispronunciations and other manglings of the language, and rejoice when their children can make themselves understood consistently.

By the age of seven or eight months, most babies understand the meanings of a few words. By three years of age, most children understand ordinary, conversational language, although they may not be able to produce it themselves. Children often understand many words by the age of one year, but they may say only a few before they are two years old, despite endless coaching from Mom and Dad. If your child seems alert and responds well to you, chances are that all is well, even if she doesn't have much to say—yet. (If you are concerned about your child's speech development, it may be helpful to talk to your pediatrician. Some children do experience delays in speech and language; therapy with a trained speech therapist can be helpful.)

It is worth knowing that children learn language best by being spoken to often and given lots of opportunities to respond. Holding a running conversation as you stroll down the grocery aisle about the bright red apples, whether or not you are out of peanut butter, or if salmon would be nice for dinner tonight does not mean you expect your four-month-old to take over shopping anytime soon. This kind of conversation allows his ear to become accustomed to language, in the same way that those age-old nursery rhymes teach children to recognize the rhythms and sounds of spoken words—and to duplicate them when the time is right. No matter how exhausting it can be, a toddler's endless stream of "why" and "how come" questions should be answered calmly. As one three-year-old reminded his exasperated mom, "That's how little boys learn!"

THE IMPORTANCE OF TALK

Language—the words you speak and the way you speak them—shapes your very thoughts. Most researchers believe that acquiring language skills is critical to the development of thinking, problem solving, and higher reasoning. Unfortunately, educators and researchers also tell us that the ability to use language well is declining rapidly among today's children. They are less able to learn, to think, and to write. It is troubling that many children are not developing the connections necessary to function well academically, to appreciate literature, and to write a logical paragraph. Why?

The biggest culprit may be our hectic, harried lifestyles and how parents choose to use the time they do have with their children. Time in which to sit and read or to talk with one another is all too limited. Children are propped in front of videos and television programs while parents fix dinner, do chores, or work at home. Children may learn the *Barney* theme song or recognize letters and numbers, but contrary to most parents' belief, they do not learn language by watching a screen. Language skills require the connection, attention, and interaction of real conversation. (You will learn more about the effects of television and other media on young children in Chapter 16.)

All too often, adults' words to children are strictly functional. "Get into your pajamas," "Eat your dinner," or "Don't hit your sister" may be all the conversation some toddlers hear. Perhaps most sadly, some children spend most of their waking hours in childcare centers where overburdened caregivers value silence and compliance, not budding language skills. (See Chapter 17 for information on choosing quality childcare.)

TEACHING LANGUAGE

Many parents believe that there will be time "later on" to teach words and language skills, but most language learning takes place in the first three years of life. What can parents and caregivers do to give little ones the best chance of learning language now—and succeeding in school later on?

Talk to Children

Most parents instinctively know the sort of verbal play that infants and young children need. Word games, nursery rhymes, and simple songs are actually wonderful ways to acquaint babies with the mysteries of language. Let children hear your voice; speak to them often. Sing the old-fashioned nursery rhymes. What you say is probably less important than giving them the opportunity to experiment with sounds and words. As your children get older, telling stories is a great way to help them follow a story line, learn word meanings, and stretch their ability to visualize and imagine, all crucial parts of later learning and school readiness.

> **How Can You Encourage Language Development?**
>
> - Talk to children.
> - Encourage children to "talk back."
> - Read lots of books out loud.
> - Turn off the television—at least most of the time.

Encourage Children to "Talk Back"

No, we don't mean that sort of back talk. But it is important to give children the opportunity to talk to you, to other adults, and to other children. At first, children's "speech" may consist of sounds, single words, and gestures, but as you encourage them ("what" and "how" questions are one helpful way), their ability to speak to you and to communicate ideas and feelings will grow. Adults sometimes are impatient with young children and rush to finish their sentences for them; do your best to be tolerant and give your child space and time to communicate.

Read Lots of Books Out Loud

Reading aloud to young children may be the most helpful activity parents can do. Even babies can be propped in your lap to gaze at the pages of a colorful board book, and toddlers usually love to cuddle up and read stories. As you read, become the characters, changing your voice and providing sound effects, and encourage your child to do the same. Don't rely entirely on picture books; include books that have more text and encourage your child to form his own pictures for the words you read.

Reading can become a favorite part of a toddler's day, and young children usually are eager to soak up the fascinating worlds books can open. Three-year-old Kevin's mother was astonished when he "read" a favorite Berenstain Bears book to her one day. He had memorized the words, the voices—and the right place to turn the pages. Barbara was thirteen months old when her favorite aunt sat down to read a book about flowers with her. Barbara gazed intently at the picture, pulled the book into her hands, and put her nose against the page for a long sniff. Her aunt was amazed at how well Barbara made the connection between the representation on the printed page and the real object.

As your child grows older, share with her the books you loved or check with friends for titles their children have enjoyed. Make reading together part of your bedtime routine. Many parents find that this cozy ritual lasts far beyond toddlerhood and provides a time of warmth and closeness for years to come.

Turn Off the Television—at Least Most of the Time

As we learned in Chapter 4, television may actually change the way a child's brain functions. The American Association of Pediatrics recommends no "screen time" for children under the age of two. At the very least we know that watching television is entirely passive; children who watch a great deal of TV show less creativity in their play. Balance may be a realistic goal; a little *Sesame Street* or the beloved Disney videos provide welcome entertainment for young children (and an occasional break for weary parents). But be sure there is more than enough time for books, music, active play, and conversation as well.

It is sobering to realize how much learning takes place in the first three years of life—and that all-too-imperfect parents and caregivers are responsible for most of it. It may help to remember that most language development takes place naturally, *when parents and caregivers make time to play and talk with children.* As we've said so many times before, raising and caring for active young children is a challenging job; providing opportunities for them to learn about feelings, words, and the world around them may seem like just one more burdensome thing to do. Take a deep breath, relax, and remind yourself to enjoy these years. It's never too late—or too soon—to begin.

11

GETTING ALONG IN THE GREAT BIG WORLD: THE DEVELOPMENT OF SOCIAL SKILLS

Did you know that a crying baby is practicing social skills? In the first months of a baby's life, crying brings adults, who provide food, comfort, and entertainment. By four months of age or so, the baby's social repertoire expands—he smiles at the adults who surround him. By five to eight months of age, the baby is giggling, cooing, and otherwise enchanting his grown-up companions.

Still, children don't truly discover that the world holds people other than themselves until they are between fourteen and twenty-four months of age. When a baby looks into a mirror, she sees an unknown being. It is well into the first year of life before a baby even recognizes the person in the mirror as "me"! Knowing this can help adults comprehend how primitive her social interactions will be for a while. When adults understand that social skills don't develop naturally but must be taught, they may be less dismayed that children often hit, bite, push, and fight as they discover how to get along with others.

Social skills like sharing and playing develop through training, practice, and mistakes—especially mistakes. The road is not smooth; emotional bumps and scrapes mark the landscape of early social experience, with an occasional real bite and scratch thrown in along the way. Knowledge of how social skills develop in young children will help parents and teachers provide both training and understanding as children learn to interact with their equally inexperienced peers.

SOCIAL SKILLS IN THE FIRST THREE YEARS

Time passes and children grow. Eventually—sooner for some than for others—your child will enter the bigger world around him. He will need social skills: to know how to get along with others, to communicate, and to choose behaviors that help, not hinder, his progress in life.

Children must learn so much in the first three years of life. They master language and learn to recognize and cope with their own emotions and those of others. They learn to choose behavior that is appropriate for their surroundings. They begin the process of believing in themselves and having the courage to venture out into the world at large.

Parents usually have questions about this stage of life—lots of them. Many parents find their toddler's behavior frustrating, irritating, and downright defeating at times. Most parents wonder what they can do to help their children get along with others, live peacefully in their families, and succeed in life.

Let's start with some of the issues that cause frustration to parents and caregivers (and their young charges) when they don't understand child development and age-appropriateness.

Sharing Versus "Mine"

Sharing is a big issue in the world of young children. Parents often expect young children to take turns, to be happy with equal portions, or to give up playing with a favorite toy. But children under the age of two are egocentric—that is, they are the center of their own world, and everything else exists only as it relates to the center (which is, to be exact, "me"). This is not selfishness—it's natural human development.

> *Mary was the first to raise her hand during the question-and-answer session at her parenting group. "My little girl, Jetta, is eighteen months old. I'm trying to teach her that everything does not belong to her," Mary said with an exasperated sigh. "She grabs my purse and says, 'Mine purse.' I try to reason with her and tell her, 'No, this is Mommy's purse,' but she just hangs on, repeating, 'Mine purse.' She does the same thing with the cereal box, the telephone, and even the dog."*

Guess what? As Mary will learn from her parenting leader, in Jetta's world everything *is* "mine." Jetta looks out at the world from its hub: herself. If you believe that the world begins and ends with you (and toddlers believe exactly that), it follows that everything in the world belongs to you. No amount of logic will change Jetta's perspective, because it is simply the way she sees her place on the planet right now.

During the "mine" stage of development, do not waste energy on debates. Try saying, "You like Mommy's purse. Want to help me carry it?" Without arguing with her and inviting a power struggle, you are giving her accurate information, offering her a way to make her own small contribution to help you, and allowing her view of the world. Until her development moves forward, this makes far more sense than holding endless arguments over ownership. If you try to correct her thinking, you will almost certainly create a power struggle, perhaps setting a pattern for the future. Cooperation promises a much healthier future for both of you.

Mary had something in common with 51 percent of parents, according to a national survey conducted by the Zero to Three: National

Center for Infants, Toddlers and Families (www.zerotothree.org/parent_poll.html). One of the questions asked in this poll was, "Should a fifteen-month-old be expected to share her toys with other children, or is this too young of an age to expect a child to share?"

They found that 51 percent of parents of children age birth to three years believe a fifteen-month-old should be expected to share. But research shows that fifteen months is too young to expect a toddler to share. The Zero to Three Center offers some sound advice. We know that fifteen-month-olds are working on learning how to share, but they point out that the process is far from complete. Children this age need *guidance* and teaching rather than "discipline" if they are having trouble sharing. Providing solutions such as finding another toy they can offer a friend, finding something else to do while they wait their turn, or suggesting (and demonstrating) ways they can play with the toy together at the same time will be most effective. After lots of practice (and with your help), by the time they are two to two and a half they can begin to do it on their own (but don't expect consistency!).

An inability to share does not portend a lifetime of selfishness. Possessiveness and ownership are normal steps before the ability to share gradually begins around the ages of three or four. Meanwhile:

• Begin teaching the process of sharing without expecting your child to understand. Kindly and firmly remove an item that belongs to someone else or that she can't have, without lecturing or shaming. Offer whatever comfort you can, but don't try to shield your child from experiencing disappointment—after all, disappointment and frustration are a part of life that your child needs to learn to cope with. You might say, "It is hard to share. You really wanted that." Empathy eases the pain and paves the way to later acceptance of sharing.

• Model sharing. Give your child bites or half of a special treat. Offer to let him hold something that is yours. Play trading games with him. "What do you want to share with me while I share this with you?"

- Support your child's need to possess. (Don't you have some posses-
  sions you don't want to share?) Help older children find another toy
  to play with, or provide more than one of the same toy.

PARALLEL PLAY

When toddlers play together, most of their play is "parallel play." They
play near other children rather than with them. Jeffrey, for instance, is
sixteen months old. At the childcare center, the caregivers feed him,
carry him, comfort him, and change him. There are other children
present, but they are more like mysterious new toys. Jeffrey has begun
to be curious about them and to
explore them; he knows they cry
when he pokes them, and when he
tried to put one child's hair in his
mouth it created quite a commotion.
For now, Jeffrey is content to do his
own thing while other children do
theirs—at least, most of the time.

It is helpful to remember that play
is the laboratory in which young children experiment with connection,
relationship, and social skills. Your
child's ability to connect with others
begins with her ability to connect with *you;* you are her first teacher in
the process of learning to trust, respect, laugh, and play with others.
Taking time to create a loving connection with your child truly is the
best way to create a solid foundation for social and life skills.

Eventually, however, other children will enter your little one's life.
Play and sharing involve two or more participants, and when one (or
more) of those participants is the center of the universe, trouble is
bound to result. Parents and teachers can help toddlers learn to share
by taking time for training. They can demonstrate sharing and give it a

name. They can encourage any moves in the direction of sharing. And adults can understand that the process takes time, so they must have patience and allow for mistakes along the way.

It helps to remember that training at this stage is mostly preparatory; as you have learned, toddlers aren't quite developmentally ready to really share. Simply redirecting a toddler's attention can effectively defuse a combustible situation. Adults may have difficulty sharing because of selfishness, but toddlers have difficulty sharing because they are toddlers. The best course of action is to begin a training program that is kind and firm, avoiding scolding and labels.

SHARING IN THE REAL WORLD OF TODDLERS

When twenty-month-old Susie grabs another child's toy, an adult can step in, remove the toy gently from Susie, return it to the other child, and carry Susie away to find some other interesting object to play with, saying, "Tommy is playing with that toy right now" or "Let's find a toy that Susie enjoys."

When Susie is two and a half and begins to attend a preschool, things change a bit. Susie is moving from a world where everything is "mine" to recognizing that the world contains other people. She no longer merely plays next to her companions but enjoys running around the playground *with* them. When Susie grabs a toy now, adults can respond differently from the way they did earlier. Susie is ready to learn and practice the social skill of sharing. A more appropriate response now is to take the toy and explore with her ways of learning to share with another child.

> *Susie and Tommy are playing in the block area when Susie grabs the toy car that Tommy has just picked up. Both children begin to yell, "It's mine! Give it to me!" Naturally, the uproar draws the attention of Ms. McGee, the children's teacher. She walks over and gently takes the car.*

"Susie," she asks, "do you want to play with this car?" "I want it," Susie agrees firmly. Ms. McGee turns to Tommy. "Are you playing with the car, Tommy?" Tommy's lower lip juts out a bit as he says, "It's mine."

Ms. McGee places the car in Tommy's hands and turns to Susie. "Susie, what do you think you could say to Tommy if you want to play with the car?" "I want to play with it?" Susie offers (with only a little sulk in her voice). Ms. McGee agrees that's one way to ask. She suggests that Susie could also try saying, "May I play with the car?"

Tommy has been watching this exchange with interest. When his teacher asks him what he might say to Susie when she asks for the car, he responds right away. "Here, you can have it," he replies, handing the car to Susie. Ms. McGee smiles. "It's nice of you to share, Tommy. What might you say if you weren't finished with the car?"

This is a new thought for Tommy. The teacher has made it clear that just asking may not be enough. She is helping Tommy learn that he has some options and can assert his own needs, but Tommy is momentarily baffled.

Ms. McGee turns to Susie. "Can you think of something Tommy can say, Susie?" Susie has just the answer. "He could say, 'In a minute.'" Ms. McGee nods. "That's a good idea. Perhaps he could say that he will give it to you in ten minutes. Would that work, Tommy?" Tommy nods, and Ms. McGee encourages him to practice saying "I'm not done yet" to Susie.

Throughout this conversation, both children were invited to explore the possibilities available to them. Sharing is a skill that must be taught and practiced (even by adults). How will a child know what to do if no demonstrations are given? This is also a period of intense language development. Providing the necessary words and ways to use them is part of the training process. Teaching and encouraging young children

Successful Strategies for Teaching Toddlers to Share

There are many ways to take time for training in sharing.

- Model sharing yourself by saying, "I want to share my cake with you" or "Let's take turns bouncing the ball. I'll count to ten while you bounce it, then we'll count to ten while I bounce it."
- Give opportunities for sharing by saying, "I know that's your favorite toy. Which of your toys would you be willing to share with Michael for a while?"
- Acknowledge children's feelings. When children have difficulty sharing, acknowledge their feelings by saying, "I know it can be difficult to share. Sometimes I don't like to either. You don't have to share all the time. I have faith that you will share when you are ready."
- Avoid passing judgment by shaming a child, labeling her as "naughty," or forcing a reluctant apology. Doing so does not encourage sharing.

to "use their words" is a wonderful way to nurture social skills. But it is important to remember that training is a process that must be repeated over and over as the developmental clock keeps ticking. It is the adults' job to guide continuously—not to expect that children will learn and remember after one experience, or a hundred. Many toddlers who had difficulty learning to share have grown up to become caring and giving people, especially if they grew up in a caring and giving environment.

Playing Let's Pretend with dolls or puppets is another way sharing can be modeled and practiced. Adults can act out a conflict between two children, showing what happened and teaching other, more appropriate responses. Then children can practice, holding the puppets and exploring both the inappropriate and the appropriate behavior. This invites children to recognize inappropriate behavior in others and, eventually, to notice and take responsibility for their own.

SHARING AND CULTURAL VALUES

Attitudes toward many social skills vary by culture. The idea of personal property is not seen in the same way by all people. Many Asian cultures, for example, believe that the needs of the group are more important than those of any one individual. In New Zealand, a Maori child is deliberately given the last serving of a special treat and told to share it, because placing the needs of the community first is a value that her culture holds in esteem.

How you transmit your values will affect the social skills your child masters and will influence your child's awareness that others often perceive the world differently from the way you do. Ultimately, a child's sense of belonging will to some degree be tied to feeling connected to the values of his culture.

HITTING AND OTHER AGGRESSION

Toddlers are short on both language and social skills, and when they play together they can easily become frustrated. When they lack the ability to express their feelings in words, hitting and other types of aggression sometimes result. When you set one toddler down to "play" with another, neither is particularly sure of what the other is all about. Watch them eyeing each other and you can guess what they might be thinking. "What is this creature? Does it break? Can I taste it? What happens when I pull its hair or examine its eyelashes?" Walking up to and hitting another child may be just a primitive form of saying hello.

Still, children under the age of two need to learn that pulling hair, poking eyes, and hitting are actions that hurt people and cannot be allowed. Firmness, coupled with removing the child temporarily and redirecting his attention to something else, works best. You can say, "It is not okay to hit Rebecca or pull her hair. Let's go find another toy to play with. When you are ready to be kind, you and Rebecca may play together." It does not help to scold or punish. How might we feel if someone scolded and punished us if we practiced a foreign language for a month but failed to speak it fluently? Social skills are a language that must be practiced, integrated, and learned at deeper levels when children are developmentally ready.

Little "Munch"kins—What to Do About Biting

One type of toddler aggression—biting—really sets off alarms for parents and for caregivers. Most biting incidents happen from about fourteen months to three years of age, which coincides with the development of spoken language. Biting often indicates frustration or anger, especially when a child isn't able to make herself understood with words.

Proponents of teaching children a simplified form of sign language claim that when children are able to communicate their needs and thoughts more accurately through signing, they will not resort to aggressive behaviors as often. (For more information see *Sign with Your Baby* by Joseph Garcia [Mukilteo, Wash.; Northlight Communications, 2002] or www.sign2me.com.) A baby as young as eight months can begin to learn simple signs to ask for food, say she wants more of something, or indicate that she is thirsty as opposed to hungry. It certainly is not necessary to teach your baby to sign, but it is an option that you may want to consider.

Other researchers believe that biting may be an angry variation of a kiss, while still others think children bite out of curiosity or to observe their victim's (and the adults') reactions. Biting may even be the result of a vivid imagination. Twenty-month-old Teddy spent two weeks biting the ankle of anyone who wandered by before an observant adult realized he was imitating the nipping actions of his aunt's new puppy.

An even more basic explanation of biting is its connection to impulse control. Young children lack effective impulse control (remember, the prefrontal cortex of toddlers is still "under construction"), making their response to frustration immediate—and usually beyond their conscious control. Impulse control develops gradually; by about the age of three, the combination of language development and a maturing nervous system will combine to reduce or eliminate most early biting. In the meantime, regardless of the reasons it happens, biting is very disturbing (not to mention painful) for the biter, the bitee (the person who was bitten), and all adults involved. We're not sure which is worse: to be the parents of the biter or the bitee. The parent of the bitee feels angry and protective. The parent of the biter feels embarrassed and protective. Both will feel a little better if they understand child development.

Biting that occurs because a child lacks the words to express feelings and frustrations will diminish as he learns the verbal skills to express himself in more appropriate ways. In addition, helping your child to express her feelings as she learns to talk, providing carrot sticks to chew on in frustrating moments, or holding a child's chin gently when he appears ready to bite may help resolve the problem. And no, biting the child back, washing out the mouth with soap, or placing Tabasco sauce on the tongue doesn't help; such responses are far more likely to escalate conflict than resolve it, and may be considered abusive.

There are no magic remedies for biting. The most helpful responses begin with one essential element: supervision. Children who bite must be watched carefully. Look for patterns. Does your child bite at a certain time of day, perhaps when she is hungry or tired or when too much is going on around her? If you spot a pattern, use your knowledge to be especially watchful during those times.

Despite the most diligent supervision, biting often continues. Once biting occurs, there are three essential steps: preventing further damage, involving both children in healing, and showing compassion to both children.

Prevent Further Injury Act at once. Separate the children and check the seriousness of the injury. Your actions should be firm and decisive, but kind. Try to remain calm, not letting your own frustration or feelings of anger fuel your response. When you understand the developmental nature of biting, realize that time usually solves the problem, and know that you are doing all you can to deal with it, it becomes easier to manage this troubling behavior. Keep words to a minimum, such as a calm "No biting."

Involve Both Children in Healing: Tend the Wound and Hurt Feelings
Biting is particularly worrisome to parents because of the possibility of blood-borne disease. Adults and children tending the wound

Biting and Hitting

Q. I have twin boys who are twenty-one months old. I know that hitting and biting can happen at this age, but one of my boys hits and bites more than the other. When he hits me, I leave the room, but he still has his brother for entertainment. What would happen if I give the one who is behaving himself lots of attention and ignore the boy who hits?

A. Dealing with two toddlers at once can certainly be challenging. Our suggestions may be shocking to people who don't understand Positive Discipline concepts: Consider paying more attention to the twin who is biting and hitting; invite him to help you comfort his brother. No, this does not "reward" the misbehavior. (Remember, children "do" better when they "feel" better.) Your little one is frustrated about something and doesn't have the skills to express his feelings. You can comfort him and teach him skills at the same time—but don't expect your lessons to "stick" without supervision. Give the hitter a hug for just a few seconds. Then say, "Look. Your brother is crying. Let's go give him a hug." (You are modeling hugging instead of hitting.) After hugging for a few seconds, teach him a skill. Take his hand and show him how to "touch nicely." If he has already bitten his brother, after a brief hug say, "Let's go get some ice and help your brother feel better." Then let him hold the ice on his brother's bite. Again you can teach to "touch nicely."

Understanding development will help you recognize why this is helpful. Toddlers can't understand abstract concepts, but they do develop a "sense of" things and begin to learn. For example, the child you rescue may develop a sense of being a victim and believe, "I need other people to take care of me." If you scold or punish the aggressor, this child may develop a sense of doubt and shame. His discouragement may actually motivate more "misbehavior."

One more suggestion: Because children of this age can't grasp abstract concepts, such as "don't hit" or "don't bite," they need lots of supervision. This is difficult for a busy mother of twins, but with close supervision you may be able to spot when one twin is getting frustrated and simply redirect both of them to acceptable activities.

should wear plastic gloves, which provide protection and teach everyone concerned to avoid contact with blood. The child most at risk is the biter, who may have ingested blood, rather than the child who was bitten (this information—along with generous helpings of compassion and calm—may be useful when dealing with the bitten child's distraught family). In addition to the physical wound, there are also feelings that have been wounded. Healing feelings requires compassion.

Show Compassion for Both Children Both children, the biter and the bitee, may feel hurt, distressed, and discouraged; both need to be shown compassion. Even the biter needs to know that you still care about him. Emotions run high after a biting incident, and the child who bites often finds himself villainized. Teachers march him to time-out and tell him to stay there all morning. Parents yell, send him to his room, and shun him. Parents frequently demand that preschools expel children who bite. It may be difficult in all the tumult to remember that this tiny person probably bit out of frustration, not evil intent. He cannot manage his impulses and probably can barely speak. What he really might need is a hug—as well as continued supervision. The child who was bitten suffers hurt feelings as well as hurt skin. It might help to ask the biter to help you comfort the child who was bitten. This provides healing for both children.

A bite happens in a split second. Even a child holding his mother's hand might manage to chomp down on the child in the next stroller before his mom can stop him. In cases where biting becomes unmanageable, reducing time spent with other children may be necessary for a while. Giving a youngster time to develop communication skills provides a needed break for everyone. If a child must be in continued contact with others, such as in a childcare setting, try having him carry a "bite-able" object. A small rubber teething ring pinned to his shirt with a diaper pin offers a temporary solution. Keep a close watch on the child while helping him learn he can always bite on his ring but he may not bite a person.

If a child continues to bite after the age of three, it may be helpful to get a speech and hearing evaluation to ensure that language skills are developing appropriately.

SOCIAL INTEREST

In this chapter we have focused on the "skills" that children need in "social" settings—those times when they interact with others. There is another social aspect of development as well, that of "social interest." Alfred Adler, a pioneer in the field of families and children's behavior, described "social interest" as a real concern for others and a sincere desire to make a contribution to society. In addition to learning and perfecting the skills needed in social relationships, children, even very young ones, learn about themselves and others through the social context of their experiences.

As children enter into the lives of their families and schools, they want very much to feel that they belong. One of the most powerful ways to achieve a sense of belonging is to make a meaningful contribution to the well-being of others in the family or group. From cradle to grave, belonging and significance are among our most basic human needs. A wonderful way to encourage social interest is by sharing the work the family does together.

For young children, there really is no difference between play and work. When a baby strives over and over again to grab a toy that is just out of reach, we say she is "playing," but actually she is hard at work, growing and developing new skills. Young children are usually eager to participate in whatever they see us doing, and the time to invite children to participate in the family is when they want to—not when they can do a task perfectly. Once you begin to see your youngster as an asset, he won't seem to be "underfoot" so much.

WHAT CAN MY LITTLE ONE DO?

Feeling capable and able to contribute to others is important. An eight-month-old hands her clean diaper to her dad when he is ready for it. A fifteen-month-old helps pile the bath toys into the tub. A two-year-old energetically helps mop up spills in the kitchen. These tasks are fun to youngsters and form the basic patterns for future learning. The next time your toddler picks up a precious vase or fragile flower, ask her to hand it to you instead of trying to take the item out of her hand. The transformation will be almost magical as she switches from resistance to willing compliance. Her response makes sense when we remember that children like to be helpful.

In fact, a recent study discovered that toddlers appear to have an inborn desire to help others. When a researcher on a ladder accidentally "dropped" clothespins, every toddler studied rushed to pick up the clothespins and hand them to the researcher. (The toddlers also picked up books and other items.) When the researcher *threw* items on the floor, however, he was on his own; the children only picked up the fallen objects when they sensed that the adult needed their help.

More critically, we are planting the seeds for healthy self-esteem when we allow children to experience a sense of belonging and contribution. Having a sense of belonging helps children feel encouraged, cooperative, and good about themselves, while not having a sense of belonging or significance leads to discouragement—and, all too often, results in misbehavior, especially as children grow older.

Children, even little ones, can do any number of things to contribute to their family's well-being. As you watch your little one during these first years of life, remember that he is watching you as well, and your example speaks more clearly than your words. Wise parents and caregivers will use a child's natural desire to imitate adult behavior by modeling desired skills and welcoming a child's involvement and help.

When we consider the idea of social interest, our example again speaks loudest. What will your child learn if you tell him to treat animals gently, then angrily toss the cat outside after it claws the furniture? Will your child learn compassion for others if he watches you sit comfortably on the bus while an elderly passenger stands nearby? Will he learn to be polite and quiet if you holler across the room, admonishing squabbling youngsters to "quit yelling"? Which lesson will children remember? Your words or your actions?

Remember those mirror neurons we read about in Chapter 4? Those neurons start lining up as soon as a child sees an action performed. That means that if you want your child to be gentle, kind, and thoughtful, you must be a parent who hugs instead of hits, who demonstrates compassion instead of impatience or retribution, and who listens instead of lashing out in anger.

Working alongside your child can give both of you a great deal of pleasure as well as countless opportunities to learn. Helping your child feel competent, resourceful, and confident will help him succeed at home, in his relationships in the outside world, and in the challenges life brings to all of us.

12

YOU CAN'T MAKE 'EM DO IT: SLEEPING

Gather any group of parents with very young children together and inevitably the conversation will turn in one of three directions. "I can't get my little girl to take a nap," one mom complains. "She's up all day, then she falls asleep early in the evening. That would be great if she stayed asleep, but she wakes up at three in the morning and wants to play. How can I get her to sleep when we do?"

"We practice the family bed, and our children sleep fine—although sometimes *we* don't sleep very well," one parent reports. Another says, "We also practice the family bed, but not because we want to. We just can't get our kids to sleep in their *own* beds."

"My son sleeps fine," a dad says, "but he absolutely refuses to have anything to do with his potty seat. He's almost three. My mother says *her* kids were all trained by the age of two. We're starting to panic."

"Well, we're still on the basics," another mom adds sadly. "My little boy thinks he can live on hot dogs and Spaghetti-Os, with an occasional cookie thrown in. I've bribed and coaxed and argued, but he just clamps his lips together when I offer him anything else. I dread mealtimes."

Most of us can relate to these beleaguered parents; in fact, you may be nodding your head as you read this. The next three chapters will deal with those perennial power struggles: sleeping, eating, and toileting. Who starts these wars? And why?

We believe that like any other parenting battle, the sleeping, eating, and toileting wars are based on a lack of knowledge, a lack of skills, a lack of faith, and a lack of confidence in yourself and your little one.

Understanding developmental appropriateness and age-appropriateness will give you needed perspective as you work with your child while he learns to master his body. Focusing on cooperation skills—especially when you face the reality that sleeping, eating, and toileting are three areas where your child is in complete control—will bring relief to both of you. It is, after all, his body!

Remember, it takes two to have a power struggle. You can't make your child sleep; you can't make her eat; you can't make her use the toilet. Only she can perform these functions. There *are* ways to invite cooperation, however, using respectful and developmentally appropriate methods.

All humans must sleep and eat to survive. Toileting is a bodily need with strong (to say the least) social significance. None of these functions becomes a battleground unless it becomes more important for a child (or a parent) to "win" than to do what comes naturally. The key is for parents to learn to support cooperation instead of engaging in power struggles.

SLEEPING: "BUT I'M NOT TIRED!"

Most babies spend more time asleep than awake during the first few months of their lives. Desperate, sleep-deprived parents usually want their demanding infants to sleep—right now—but many power struggles over sleeping can be avoided if you help your child learn to fall asleep by herself as early in her life as possible. This means putting her in her crib just before she falls asleep. (We know this isn't always possible with tiny babies who doze off after a few sucks on the bottle or breast, but making an effort will promote healthy sleep patterns.)

Some parents find they are afraid to lay down a drowsy or sleeping baby for fear of waking her, but waking up and being allowed to go back to sleep after a little fussing is fine. It may help to add a gentle pat on the back to soothe her back to sleep.

"But isn't it just easier to hold her while she sleeps and get a few moments of quiet for myself?" you may be asking. Adults often try to take responsibility for getting the baby to sleep and then managing the environment to keep him asleep ("Shh! The baby is *asleep!*" they anxiously stage-whisper), then feel guilty, frustrated, or annoyed when they fail to ensure uninterrupted snooze time.

With time and practice, you will learn what works best for your child: you can explore the relative virtues of darkness versus night-lights, music versus silence, warm rooms versus cool ones. Still, *sleeping is the baby's job*. You will invite a battle if you try to make his sleep your responsibility.

Sleep patterns are different too. Some babies are born with more active temperaments, while others may have colic or other physical problems. These infants may require more holding and comforting during the first three to six months until you (and your doctor) know your baby well enough to know if the problems are physical or not. Establish good sleeping habits as soon as you feel confident that your child does not have any physical problems.

CREATING A MORE PEACEFUL BEDTIME

Most parents and children will wrestle with bedtime at some point during their journey together. Here are some ideas that may help you make bedtime a soothing—instead of seething—time of day:

Sleeping Single

Q. My two daughters (twelve months and almost three years old) will not fall asleep by themselves. I have to lie down with them until they fall asleep. Usually I fall asleep, too, and the whole evening is shot. Actually, the whole bedtime routine is a battle. They scream about having a bath, getting into their jammies, and going to bed. My older daughter tells me she isn't tired. I try to convince her that she is. When I finally get them to bed and read a story, they cry for more. I'm a stay-at-home mom, so my children get plenty of attention, but it never seems to be enough. Help!

A. When children do not learn to fall asleep on their own, they are not learning "I am capable." Parents usually suffer more than their children do while helping their children learn they can go to sleep by themselves. Are you willing to suffer to help your child? In truth, your child's resistance may be much harder on you than it is on her!

Your daughters probably will cry for three to five nights until they get used to the fact that you know what is best for them and that you are going to stick to your resolve with confidence. Use your intuition to decide if you want to help them learn cold turkey or in stages (going in to let them know you are there after five minutes, then ten minutes, then fifteen minutes, and so on, but not lying down, cuddling, or coddling). You may question whether a baby knows the difference between five minutes and fifty, but the important thing is that she experiences consistency in finding you when she wakes up. This may be the only way some parents can handle this

- Establish a bedtime routine. The predictability of the night's bath, toothbrushing, and bedtime stories will ease the transition from day to night. Consistency creates a feeling of safety and reassurance—the ideal atmosphere for a restful night's sleep. Many busy families report that bedtime is seldom the same from one day to the next. While older children may be more flexible, consistent bedtime routines are essential for little ones.

- Create a bedtime routine chart together. As children grow older, the night's routine can be made into a visual chart. List all the things you do before sleep time, limiting this list to no more than three to adjustment; others see this as a way of teasing the baby and making separation more painful for both parent and child. In either case, parents who go cold turkey and parents who go in for a few seconds of comfort agree that it takes three to five days for children to learn to fall asleep by themselves.

There are two main ingredients for success in helping your children learn to go to sleep by themselves:

1. Your understanding that this is the most loving thing you can do for your children. It is not helpful to teach them, even inadvertently, that they are not capable except to manipulate others.

2. Your confidence. They will feel this from your energy and from your body language. Energy is very readable. Children feel safe and trusting when parents are confident. When you are confident, it will be easier for you to be kind and firm.

In the end, sleep will triumph. Your children receive plenty of love during the day, and they see you every morning. We do not believe they will feel unloved or abandoned if they have to cry for a while as they learn to fall asleep by themselves, and it is actually empowering and loving to teach children the skills they will need to become healthy, responsible people.

Crying or resistance does not mean that you have made the wrong choice. Your job as a parent is to make choices that are in your child's best interest, but that does not mean those choices will always be popular. How will children learn that they can solve problems or develop resilience if they aren't allowed opportunities to try?

five items. Find pictures in magazines or take photographs of your child performing each task. Make this fun: Decorate your chart with glitter, markers, and stickers, and then post it in a prominent spot. Now the routine chart becomes the boss. Start the routine early enough to avoid feeling rushed. Ask your child to check the chart for the first thing he needs to do. Continue to have him show you what is next on the chart as he progresses through the list. This puts him in charge and encourages feelings of capability.

• Encourage your child to take an active role in bedtime preparations. If your child is old enough to manage, don't put his jammies on for him (remember, two- and three-year-olds are working on autonomy and initiative). You might want to let him set a timer to see how quickly he can get his jammies on. Do this in a spirit of fun, not as a means of pressuring or hurrying your child. Encouragement is the key element whenever we promote independence and autonomy in young children.

- Practice bedtime behaviors at other times of the day. You may want to play Let's Pretend to prepare your child for what is going to happen. Try role-playing going to bed crying and going to bed happy. You might want to show her what each one looks like, and then let her do it. This exercise is intended to teach. Pretend she is getting her jammies on. Tell her you have faith in her to do it herself. Let her practice telling you she has her jammies on and has chosen a book for you to read to her.

  You can also pretend to be the child and let her be the parent (children love this, especially when the adult "child" misbehaves). This gives her the opportunity to show how much she really understands about appropriate bedtime behavior. Model cooperation and do remember to have some fun doing it. (No one ever said parenting had to be boring!)

- Avoid power struggles. If your child says, "I don't want to go to bed," don't argue the point. You might say, "You'd really like to stay up later," or "You don't want to go to bed yet." These statements acknowledge her demands and help her to feel listened to, even though it is still bedtime. Practice being kind and firm at the same time. Trying to convince her that she is tired or telling her that she is cranky is not helpful. This only invites argument, and is a surefire recipe for a power struggle.

  In a power struggle, if one participant wins, the other loses. In this case, though, you both lose because you will both end up exhausted and frustrated by the time she finally does what she needs to do. It is your job to step out of the power struggle and create a win/win solution. Be kind but firm. Continue with the routine. Ask, "What's next on our chart?"

- Decide whether bedtimes are the same. If you have more than one child, do you want them to go to bed at the same time or at separate times? It probably won't take as long as you fear to do two routines when you combine part of the routines for both children. For instance, you may decide to have bath time and playtime together. One partner can play with an older child while the other gets the baby dressed. Or an older child can help by entertaining baby while baby gets his diaper changed. This contributing role will help the older child feel involved instead of ignored and promote her cooperation when it is her own bedtime.

- Decide what you will do—then do it. Agree to read one book or two, then stick to the agreement. Don't get involved in a debate. Children learn best from actions that are kind and firm. If she keeps begging for one more story, give her a kiss good night and leave the room. Yes, she may cry, but your kind, respectful action will teach her that manipulation is not an option.

- Make bedtime a time of sharing. Once your child can talk, you might say, "It is time to tell me the happiest and saddest thing that happened to you today." You can also share your own happy and sad moments. This is a wonderful way to develop closeness. (Remember, today, yesterday, or last week are measures of time that children under four or five do not fully understand. Her happy moment might be something that took place months ago. Don't argue the details; simply enjoy the sharing.)

- Give a big hug—and leave. The more confident you are, the easier it will be for your child.

Trust yourself to modify these suggestions to fit your style; you may want to add prayers, a song, or some other special item to your routine chart. Bedtime may be difficult sometimes, but you can feel confident that you are helping your child learn to go to sleep by himself, to get the rest he and you need—and building his confidence and self-esteem in the process.

DOES IT WORK?

Tara tried one more time to stuff her small son's arm into his pajama sleeve and gave up in frustration as he wailed and wriggled free again. Ever since baby Sean had been born, bedtime had meant a battle with two-year-old Tyler. Tara knew that children sometimes struggled with the addition of a new sibling to the family, and she thought she and Miles, her husband, had prepared Tyler well.

Ever since Sean had come home from the hospital, however, Tyler had refused to fall asleep without a parent in his bed. He woke up several times a night, and he resisted the whole bedtime process. Tara sighed and picked up the pajama top again. Tomorrow, she resolved, she would dig out the notes from her parenting class. It was time to declare a cease-fire in the bedtime wars.

The next morning was Saturday. Tara waited until Sean was napping, and then called Tyler to her side. "I have an idea," she said with a smile. "I need some help remembering how to do bedtime with you. Could you help me make a chart so we can remember everything we're supposed to do?" Tyler liked being consulted by his mom and agreed to help, watching with curiosity as Tara gathered poster board, markers, the camera, and stickers.

"Now," she said, uncapping a marker, "what's the first thing we do at bedtime?" Working together, Tara and her small son listed the bedtime tasks and illustrated each one with a picture.

When the chart was complete, Tara wrote "Tyler's Bedtime Routine" in big letters and helped him sprinkle glitter on squiggly lines of glue. Tyler dashed off to show his creation to his dad.

Miles admired the bright chart, amused by his son's enthusiasm, but he looked dubiously at Tara. "I don't know," he said. "How can that make a difference?" But that night, Miles and Tara were both surprised by how well Tyler responded to the chart.

Later that week, Tara shared the results with her parenting group: "Tyler still doesn't want to go to bed sometimes," she said, "but when he knows I mean it, he immediately asks, 'Where's my chart?' We have to follow every step in order and he corrects me if I make a mistake. I tried to read only one book last night and Tyler reminded me that the chart says he gets two. He's been falling asleep without a whimper and sleeping through the night almost every night. His grandpa was so charmed by the bedtime chart that he asked if he could keep it as a memento after Tyler has outgrown it!"

It is wise to remember that nothing will work all the time for all children but most toddlers thrive on routine, consistency, and encouragement. You may be surprised at how well your own toddlers respond.

SLEEPING WITH PARENTS

Many parents wonder whether or not they should let their children sleep with them. There are differing opinions on this issue. Books have been written about the "family bed" and the benefits of allowing children to sleep with their parents. Some people believe children feel more loved and secure when they sleep in their parents' bed. Other experts believe children become demanding and dependent when they sleep with their parents and that children have the opportunity to learn more cooperation, self-confidence, and autonomy when they sleep in their own beds. In *Positive Discipline A–Z*, Jane Nelsen, Lynn Lott, and H. Stephen Glenn (New York: Three Rivers Press, 2007) write, "If your children are in your bed by choice, that is one thing. . . . However, most parents allow their children to sleep with them not by choice but by default and they are not happy about it. When this is the case, it is disrespectful to let your children sleep in your bed with you." This excerpt raises an important distinction and one that can help you sort out what is really going on in your situation.

The first thing to consider is what works for you. Follow your heart *and* your head. Do you find it difficult to sleep with your children in your bed? If you are a single parent, it is vital to consider the implications of a potential new partner entering the picture and ask yourself how committed you might wish to remain to sharing your bed with an infant, toddler, or preschooler in such an eventuality. Some couples find it hampers their relationship (emotional and sexual) and don't want to give up time for adult conversation after slipping under the covers, a quiet moment to read a book, and/or the chance to make love before going to sleep. (We purposely left out watching television, which can create a bigger wedge in a relationship than children in the bed.)

On the other hand, if you believe that sharing the family bed fosters emotional closeness, then do so with safety considerations in mind. (The American Academy of Pediatrics advises against infants sleeping in an adult's bed because of the risk of suffocation and an increased risk of SIDS, though not all experts agree with this advice.)

Aside from philosophical, emotional, and safety concerns, remember that each child and family is unique. How does sharing a family bed work for your children? Does it help or hinder their development of autonomy, self-confidence, and self-reliance? Each family must find its own answers to these questions. We don't claim to have "the" answer, but we do believe that parents will be able to sense when their child becomes overly demanding or is developing excessive dependence (instead of healthy independence).

Alfred Adler believed that there is a strong connection between daytime misbehavior and nighttime misbehavior. In other words, children who create difficulties during the day also tend to create difficulties at night. Adler told the following story about a woman who came to him with a "problem" child. After hearing the woman's complaints about her problems with the child during the day, Adler asked, "How does the child behave during the night?" The woman replied, "I don't have any problems at night." This surprised Adler because of his theory that daytime and nighttime behavior are related. After a bit more discussion, Adler asked again, "Are you sure you don't have any problems during the night?" The woman assured him, "Oh no, I don't have any problems at night." Finally Adler guessed what might be happening at night. He asked, "Where does the child sleep?" The woman replied, "Why, she sleeps with me, of course."

Adler explained to the woman that the sleeping arrangement was part of the problem. Of course the child was not creating any problems at night, because in bed she had her mother's undivided attention. During the day the child was only trying to get the same level of attention she received at night, and she created problems when her mother did not cater to her as she did at night.

If your child is sleeping in your bed and seems overly demanding and dependent during the day, you might want to consider weaning her from the family bed. This decision can be difficult. As H. Stephen Glenn and Jane Nelsen point out in their book, *Raising Self-Reliant Children in a Self-Indulgent World,* "Weaning has never been easy for the weanor or the weanee, but it is necessary for the survival of both."

Some parents don't allow their children to sleep with them during the night but welcome them into their bed on weekend mornings for "morning snuggles." Other parents have a routine of lying down on their children's beds for story time. They make it clear to their children that they will leave when the story is over. They want to avoid the habit many children quickly adopt of insisting their parents stay in their bed until after they fall asleep.

Again, use your wisdom to decide what works best for you and your children. Each family is different; many parents find that allowing a child to snuggle in their bed is the best cure for occasional fears and nightmares—or the best time for quiet confidences. If you are weighing your own needs against the skills your child will eventually need to develop, chances are excellent that you'll make the choice that is best for both of you.

Whatever the choice, be sure that the adults involved agree on it. Children ought to bring families together, not split them apart. If you are part of a couple, listening and respecting each other as you make parenting choices will benefit your relationship, which will in turn benefit your children and your life together as a family. Balance is better than a battle.

A WORD ABOUT BEDS

As if there weren't enough to consider, there are many choices for beds for children today. Should a child be in a crib or on a mattress on the floor? Proponents of each of these styles have strong opinions and reasons to back them. The key is balance. What works for your family?

Speaking of balance, one unique sleeping choice is a rocking hammock that fans claim is especially helpful for babies who have colic. Even without colic, this choice appears to be very comfortable and makes it easy to keep a baby on her back, a position that may reduce the risk of SIDS.

Any bed can be placed in a parent's room or in a separate room. Again, balance your baby's needs with your own. Monitors make it easier to have a child in a separate room, providing reassurance to a nervous parent of a child's safety.

WEANING

"What if it is too late?" you may be asking. "I have already allowed some bad habits to develop, and my child is now very demanding. She won't go to sleep at all unless I lie down with her or let her sleep with us. When I try to break her of the habit, she screams—and I can't stand it. I always give in. It has created all the problems you have discussed, but I can't stand to listen to her cry."

Knowing in advance that weaning is difficult helps—but only a little. Here are some tips to help you survive the weaning process.

- Give up your "guilt button." Children know when they can push that button; they also know when it is gone. (Don't ask us how they know—they just do!) Guilt is rarely a positive, helpful feeling. Knowing why you are doing something will help you do what is necessary for the ultimate good of your child.

- Tell your child what you are going to do. Even if your child is preverbal, he or she will understand the feeling tone behind the words. A little warning and time to prepare will help both of you avoid unpleasant surprises.

- Follow through. If you say it, mean it; and if you mean it, follow through with action that is kind and firm.

- Take time during the day for lots of hugs and other special time with your child. Make sure this isn't "guilt penance" time but time for reassurance and enjoyment of your love for each other.

- Hang in there. If you've followed the above steps, it usually takes at least three days for your child to believe that you mean what you say. This means that she will try very hard to get you to maintain the old habit. She may cry (or scream) for at least three nights. Decide beforehand how you will handle such resistance. (The crying time will probably get shorter each night, even though every minute might still feel like an eternity.)

Allowing a child to "cry it out" is always a dilemma for parents. Remember that crying is a form of communication. Of course, you want to respond to your child's cries. The challenge is to be able to discern whether the cry is communicating a need or a want. Children need to be fed, diapered, and given love. They also need sleep. On the other hand, a child may want to stay awake, even if his body is exhausted. When this is the case, a bit of crying to express disappointment or a sense of being overwhelmed by fatigue may be necessary to

---

Bedtime ABCs

Acceptance: Accept your child's limitations and your own.
- Accept that a child's resistance does not make an adult's choice wrong.
- Be aware of a child's developmental abilities; be sure your expectations are reasonable.
- Concede that you cannot make your child sleep—that's his responsibility.

Balance: Maintain a balance between your child's needs and the needs of the rest of the family.
- Acknowledge your needs, including your need for rest.
- Balance your child's needs with the needs of all family members.
- Create a restful environment that is comfortable, safe, and secure.

Consistency: Yours will lead to your child's.
- Allow time for each child to prepare for the transition to bedtime.
- Be consistent: maintain routines and follow through on agreements.
- Create a bedtime routine that progresses toward that final tuck-in time.

---

meet his true need for rest. If you interrupt this need for sleep by staying with your baby and keeping him stimulated, neither you nor your child will get the rest you need.

Sometimes parents worry that letting a baby cry is traumatic and will scar him for life. We believe it may be more traumatic for a child

to develop the belief of "I'm not capable," which may happen if she doesn't learn independence in small doses. Sometimes adults don't get what they want—and sometimes they, too, have temper tantrums! But they soon recover and life goes on. The more confidence you have in your decision, whatever that decision may be, the easier it will be for your child to recover from the disappointment of not getting her way.

Keep in mind that children do not always know what is best for them. The baby bird does not enjoy being pushed out of the nest, but the mother bird knows it is essential. Bedtime hassles are common. Most families survive them, however. Bedtime brings up difficult issues for many reasons, but we are confident that with a little thought and planning, you can discover a process that works for you and for your children.

13

YOUR TODDLER AND EATING: "OPEN WIDE . . . PLEASE?"

Food is not only something we humans need to survive, but something most of us enjoy. (In fact, some of us enjoy it a bit too much!) So why do mealtimes become such a struggle for the parents of so many toddlers?

Eating is a process entirely controlled by the person doing it. Even if you manage to squeeze, poke, or slide a bit of unwanted food between your child's lips, can you make him chew it? Swallow it? If you've ever tried, you undoubtedly know the answer. Let's explore when and why the battles begin.

Eating begins when you offer an infant a bottle or the breast. Adults often argue over which is better. We encourage every mother to get as much information about the advantages and/or disadvantages of both methods and then to choose the one with which she feels most comfortable. Your confidence is the key. Remember that a confident mother is better able to foster a sense of trust in her baby. Either choice, bottle or breast, can supply the nurturing (and nutrition) an infant needs.

Babies are programmed by nature and their own reflexes to suck for nourishment and comfort, and they usually want to eat frequently. There are many different opinions about how to satisfy this basic need. The debate centers on breast-feeding, bottles, and formula. Not too many years ago, many doctors discouraged breast-feeding, because formula, the product of science, was believed to be better. Now we understand that babies benefit in many ways from their mother's milk. Whichever choice you make, adapting to your baby's needs can be challenging.

In the following section, Jane, one of the authors (and mother of seven children), shares her nursing story and what it taught her about trusting her own instincts.

NURSING

How I wish I'd had more information on nursing from the beginning; I wouldn't have created so much pain for myself and my children as I learned. My first child was born in 1956, when doctors were advocating a strict feeding schedule of every four hours. I didn't even question their reasoning. I just assumed they had to know what they were talking about. Baby Terry would nurse for a short time and fall asleep. Often, during the afternoon, he would wake up after an hour and start crying. I would think, "Oh no! Three more hours before he can nurse." I would walk the floor with him and try to comfort him, but he would just cry until he was screaming. I tried pacifiers and water. They would work for a few minutes, but soon he would be screaming again. (It is painful for me to even remember this.)

Finally, after two hours, I would "cheat" and nurse him before the four hours were up. He was so exhausted from crying that he would nurse for a minute or two and then fall asleep. How could I have been so ignorant that I didn't know he couldn't get enough in two minutes? I was so intimidated by the doctor's advice that I didn't think. I just assumed that I had to wait another four hours. Terry would wake up hungry in about an hour and we would go through another agonizing two hours before I would "cheat" again.

Because of my lack of information about nursing, I believed many myths. I believed that if my breasts weren't engorged, I didn't have any milk, that my milk could not have been rich enough because it wasn't "milky white," and that Terry cried because I didn't have enough milk. The truth was that he cried because he wasn't nursing long enough to get enough nourishment and to build up my milk supply in the process. Another mistake was introducing him to cereal at two weeks (based on my doctor's suggestion) to fill him up. I didn't know that would only keep him from nursing long enough to build up my milk supply. I gave up in frustration after three weeks and put him on a bottle.

I tried nursing with my next three children—Jimmy, Kenny, and Brad—and even though I didn't wait four hours between each feeding, I still believed they needed cereal, apple juice, and baby food and that I didn't have enough milk unless I was engorged. I gave up after a few weeks each time, thinking my milk just wasn't good enough.

When my fifth child, Lisa, was born, I tried nursing again. I was on my way to failure once more when my sister-in-law told me about La Leche League and their book, The Womanly Art of Breastfeeding. *She told me there was no such thing as bad mother's milk, that engorgement wasn't a sign of "enough" milk, and that I should throw away all the formula bottles and supplemental foods and just nurse whenever my baby wanted to in order to build up my milk supply. I read the book, threw away the bottles and solid foods, and began a successful nursing experience.*

I don't know when I have ever been happier! I loved nursing on demand. There were times when Lisa would sleep five or six hours. In the late afternoon and evening she would sometimes nurse as often as every hour—or sometimes every fifteen minutes! By the time she was three and a half months old, she had regulated herself to a three-hour schedule during the day and would sleep through the night, even without cereal to "fill her up."

The Womanly Art of Breastfeeding answered so many questions that it became my bible. I became confident that Lisa didn't need supplemental foods; many babies don't until they're six months to one year old. Every month, my pediatrician would tell me I could introduce a new baby food, and I would just smile. The next month he would ask me if I had introduced the foods, and I would tell him I hadn't. He would suggest that maybe I should, just to make sure she didn't get anemic (iron is the only thing missing from mother's milk, although the baby is usually born with a year's supply of iron). I would ask him if he would like to take a blood test to see if she was in danger of anemia. He would say, looking sheepish, "I can tell from looking at her that she isn't anemic." He really was a wonderful doctor whom I trusted for the health care of my baby; I just knew that he didn't know as much as I did about nursing.

Most mothers find they occasionally have questions about nursing, feeding, bottles, and their babies' nutritional needs. One of the wisest things mothers can do is to begin right away to build a support and resource network. Many hospitals and maternity centers offer breast-feeding support; in fact, some even offer twenty-four-hour phone lines to call when you have questions. Churches, childcare centers, and pediatricians may have information on new mothers' support groups, which can be invaluable in answering questions and boosting your confidence. Remember, no question is ever "stupid." Ask for help when you need it, and have confidence in your own wisdom and growing knowledge of your baby.

LISTENING TO YOUR OWN HEART

Jane's story eloquently demonstrates the need to listen to your own heart when making decisions as a parent. Another mom tells this story—with a very different nursing outcome. She, too, had to listen to her heart.

> *Barbara had nursed her first child for three months but the experience had been difficult—not because of the nursing, which Barbara loved, but because of its inadvertent effect on her own health. Barbara had taken a daily medication for years, one that helped her to maintain her health, but she had discontinued it during the months of pregnancy and nursing. The result was that Barbara's health began to deteriorate, making it even more stressful to take care of her young baby.*
>
> *When Barbara became pregnant with her second child, she made the decision to nurse him only a week or two before switching him to formula. Barbara then was able to resume her medication, ensuring her own health needs were met. She felt healthier and had more energy to care for her newborn son as well as her older child, who was now a toddler.*

As Barbara's story illustrates, each parent must weigh the health and needs of all family members, including his or her own. There are lots of possibilities, but no one "right" choice that will work for all. Although we encourage breast-feeding for its many nutritional and emotional benefits, it is not mandatory. Many emotionally and physically healthy babies have been raised on formula and baby food. When

Pulling Hair While Nursing

Q. I know my eight-month-old daughter is too young for much active discipline, but I'm concerned that her roughness will become a habit and I won't be able to alter it in the future. She's extremely active, energetic, and highly sensitive. She has been hitting, gouging, and yanking hair for a few weeks now, usually when nursing. I've tried taking hold of her arm and demonstrating how to be "gentle" (while reinforcing the idea with words) over and over, but I don't seem to be making any progress. Our poor cats are at their wits' end, as she yanks on them too! Do you have any ideas, or is it too early to worry about this sort of thing?

A. Please read the section in Chapter 8 about what your child really knows about "no." This will help you to understand why supervision and distraction (over and over) are about the only things that are effective at this age—at least regarding the cats. When she pulls your hair while nursing, however, it can be effective to immediately (kindly and firmly) remove her from your breast and wait about a minute before nursing again. She may cry for that minute, but children at this age learn more from kind and firm action than from words. If she is hungry, she will learn that you will stop nursing when she pulls your hair. There is another solution as well: Tie your hair back when you nurse.

you have knowledge about and have considered all choices with care, you will feel confident in whatever you decide.

INTRODUCING SOLID FOODS
AND SUPPLEMENTAL BOTTLES

Eventually all children are ready to be weaned from bottle or breast and to move on to other foods. Here Jane continues with her own experience.

Introducing solid foods to Lisa was easy. When she was seven months old, we occasionally offered her some mashed banana or mashed potato. I might blend other fruits or vegetables in a blender with some liquid. I say "might" because sometimes we did and sometimes we didn't. We didn't feel any pressure, because we knew she was getting all she needed from breast milk during the first year. We saved a fortune (at least, it seemed like a fortune to us) on what we would have spent on formula and baby food. By the time she was one year old, she could eat many of the foods we cooked for our own meals if we mashed, chopped, or blended them for her to eat.

Babies often thrive on nursing for the first year. If you plan to be away from your baby, however (and an occasional night away is good for your own mental and emotional health, as well as your partner's), it is easier if she is comfortable taking a bottle.

I made the mistake of not introducing my last baby to a bottle until I needed to leave her with a babysitter when she was three months old. It took me three days of almost constantly pushing a bottle of apple juice in her mouth before she would finally take it.

La Leche League suggests expressing (that is, pumping) breast milk into a bottle and freezing it so it is available when a mother needs to be away from the baby. This can allow Dad the opportunity to take turns with night feedings or other much needed "mommy breaks." Expressing breast milk also makes it possible for nursing to continue when a mother returns to work and must place her child with a caregiver. With time and practice, parents will learn to gauge the needs of their baby. Some babies do well on a combination of nursing, formula, and solids; some babies never need anything but breast milk. Babies, like adults, are unique individuals. Patience and a bit of trial and error will help you learn your baby's requirements.

WEANING

Lisa weaned herself by her first birthday; she simply refused to nurse anymore. Many mothers believe weaning can't be that easy, but it can be if mothers are willing to watch for the signs of readiness in their babies. Somewhere between the tenth and twelfth month, many babies lose interest in nursing (or in taking a bottle). Many mothers ignore the signs and push the bottle or breast at the baby until they give in and start taking it again (unless they are as stubborn as Lisa). Mothers do this for one of two reasons: (1) They are not aware that a loss of interest during this window of time may be a natural phenomenon that indicates a readiness for weaning; and (2) mothers sometimes want their babies to keep taking the bottle because it is an easy way to calm them when they are fussy and/or to help them to go to sleep.

Keeping babies on the bottle or breast after they are ready to stop may squelch the first blossoming of their sense of autonomy. It is important to realize that once the window of readiness to wean passes, nursing or taking a bottle may become a habit instead of a need. (This distinction between habit and need can help adults determine timing in many areas of development, not just nursing.) But missing this opportunity for weaning isn't a traumatic, life-damaging experience. Many parents have been unaware of the signs of readiness for weaning and have allowed their children to develop the bottle or nursing habit. These parents have just had to learn (from hard experience) that weaning is more difficult when it has become a habit. You and your baby will survive, however, even if you miss this one factor that could increase autonomy a little and make weaning much easier.

Some people disagree with this point of view. We know people who advocate nursing children as old as six or eight years old. This may feel right for some, but we want to encourage parents who are miserable with extended nursing to follow what is right for them. As we have said before, parents will enjoy their role much more when they have the knowledge and the confidence to follow their hearts.

Weaning Is Difficult

Weaning is never easy for the weanee or the weanor, but it is necessary for the ultimate good of both. Weaning is part of the larger, lifelong process of letting go and is vital to helping children develop their full potential. Weaning (and letting go) should not be confused with abandonment. Children need a lot of loving support during the weaning process. When parents begin the weaning process and let go with love at developmentally appropriate times, children are encouraged to trust, to learn confidence, and to develop healthy self-esteem.

Betty's son, Ben, began preschool at age two and a half. He proudly carried his own lunch box to school with him. But his bravado turned to dismay when snack time came. He wanted his bottle, while everyone else was using a cup. Ben's teacher soon realized the cause of his tearful whimpering. That afternoon, she spent some time discussing the situation with Betty. They agreed to allow Ben to use a bottle when he sat at the snack table and when he was lying down for his nap, but the rest of the time the bottle would be kept in the refrigerator. Also, the bottle would contain only water. This plan was relayed to Ben. At the same time, Betty decided to limit the contents of Ben's bottles at home to water. She chose not to reduce their availability, allowing him to use the bottle with fewer restrictions at home.

Several times over the next week, Ben tested his teacher to see if she would give him his bottle at other times of the day. The teacher was sympathetic, offered to hold or hug Ben if he wished, and reassured him that he could have his bottle at snack or rest time but held firm to the plan she had made with Betty. By the second week, Ben stopped asking for his bottle throughout the day. Within the month, he had lost interest in the bottle at other times as well.

Ben continued to use his bottle at home. When Betty saw how successfully the plan at school had worked, she set similar limits at home. After another week or two, she happily gathered up the forgotten bottles and packed them off to a charity program serving infants.

Betty and Ben's teacher used a gradual approach to weaning. Betty could have just refused to bring in any bottles, but Ben, his teacher, and his classmates might have had a much more stressful few weeks. In the end, Ben would have given up his bottle either way. Being firm does not mean that "cold turkey" is the only way to break lingering habits.

EXTENDED NURSING

Some parents do choose to delay the weaning process, allowing children to nurse well into their preschool years. There are at least two sides to the story of extended nursing. We encourage you to become educated and aware before you decide what works for you and your baby. La Leche League and other groups encourage nursing for as long as it feels right for the mother and her child. If you decide you want to nurse for an extended period of time, La Leche League offers classes and support. (The support can be very helpful, since many people will be critical.) If you choose to extend nursing, you will have more confidence if your decision is based on education and awareness.

AVOIDING "FOOD FIGHTS"

"If you don't eat your vegetables, you won't get any dessert!" "If you don't eat your oatmeal for breakfast, you'll get it for lunch!" "You are going to sit there and eat until you finish your dinner if it takes all night!"

These parents seem to believe they can make a child eat, but we have seen just as many kids demonstrate that you *can't* make them eat. We've known children to throw up, sneak food to the dog, glare at the oatmeal through breakfast, lunch, and dinner, and sit there all night— or at least until the parent gives up in despair.

As we've seen, insisting on a particular course of action or behavior is an invitation for most toddlers to engage in a power struggle. It may also be helpful to realize that it isn't usually necessary to force exact quantities of healthy foods down your child's throat. Unless he suffers from a metabolic disorder or requires a special medical diet, many pediatricians believe a young child will tend to choose, over time, the foods his body requires, although this may not happen in one meal or even one day. A parent's task is to prepare and present healthy, nutritious foods; it is a child's task to chew and swallow. Of course, it doesn't hurt to include foods you know your child likes as well.

INVITING COOPERATION AT MEALTIMES

Most people who lived during the Depression report that battles about food and picky eating simply didn't happen. Parents didn't make a fuss when a child didn't want to eat, because there often wasn't enough to go around. When children didn't get any mileage out of being picky or resistant, they ate what was available or went hungry.

In these days, when many of us have so much (and when, as research tells us, most of us eat out several times each week), it's easy to lose sight of the simplicity of eating. Some parents have been so thoroughly hooked by their demanding toddlers that they prepare two or three different meals for dinner: one menu for adults, peanut butter sandwiches for the preschooler, hot dogs for the toddler.

Have children really gotten pickier? Simply put, children do what "works." If refusing to eat what Mom puts on the table gets them the meal of their choice (and the feeling of power that goes along with it), they'll continue to refuse family meals, harried parents will continue to prepare alternatives, and no one will enjoy mealtimes. There are, however, any number of ways to invite cooperation and harmony at the table. As with so many other issues in early childhood, parents can decide what they will do, give up the notion of control, remain kind and firm—and teach children to be responsible, cooperative, and capable.

"Sounds too good to be true," you may be thinking. And in reality, there is no one simple answer to mealtime hassles. Children (like adults) sometimes just aren't hungry. Their food preferences change over time and they may not always want to eat on your schedule. Still, some of the following suggestions and ideas may help you keep food from becoming a fight in your family.

- Don't force-feed. Insisting that children eat particular foods in particular quantities at particular times will only create power struggles—and most parents of toddlers find they have lots of those already! If your baby spits food at you, it may be a clue that she's had enough. Don't insist on feeding more; get a sponge and let her help mop up the mess.

- Presentation counts, even for little ones. Good nutrition is important, but distasteful foods can sometimes be offered in tasty ways. Rather than forcing your child to stare at the soft-boiled egg congealing on his plate, serve eggs by including them in a slice of French toast or a cheese-filled omelet. Include extra fruits and vegetables by pureeing them and adding them to milk or yogurt, or blend and strain soups so that they can be sipped from cups. Serve healthy meals; include a variety of foods as well as familiar ones you know your toddler likes, and then relax with the reassurance that even if he doesn't eat everything, whatever he does eat will be nourishing.

  (Tip: To make it easier to offer a balanced variety, serve foods that are different in color, such as slices of red-skinned apples, bright green peas, and sunny orange sweet potatoes and carrot sticks.)

- Learn your child's needs and preferences. Your little one may have no trouble eating on a regular schedule, but some children do better eating small amounts of food throughout the day. You and your toddler may feel better about her eating if you allow her to do what feels natural. If your child is a snacker, make healthy snacks available. One family set aside a kitchen drawer for their little snacker. Whenever Patrick felt hungry, he could go to "Patrick's drawer" and eat anything he found there. Patrick's mother kept the drawer stocked with crackers, pretzels, raisins or other dried fruits, and an occasional cookie or treat. Patrick loved to see what turned up each day in his drawer, and his mother enjoyed not arguing about meals.

As long as your child is gaining weight and growing (well-child checkups are a must), he is probably doing just fine.

- Learn to read the labels on foods. There are a surprising number of hidden sugars and fats in the prepared foods young children love (breakfast cereals are a prime example), and too much sugar can wreak havoc with a child's appetite for nutritious food. Balance is the key: Your child needs a certain amount of fat to grow and be healthy, so the low-fat, low-sodium diet you may be following is not a good idea for her—nor is it necessary to always substitute carrot sticks for holiday candies and treats. Don't be afraid to serve the same favorites over and over again; children aren't usually as fond of variety as their parents are. But do continue to offer new foods as well. In fact, one way to get a suspicious eater to try new foods is to serve the "strange" item often. The food becomes familiar and children are more willing to sample it. Your pediatrician can answer your questions about specific foods and help you feel confident that your child is healthy and growing.

- Use mealtimes to invite contribution. While toddlers may resist force, they usually enjoy being invited to help Mom or Dad in the kitchen. Even young children can place napkins on the table, rinse lettuce for a salad, or place slices of cheese on hamburger buns. Children are almost always more competent and capable than adults think they are; we know two-year-olds who spread peanut butter on crackers and help stir together muffin recipes (with child-safe utensils and a parent's close supervision, of course).

  Teach children how to make simple sandwiches or spread beans and cheese on a tortilla. Include them in the planning and preparation of meals. If an older toddler doesn't want to eat what is on the table or complains about a meal, simply ask, "What can you do about that?" Then, without making a fuss, sighing, or rolling your eyes, let him choose to prepare the crackers, sandwich, or tortilla he has learned how to make.

Inviting your child to help plan meals, choose ingredients at the grocery store ("Can you find the yellow bananas we need for your pudding?"), dish up servings, and help in the kitchen will not only take some of the struggle out of eating but will also help you create a more resourceful, confident child.

- Hang in there. Most children change their eating habits over time, and the toddler who turns up his nose at veggies today may well love them next month. This miracle usually happens a great deal sooner if parents aren't shouting, lecturing, and pushing. Be patient; offer new foods occasionally, but don't insist. Enjoy mealtimes as an opportunity to gather your family together and share one another's company. In other words, relax a bit. This, too, shall pass!

THE MEDIA AND THE BATTLE AGAINST UNHEALTHY FOODS

One of the real challenges parents face is that of advertising targeted toward children, in particular the promotion of foods that are either unhealthy or low in nutritional value. The Institute of Medicine, a well-regarded scientific-advisory body, has linked television advertising to obesity in children under the age of twelve. The simplest way for parents to prevent unhealthy media influence is to shield a child from such advertising by simply turning off the television (a choice that is in accordance with the American Academy of Pediatrics, which recommends against television viewing for children under the age of two).

The second thing you can do is resist buying unhealthy foods, especially when they are associated with a cartoon or media character. Nutrition, even for a "picky" eater, will be of less concern if all the foods available to him are nutritious and food doesn't become a toy or satisfy a playtime urge.

There are two more ways to protect your child and encourage the development of healthy eating habits. First, model healthy eating. It is hard to convince your child that she shouldn't eat high-fat chips or sugar-laden candy when she sees you polishing off a bag of nacho cheese crisps or eating chocolate bars. She will want to eat what you do, especially if it's sweet or salty.

You can also let manufacturers know when you disapprove of inappropriate foods being marketed to young children or identified with popular entertainment figures. Send letters to manufacturers and marketers. Complain to the manager of the restaurant that only offers high-fat choices such as french fries or macaroni and cheese on the "children's menu," with no healthy alternatives available. Businesses want to sell their products, and when customers question those products, they listen.

Positive Discipline includes encouraging the self-discipline you want your children to develop, and food and eating habits play a large role in this. Prevention of poor eating habits and future obesity are important goals, ones that you can promote through your actions, awareness, and thoughtful consumer choices.

Learning that you "can't make 'em do it" takes most parents until their children are well into adolescence—and sometimes even beyond. Eventually, children will have to manage their own eating habits. They will need to know what constitutes a healthy diet, how much to eat and at what time, and when to stop. Parents can allow their children to explore these concepts right from the beginning, acting as guides and teachers rather than enforcers. Mistakes, as we have said so often, are opportunities to learn—for parents and for children. Life with energetic young children will hold lots of challenges; mealtimes don't have to be among them.

MORE THAN FOOD

Remember that meals are about more than food. They provide a time and place for families to connect, and can also represent the important cultural or familial traditions you may want to pass along to your children. Recent research also tells us that one of the best ways to prevent behavior problems, especially as children grow older, is by having regular family meals. Because of these vital larger roles, making mealtimes pleasant is important. Your special rituals and traditions—holding hands before eating, offering a prayer, or sharing something you are grateful for—will enrich your time together.

When you make mealtime an opportunity to come together, not just to share food but to share your lives as a family, you will feed both bodies and spirits.

14

TOILETING:
"IT'S MY JOB, NOT YOURS"

The struggles parents encounter with sleeping and eating pale in significance when we move to a discussion of toileting. No other topic in the world of raising young children arouses such strong emotions, it seems, as potty training.

The issue of toilet training has been blown out of proportion in our society. It can be the origin of feelings of guilt and shame, power struggles, revenge cycles, bids for undue attention, and competition between parents. But here's the truth: *Even if parents didn't worry about it at all, children would still become toilet-trained in due time just because they would eventually want to copy what everyone else does.* It is adults who create the power struggles that sometimes make it more important for children to "win" than to "cooperate" (which may feel like losing to them).

Paula took a great deal of pride in the fact that her first child was using the toilet at the age of eighteen months. She was so pleased, in fact, that she thought about writing a book about toilet training to help other, less fortunate families. Before she could get around to it, however, her second child was born. Much to Paula's surprise, this child wanted nothing to do with her prize-winning toilet-training techniques. In fact, despite being placed on the potty for long periods of time, this child was almost three years old before the "training" worked.

So much for genius. The reality is that children will use the toilet when they are ready to do so. You can cheer, beg, and threaten, but hang on to your diapers. Each child has his or her own unique schedule—and absolute control. What can parents do to set the stage for this important developmental milestone?

READINESS

Perhaps the real question is *who* is ready for toilet training. Is it *you*? Are you ready to be done with diapers? Are you ready to compete with the neighbors who claim their eighteen-month-old is already potty-trained? And who is actually training whom?

If you could observe closely in most homes where parents claim their toddlers are trained, you might notice that it is the parents who are trained. They are trained to watch the clock and take their little ones to the potty chair, usually offering candy bribes and stars on charts for a tinkle or poop in the potty. They monitor how much their children can drink—especially before bedtime. Many wake their toddlers up in the middle of the night and prop them, half-asleep, on or in front of the toilet and turn on the sink faucet in hopes that the sound of running water will coax some water from their sleepy ones.

So when *are* toddlers ready for toilet training? There is no precise age at which children are ready to use the potty. Few children master control before eighteen months; most do so by age four. Complete nighttime success can take slightly longer and still be within the typical developmental range. When children are truly ready, the process often takes only a few days or weeks. Physical readiness, emotional readiness, and environmental opportunities set children up for success.

Physical Readiness

Children give us a number of clues when they are physically ready to begin toilet training. Observe your child's behavior and ask yourself the following questions: Do long periods elapse between your child's diaper changes? Is her diaper dry after nap time? Does she stop what she is doing and get a look of concentration on her face when she wets herself? These things indicate increasing bladder capacity and awareness and mean that your child is becoming more able to connect her physical sensations with the need to use the toilet.

Children with regular bowel movements experience early success when their parents or caregivers tune in to those rhythms. As we have mentioned, however, adults may need more "training" than the child. Many parents know their child's patterns or facial clues and train themselves to put the child on the potty in time to catch the droppings in the toilet. This is one approach that helps a child become aware of her behavior and know what to do in response. After all, nothing succeeds like success.

Keep in mind that every child is different. In one family Mom and Dad became very familiar with the different physical capacity of their three children. Mom and Dad knew that when driving in the car, they had about twenty minutes to find a place to stop when Kenny said he needed to use the bathroom. If Laura needed the bathroom, they had about ten minutes. If Brad said he needed to "go," they immediately pulled off the road and hoped a bush was nearby.

Emotional Readiness

Q. I have a son who needs to be potty-trained. He turned three years old two months ago. He does not like to use the potty. He does not show me signs when he has to go, but he will tell me when to change him. Please, I need some advice!

A. It does not take great intuition to recognize your desperation. It is hard to keep changing diapers as children grow older. Your son's reasons for not using the potty probably are magnified by your own discouragement. Take heart. He will succeed, but it may take more patience than you think you have. (Does it help to know that he probably won't still be wearing diapers when he goes to college?)

Here are some ideas to keep in mind:

- Try to deemphasize the whole issue. When parents insist on a certain behavior, power struggles may ensue. Remaining calm and kind and refusing to argue over the toilet will ease the process for everyone concerned.

- Sometimes a discussion of safety regarding the flushing toilet eases a child's mind. Help him see that he is too big to fall through the toilet seat, allow him to flush the toilet to reassure himself that he is in control of this powerful, gulping monster, and reassure him that nothing scary will happen to him. Of course, using a small potty chair avoids this problem altogether for a while.

- Don't become so focused on the bathroom that you lose your ability to enjoy the rest of your lives together. Express your confidence in him; tell him that you know he will manage using the potty successfully one day. He, too, needs encouragement.

- There are many ways to set the stage emotionally for successful potty training. Young children often dislike having to lie still while being changed. Use this time to talk to your child, engaging her interest and thereby distracting her attention. Consider hanging a toy above the changing area, using a strip of elastic. Your child can swat, reach for, and handle the toy while she is being changed. This sort of distraction creates a more cooperative atmosphere, avoiding emotional resistance later on when potty training is begun. Hang a musical mobile above the area or tape a fun picture on the ceiling. Changing these items periodically sustains children's interest.

- As your child matures, invite him to help with the job by handing you supplies, holding the clean diaper in readiness, or laying out the changing mat. This increases opportunities to develop autonomy and sends the message that you believe your child is competent and capable. When he needs to be changed, show him ways he can help out. He can wash or wipe himself off, help empty the stool into the toilet bowl, and practice washing his own hands afterward. Inviting his participation also invites cooperation, an important ingredient for success. Changing older children while they stand up often invites more cooperation. Be sure to change a standing child on the floor or perhaps over the bed, so there is less danger of falling.

- Lighten up and make toilet training fun. One parent emptied the toilet bowl and painted a target in the bowl. His son could hardly wait to try to hit the bull's-eye.

- Avoid rewards and praise like stars on a chart or candy treats. Rewards can become more important to your child than learning socially appropriate behavior. Allow your child to feel capable within himself instead of getting hooked on outside validation.

As with most skills, there will be accidents or mistakes during the process of mastering bladder and bowel control. Treating toilet accidents calmly and respectfully makes it less likely that power struggles, resistance, and lack of cooperation will result. Don't humiliate or shame your child when he has an accident; don't put him back in diapers. Simply help him clean up. Say, "It's okay. You can keep trying. I know you'll get it soon." With time and patience, the skill will be mastered.

Here is another suggestion on toilet training from the book *Positive Discipline A–Z,* by Jane Nelsen, Lynn Lott, and H. Stephen Glenn (New York: Three Rivers Press, 2007):

Action Please

Toilet training usually coincides with another toddler milestone, the ability to say no. What will most toddlers say when asked, "Do you need to use the potty?" "No" is a pretty safe guess. A better plan might be to pay attention to your child's facial expression and body language, or to set a reasonable schedule and say, "It's time to go potty," then act. Take his hand and walk to the bathroom, then help him to sit on the toilet or potty seat. Consider letting him sit on his potty while you sit on the big one nearby. This might be *too* much togetherness, but if you are comfortable with it, your little one will probably love the chance to be "just like Mommy or Daddy."

If your child is still not toilet trained by the time she is three years old, be sure to get a doctor's evaluation to see if there is a physical problem. If there is not a physical problem, you may be involved in a power struggle. Guess who will win! One thing you can't control is a child's elimination functions. It takes two to engage in a power struggle. Stop. Allow your child to experience the consequences of his choice with dignity and respect. Teach your child to change his own clothes during a calm time. When the pants get wet or soiled, kindly and firmly take your child to his bedroom to find new clothes. Then lead him to the bathroom and ask if he would like to change alone or with you there to keep him company. (Do not do it for him.) It is unlikely that he will refuse if you are kind and firm and if you have truly dropped the power struggle.

ENVIRONMENTAL OPPORTUNITIES

Some of today's diapers make it difficult for children to respond to their own natural clues. Disposable diapers may do such a good job of absorbing moisture that children do not notice when they are wet. Give children opportunities to notice what happens when they "go." You can use training diapers that provide less complete absorption, or cloth training pants—with lots of clothing changes nearby.

Allowing a child to go diaperless in the backyard on a warm day often provides an eye-opening experience. You can almost read her mind: "Wow! Look what I can do." The awareness of what happens physically often leads to mastery. Some parents have found it helpful to wait until the summer after their child reaches two and a half years old, and then spend some time in the backyard with a naked child and a potty chair, making it a game to pee and poop in the potty. One family found that their son became potty-trained during the week of their family's camping vacation. Urinating in the woods with his older brother beat diapers any day!

Make the process as easy as possible. Switching to training pants or pull-ups eases the transition from diapers. Small potty seats or conversion rings for adult toilets with a small stool for climbing make perfect modifications. Be sure your child is wearing clothing that helps rather than hinders; elastic waistbands and loose articles are easier for small fingers to manage than snaps, buttons, and bows. The easier the on-and-off process, the more successful your little one will be.

Again, a parent's patient confidence makes a difference. Take young Andrew, for instance.

> By the age of three or so, Andrew was ready to give up his diapers. Because he'd decided it was time, his mom and dad found the process delightfully easy: in just one day and two nights, Andrew was completely trained and accident-free.
>
> Imagine, then, how surprised Andrew's mom and dad were when he demanded his diapers back after just one week. In checking out their son's request, his parents learned that Andrew had observed an interesting fact. Going to the bathroom, undoing his clothes, sitting down, cleaning up, and dressing again took more time away from important play than he was willing to spend. Andrew had discovered that diapers were simply less time-consuming, and he wanted to go back to

them. When Andrew found that his parents weren't willing to provide any more diapers, he sighed—and remained in his "big boy pants," entering the grown-up world of bladder-regulated inconvenience.

If your little one wants to change his mind after the training process has been completed and celebrated, don't despair. Remain kind and firm, and the situation will undoubtedly resolve itself. And remember, each child will master toilet training—on his own timetable.

15

BUILDING HEALTHY SELF-ESTEEM THROUGH ENCOURAGEMENT

Learning the fine art of encouragement is one of the most important skills of effective parenting. Experts who study human behavior and development tell us that a healthy sense of self-esteem is one of the greatest assets a child can have, and parents who know how to encourage, have faith, and teach skills are best able to help their children develop self-esteem.

WHAT *IS* SELF-ESTEEM? WHERE DOES IT COME FROM?

Self-esteem is, quite simply, the confidence and sense of self-worth each person has in himself or herself. Self-esteem comes from feeling a sense of belonging, believing that you're capable (because you have experienced your capability—not because someone else tells you that you are), and knowing your contributions are valued and worthwhile.

Self-esteem gives children the courage to take risks in life and to welcome new experiences—everything from tackling the stairs with unsteady steps to making friends at the childcare center to trying out for the football team or honors orchestra later in life. Self-esteem helps children feel comfortable in their own skin, whether they prefer just one friend or many. Children with healthy self-esteem have learned that it is okay to make mistakes and learn from them, rather than thinking a mistake means they are inadequate. Children who lack self-esteem fear failure and often don't believe in themselves even when they possess wonderful talents and abilities.

Self-esteem doesn't just happen in children; it evolves from their beliefs and experiences. Parents can't give children self-esteem; children must develop it for themselves. How can you help your little one begin this important process?

MISTAKES PARENTS MAKE IN THE NAME OF SELF-ESTEEM

Parents (and teachers) are usually well aware these days that children need a healthy sense of self-esteem. They may try to nurture this quality in the children in their care, often through praise and by teaching children to parrot slogans such as "I am special." Remember, though, that children, even very young ones, are making decisions about themselves and the world around them. All too often, these misguided efforts backfire, leading children to form beliefs that are not in their long-term best interest. Before we look at effective ways to build self-esteem, let's look at some methods that don't work.

Trying to Give Children Self-Esteem Through Excessive Praise
Praise can actually be discouraging instead of encouraging. When parents constantly tell a child, "You are such a good girl! I'm so proud of you," that child may become an "approval junkie." Instead of devel-

oping self-esteem, she may decide, "I'm okay only if someone thinks I am." She may feel pressure to be perfect in order to avoid disappointing her parents. Or she may give up because she believes she can't live up to the praise and the high expectations that usually go along with it. In the long term, praise doesn't have the positive effect most people think it does. A little praise may not hurt—but it probably won't help much, either.

> ### Ineffective Methods for Building Self-Esteem
>
> - Trying to give children self-esteem through excessive praise and pep talks.
> - Overprotecting or rescuing children.
> - Wanting children to be "better" (or just different).

Overprotecting or Rescuing Children

Many parents are afraid their children will suffer if they have to deal with discomfort or disappointment, but the opposite is true. Overly protected children may decide, "I can't handle problems. I can't survive disappointment. I need others to take care of me and rescue me." Or they may decide that it's easier to let others take responsibility for them. Either way, overprotected children rarely develop the competence and self-confidence that might help them handle life's challenges as they grow.

Wanting Children to Be "Better" (or Just Different)

Since the primary goal of all children is to feel that they belong and are significant, it may be devastating when a child discovers that her parents don't love her unconditionally. When the mother of Travis, an active, high-energy child, says, "I wish you were as calm and well behaved as Johnny," Travis may decide, "I'm not good enough. It really doesn't matter what I do—my mom doesn't like me." This kind of discouragement is the foundation for most misbehavior. Remember, a misbehaving child is a discouraged child. There is nothing as encouraging and effective as loving, unconditional acceptance. This does not mean that parents must applaud their children's misbehavior and weaknesses; it does mean that parents must realize that they help their children best when they accept them for who they are, with all their unique strengths and weaknesses. Parents also help by practicing kind, firm discipline, teaching skills, and offering encouragement, providing experiences that help children grow into capable, confident young people.

KINDNESS AND FIRMNESS

The best parenting approach is undoubtedly to be kind and firm at the same time. Notice how this phrase fits as you look at the mistakes listed above. Teaching children that they are loved only when they behave in ways that are cute, sweet, or undemanding is not kind. Kindness shows unconditional love. Firmness provides guidance and real teaching. An example of fusing the two is switching from giving commands to inviting cooperation. If your little one grabs a breakable vase, instead of telling her to put it down, try asking, "Please hand me the vase." You will avoid a power struggle and provide an opportunity for her to feel that she is competent instead of a "naughty girl." Kindness and firmness at the same time provides children with many opportunities to develop self-esteem. Let's look now at other ways to help children develop healthy self-esteem.

ENCOURAGEMENT

Praise is like junk food; it is mass-produced and often is neither personal nor meaningful. Little smiley faces that say "great kid" can be stamped on any child's hand. Real encouragement is more selective because it notices and validates the uniqueness of each individual.

Little Amy waited until her twelfth month to make her walking debut. Her family had traveled across the country to visit grandparents in Florida. One afternoon, with her parents, grandparents, and siblings gathered around, Amy decided the time to display her skills had arrived. She grinned at her family, then relinquished her hold on the sofa and with heart-stopping

*wobbles took her first steps—straight into Grandma's eager
arms. Her family was ecstatic. "You can do it!" they called,
their faces wreathed in smiles. "That's it. Just take it slow. Just
a little farther. Go Amy! You've got it! Hooray!"*

*Amy's grin almost split her face in two as she basked in her
family's love. Now, that's encouragement!*

The praise version might have sounded more like this: "Good girl!
I'm so proud of you."

Many parents become confused about the difference between praise
and encouragement, so let's take a closer look. In the scenes described
above, encouragement focuses on the task, while praise focuses on the
person. Many children, when praised, form the belief that they are
"good" only if they accomplish a task. Praise usually requires a successfully completed task, while encouragement speaks to the effort. In
other words, praise is often conditional, while encouragement is
unconditional.

Also remember that, oddly enough, too much of a good thing can be
discouraging. When children receive cheers for every little thing they
do, it is easy for them to develop the belief: I'm okay only when others
are cheering and clapping.

An important clue that will help you understand the difference
between praise and encouragement is to get into your child's world.
Notice if your child is depending too much on the opinion of others—
a dangerous result of praise. On the other hand, little ones love an
audience and often enthusiastically invite you to "Watch me! Watch
me!" It isn't necessary to worry too much about the difference between
praise and encouragement. Just be aware of the decisions your child
may be making about your feelings. Do your statements convey conditional or unconditional love and support?

One approach is to ask yourself if your words could only be said to
this person at this time. You can say "Great job" to the barber, the
dog, and your spouse, all in the same breath. You can't use "Thank
you for giving me such a flattering haircut," "You found your bone—

how yummy," or "That color of blue looks really nice on you—it's different from the shade you usually wear" interchangeably. If your words are unique to the person, place, or situation, they are more likely to be encouragement.

Showing Faith

Amy's family offered her encouragement most effectively by allowing her to experiment with the process of walking—and by not intervening unnecessarily. Amy's family might have chosen to rescue their fragile baby. Grandma might have called out, "Be careful. Quick, someone, catch the baby." Mom or Dad might have swooped in to hold Amy's hand, block her path, or pick her up. Older brother might have grabbed Amy from behind to steady her.

There was a risk that Amy might fall, but Amy's family gave her the chance to take that risk. Risks imply the possibility of failure, but without risk there can never be success. Amy took a risk and managed her first steps. No praise could replace her feeling of accomplishment in that moment. Self-esteem is that experience of "I can do it!" You help your children build self-esteem when you balance your need to protect them with their need to take risks, tackle new challenges, and explore their capabilities.

Balance, however, is essential. Imagine a parent believing that her child should never be discouraged from exploring his environment. Perhaps she feels that limiting his activities will frustrate his curiosity. So when little Michael heads into the street, she runs to the intersection and flags the cars to a stop, allowing Michael to stroll contentedly among the fenders. This is not encouragement. What Michael needs is supervision and lots of teaching about the danger of intersections, lest he decide to try crossing the street when his mother isn't there to play traffic cop.

Encouragement does not mean remaking the world to fit your toddler's every whim. Kindly and firmly removing a child from the street does limit his exploring; it also protects him from danger and does not allow him to believe wandering in the street is safe. Wise parents weigh their children's choices and environments to determine which experiences offer opportunities for growth and which are simply too dangerous. Allowing a child to take reasonable risks and learn new skills is encouragement. Facing challenges and experiencing success builds self-esteem.

Excessive Encouragement

Some parents seem to think they need to clap wildly while shouting "Yeah" every time their child accomplishes a task. This response could teach children that they need attention for everything they do. Also, too much attention for every accomplishment may diminish a child's inner sense of pride in his accomplishment. Have we mentioned balance? Here it is again. You will encourage your child most effectively when you consider what he might be thinking and deciding. After all, these decisions will become the foundation of his approach to life.

LOVING THE CHILD YOU HAVE

Most of us have dreams of who our child will be. We may hope for a child who is quiet and dreamy, one who is energetic and outgoing, or one who possesses some other combination of qualities and talents. We may even want a child exactly like ourselves. (Parents and children do not necessarily come in matched pairs!)

> *Janice had dreamed of her child's babyhood. She was delighted to have a little girl, and she had painstakingly furnished the nursery in pastel-colored lace and ruffles. She bought ribbons and bows for her daughter's almost-invisible hair; she filled drawers with adorable little dresses. She cleaned up her own favorite dolls and added several more, preparing herself to share all sorts of blissful times with her daughter.*

The little girl in question, however, had other ideas. She was not a cuddly child and squirmed and wriggled constantly. She crawled and walked early and was always into something, much to her mother's dismay. She delighted in pulling the vacuum cleaner attachments apart and emptied the kitchen cabinets time and time again. The dainty dresses were a nuisance; the baby seemed to have a gift for tearing and staining them.

Things only got more difficult as she grew. She preferred to be called Casey rather than Katy; she thought dresses were silly. She had no patience with dolls and tossed them into the darkest corner of her closet or undressed them and scribbled on them with ink; she insisted on "borrowing" her older brother's trucks and guns. Her favorite game was Army, and as soon as she was able, she joined the older boys (despite their howls of protest) in their games, showing an astounding talent for street hockey and climbing trees. She even liked lizards and snakes. Janice tried offering ballet lessons and even gymnastics, but to no avail: Casey refused to be Katy. (It is interesting to note that when Casey had a little girl of her own, her daughter didn't follow in her mom's footsteps. Little Diana delighted her Grandma Janice by loving dolls, dresses, and makeup—even as a toddler.)

Does Janice love her child? Undoubtedly she does. But one of the most beautiful ways of expressing love for a child is learning to love that child—not the child you wish you had.

THE POWER OF UNCONDITIONAL LOVE AND ACCEPTANCE

All parents have dreams for their children, and dreaming is not a bad thing. But we must love our children unconditionally in order for them to feel the acceptance and self-worth that will lead to success. If you are to encourage your child and help him develop a sense of belonging and significance, you should keep several ideas in mind.

Accept Your Child as He Is

Children have their own unique temperaments. They have abilities you may not have expected and dreams of their own that don't match yours, and sometimes their behavior is a real disappointment. It is all too easy to compare your offspring with the children down the street, with their cousins, or even with their own siblings, and to find them lacking in some way.

We humans are not good at unconditional love, yet children need to be loved unconditionally. Parents must learn to love the child they have, which is sometimes easier said than done—and which takes time and patience. You must remember that even the youngest child has an amazing ability to sense her parents' true feelings and attitudes. If she knows she is loved and accepted—if she feels the sense of worth and belonging she craves—she will thrive. If she senses that she doesn't belong, that she is a disappointment or a nuisance, her budding sense of self will wither, and you may never get to know the person she could have been. Encourage your child to be the best person she can be, not to be someone she is not.

> **Effective Methods for Building Self-Esteem**
>
> - Accept your child as he is.
> - Be patient with your child's development.
> - Provide opportunities for success.
> - Teach your child skills.
> - Be aware of self-fulfilling prophecies.

Be Patient with Your Child's Development

Developmental charts are a wonderful way to keep track of the average time span during which children do certain things. The problem is that there are no average children! Children develop—crawl, walk, talk—at their own pace, and many early-childhood conflicts stem from parental impatience. Your child will walk and use the toilet when he's ready;

after all, have you ever seen a child crawl off to kindergarten in diapers? If you have serious concerns about your child's development, a word with your pediatrician may set your mind at rest—and save both you and your child a great deal of discouragement.

Provide Opportunities for Success

Far more powerful than even the most loving and appreciative words are experiences that teach children they are capable, competent people. Begin early to look for your child's special gifts and talents, her abilities and strengths, the things that make her bubble inside. Then give her chances to try those things.

Provide opportunities, too, for her to help you and to take on the little responsibilities she can handle. Early successes and experiences that say "I can do this!" are powerful builders of self-esteem.

Teach Your Child Skills

Real self-esteem grows when children have "competency experiences"—that is, when they learn skills and develop confidence in their ability to accomplish a task "all by myself." Yes, toddlers are young, but you might be surprised at how much your little one can do. Your child can place napkins on the table, rinse lettuce leaves in the sink, and mop up spills with a sponge. She can place slices of cheese on hamburger buns, learn to dress herself, and pour her own juice. Will she do these tasks perfectly? Of course not—which is a good reason for you to have realistic expectations, lots of patience, and the willingness to teach these skills more than once. Still, skills are the foundation of healthy self-esteem and self-confidence. When you teach your little one, you help her become a more responsible, self-reliant person.

Be Aware of Self-Fulfilling Prophecies

It is interesting to wonder just how terrible the twos would be if parents weren't forever telling each other—and their children—about them. Children have an uncanny ability to live up (or down) to their parents' expectations. If you call your rambunctious toddler a "little monster," don't be surprised if he does his best to be what you expect. In the same way, you can build self-confidence in your children by letting them know you love and accept them and believe in their ability to succeed.

Are your children always going to live out your predictions and expectations? No, of course not. But remember how powerful your words and opinions are to your child. If you tell him that he's bad, or lazy, or stupid, or clumsy, don't be surprised if you reinforce the very behavior you dislike. By the same token, if you look for what's positive in your child, you can choose to reinforce those positives—which leads us to one of the most powerful tools a parent has for helping a child develop a sense of healthy self-esteem: looking for the positive.

LOOKING FOR THE POSITIVE

The next time your toddler is playing quietly, peek in for just a moment and watch. What do you see? You may notice your child's glowing smile, his ability to build tall towers with his blocks, or his wonderful creativity and imagination. Whatever it is that you see, make a note to share that observation with your child, and then watch what happens. Behavior that is noticed and appreciated is often repeated!

All human beings long to be appreciated. Young children who are just learning about their world and their place in it have a special need to be encouraged, to have their progress noticed, and to feel they are valuable people.

It is easy in this world of ours to focus on what's wrong. We have no trouble making long lists of what we dislike about ourselves, our spouses, our jobs—and our children. Think for a moment about how you'd feel if your boss at work never did anything but point out your errors and shortcomings. How motivated would you feel to try harder?

Some young children hear a constant litany of "No, no, do it this way" or "How many times do I have to tell you?" or "Here, let me do it." It's no wonder they get discouraged, and as we've already learned, discouragement usually leads to misbehavior.

CELEBRATE THE POSITIVE

Take a moment sometime soon to make a list of what you really like about your child. Hang the list where you can see it (the refrigerator or the bathroom mirror work well) and add to it when you think of something new. Then find an opportunity each day to appreciate your child

for something on the list. Children often bloom amazingly in the steady light of love and encouragement. Don't worry if your child is too young to understand the words you're saying; your warm tone of voice, smiles, and hugs will send the message loud and clear.

The Virtues Guide, by Linda Popov (The Virtues Project, 1995), lists many of the character traits parents hope to pass on to their children. One suggestion is to focus on a different trait each week. You may want your children to be honest, compassionate, and cooperative—but do they know what these traits mean or feel like? As your little one learns words, introduce a few of these concepts and let him know when you see him demonstrating them.

Encouragement means noticing progress, not just achievement. It means thanking your small son for picking up most of his cars, even though he missed a few in the corner. It means giving a hug for an attempt on the potty seat, whether or not there was a result. It means smiling with a child who has put on her shoes, even though they're on the wrong feet. Encouragement says to a child, "I see you trying, and I have faith in you. Keep it up!"

Looking for the positive in your children and encouraging it is a skill that will serve you well throughout their childhood and adolescence. It will help your children to feel good about themselves.

PREVENT PROBLEMS WITH ADVANCE PLANNING

Some problems may be prevented when you let your children know how to deal with new situations by taking the time to prepare them for what will happen—which might make the experience much more pleasant for all concerned.

Patsy was on her way home from picking up her two-year-old son, Eric, when she decided to stop in at the jewelry shop to get her watch, which had been repaired. She hurried in with Eric tagging along behind her and went straight to the counter to present her claim check.

Eric stood clinging to his mother's coat. He had never been in a shop like this before, and there was a lot to look at. He was gazing about him when suddenly an open display shelf near a window caught his eye and utterly dazzled him.

The late-afternoon sunlight was glinting off a collection of the most fascinating objects Eric had ever seen. They were small crystal figures—little animals and people, and even a perfect, tiny castle atop its own crystal mountain, exactly like the one in Eric's favorite storybook—and every movement of Eric's head created rainbows of bright light.

Before Patsy had time to realize what was happening, Eric was off toward the shelf as fast as his short, round legs could carry him. He reached for the wonderful castle, but his small fingers were only strong enough to drag the castle off its shelf and onto the tile floor, where it splintered into pieces.

Eric howled in fright. Patsy was embarrassed, apologetic, and angry—the crystal castle turned out to be shockingly expensive.

What are Patsy's options? Unfortunately, at this point she doesn't have many. She can pay for the broken castle and whisk her small son out to the car, vowing never to take him anywhere again. She can explore with Eric what happened and hope he remembers next time. (Notice that we haven't mentioned punishing Eric; it is doubtful a slap or a time-out would make things any better, especially since Eric had received no guidelines beforehand.)

It's impossible to keep children from exploring their world; it's up to you to prevent disasters. Patsy could have thought things through before entering the store and taken the time to teach. She could have gotten down on Eric's level, perhaps placing her hands gently on his shoulders or taking his hands in hers, and explained that there would be many pretty things in the store but that touching and holding them might break them; Eric could look but not touch. Patsy could have made sure that Eric had something to occupy him while she was busy with the clerk. She probably should have planned on holding his hand anyway, because it is too much to expect that a child will not want to explore at that age, no matter how much teaching takes place. Or she could have decided that discretion was the better part of valor and picked up the watch at a time when Eric could be elsewhere.

You may have noticed recent stories in the news about restaurants and other public places that require children to "use indoor voices" and behave appropriately. Some parents have chosen to regard these requests as "antichild" and boycott the businesses that post such notices. It may be more helpful to remember that as your child grows, he will need to know how to behave in public places. Taking a moment to teach, to talk quietly about behavior, and preparing by packing a few small, quiet toys, will help your child develop skills and confidence—and will earn you the gratitude of your fellow diners and shoppers.

THE IMPORTANCE OF HUMOR AND HOPE

The ability to laugh and the ability to hope and dream are among the greatest gifts parents can bestow on their children. From the earliest games of peekaboo with your infant, laughter creates one of the closest bonds between you and your child. Babies and young children are a wonderful source of joy; every day can be an adventure, a chance to laugh and love together. Learning to share a smile, to make funny faces, or to find the humor in situations can carry your family through many tough times.

Rules and limits have their place, and we couldn't function well without them. But try the following experiment sometime: Notice how often you reprimand your child, make a demand of him, or warn against danger or an infraction of the rules. Then count how many times you admire his skills, encourage his explorations, or chuckle together over some amusing incident. Which do you do more often?

A research project many years ago found that toddlers hear many more negative statements a day than positive. This would send most adults into deep depression. It is amazing how resilient little ones can be—but these negative statements do take their toll in later life. Could this explain why so many adults are fearful of mistakes? Is this why adults have such a difficult time with any kind of feedback and see it as criticism, even when criticism is not intended?

An awareness of the impact of negative statements might convince you to be more encouraging to your children. Focus on the positive. Allow time for relaxing a bit, for allowing a child an extra hug or a few extra minutes of talk before bed. You may find it much easier to get dinner on the table at the end of a busy day when you take a moment to reconnect with your child first, rather than reacting to her whining and endless bids for your attention. There are times when the best medicine truly is laughter and play.

FIRST STEPS

Children take many first steps—and only a few of them involve walking. Your child needs your unqualified support; he needs to know you have faith in him. He needs opportunities to practice new skills and to take his first steps, no matter how wobbly. He needs to know he can make mistakes without risking the loss of your love. When children live in an environment rich with encouragement, are allowed to learn from their mistakes, and experience kind and firm support, they will learn to believe in themselves. Self-esteem is inherent within each human soul, and like any young seedling, it needs nurturing, warmth, and encouragement to thrive.

16

THE WORLD "OUT THERE": DEALING WITH THE INFLUENCE OF TECHNOLOGY AND CULTURE

It's hard to imagine, but there was once a time when television did not exist and families gathered around a mysterious new device called the "radio" to hear music, drama, and news. Earlier still, radio had yet to be invented and families entertained themselves by reading books, gathering around the piano to sing, or telling stories aloud. You may be thankful for modern conveniences, or you may find yourself wishing for simpler times, but like it or not, there is no going back. Television, computers, the Internet, digital music players, and video games are here to stay, and new devices are undoubtedly just around the corner. At some point in your child's early years, you must make a decision about the place these technologies will occupy in your home.

You may feel a bit surprised that the subjects of technology and culture are included in a book on the first three years of your child's life, but consider the following facts:

- The average American family has 2.75 television sets.

- Sixty-six percent of American children have a television in their bedroom (including 20 percent of children between two and seven years old).

- Average viewing time per week for children and adolescents in America is more than 21 hours per week, or nearly one-fifth of a child's waking hours.

- Television viewing may affect attention span by conditioning children to short bits of information delivered in rapid succession.

- American advertisers spend approximately $15 billion each year marketing products to children.

- Having a television on in the background appears to hamper a child's ability to learn language.

- Increased television viewing is directly linked to obesity; the more time children spend in front of a screen, the less time they spend running, using their imaginations, or learning social and life skills.

- Exposure to TV violence in childhood is linked to aggressive behavior for both male and female young adults.

Even toddlers gravitate toward the television; many children learn to operate sophisticated remote controls before their third birthday and sit mesmerized in front of the screen to watch a cartoon or video. In fact, many parents include television as part of a child's bedtime routine, unaware that television viewing before bed may disturb children's sleep patterns. Some children even routinely fall asleep on the floor in front of the television rather than in their own beds. Because young children learn by imitation, your toddler may be quick to learn how to use your cell phone or personal digital assistant—or at least how to punch lots of buttons. (In this chapter we refer to "screen time," which includes television, computers, video games, and other electronic devices.)

Software designers are quick to promote "educational" programs for very young children, urging parents to start early to teach computer literacy to their small fry. And while commercial tie-ins to children's programming have been limited in recent years, children still clamor for toys and products (often junk food, candy, or sugary beverages) bearing the image of their favorite television or video characters. Wise parents learn to thoughtfully consider whether they will have the strongest influence in a child's life—or whether that influence will be handed over to advertisers and marketers. Who is most likely to have your child's best interests at heart?

TELEVISION: FRIEND OR FOE?

Q. I have two boys; the older one is eight years old and my youngest is almost three. My three-year-old loves to watch television with his brother. He also loves to watch the video games his brother plays. We monitor their viewing and will not allow either boy to play violent games. But so much of "children's programming" these days involves scary subjects, fighting, and disrespect. My little boy recently aimed a karate kick at me when I asked him to take his bath—just like his favorite TV character. Should we unplug the television completely?

A. Experts have spent a great deal of time over the past decade or two studying the effects of television and video game violence on young children. (For examples, as well as ratings for games and other programs, check David Walsh's excellent website, www.mediawise.org.) They have discovered that television and video violence may have a stronger effect on young children than previously thought. In fact, a forty-year longitudinal study funded by the National Institute of Mental Health and conducted by the Institute for Social Research at the University of Michigan found compelling evidence linking a child's exposure to media violence to a lasting tendency for violent and aggressive behavior later in life.

Toddlers and preschoolers learn a great deal about behavior and attitudes by imitating others. As discussed earlier, young children cannot tell the difference between reality and fantasy in the same way older children and adults can. They also may be more likely to imitate aggressive behavior, especially aggression that goes unpunished or is performed in the service of "good" (as in superhero cartoons or movies). One recent study found that between 60 and 90 percent of the most popular video games have violent themes. Children who see screen violence are less likely to develop empathy for others; after all, if people on TV get shot and kicked and punched and are still okay (and they usually are), what's the problem?

The best ways to deal with the effect of video and television violence on your sons is to limit their exposure and to do lots of teaching. Watch programs or games *with* them and be sure you teach them the values you want them to adopt. It may be helpful to remember that television viewing encourages passivity. Critical thinking and learning occur only when dialogue takes place. Let your child know kindly but firmly that kicking, punching, and hitting are not acceptable in your family and that real people suffer pain and harm when they are kicked or punched. Most important, put a cap on the time they spend in front of the screen—any screen—and substitute time for active play and conversation, with one another and with you.

COMMERCIAL INFLUENCE

It is no accident that advertisers target children for their products. Young children may not have much spending money but they certainly know people who do—and children are often able to whine, beg, and manipulate parents into buying the toy, product, or snack food of the moment. Most snack foods marketed in this way are not healthy. In addition to other safeguards, consider becoming more proactive by letting advertisers know when you object to their marketing to young children. There are some products that should not be made attractive to small children, such as cigarettes, alcohol, and anything dangerous. If you feel that advertisers are specifically targeting children for something inappropriate, tell them so. Your voice does count.

THE CULTURE OF DISRESPECT

Television, music, movies, and the culture in general have a subtle but pervasive influence on family life. Not too many years ago, the after-dinner hours were considered "family time"; programming was intended for children as well as adults, and profanity, sexual innuendo, and other adult influences were forbidden. Now think about the programs that are broadcast regularly in "prime time." What messages do they teach about respect for adults, courtesy, and cooperation? In many popular programs, children and teens are presented as "cool" and smart, while adults (especially parents) are pathetic, dumb, and hopeless. Even the evening news programs routinely deal with subject matter that most parents find inappropriate for young children.

Certainly there are exceptions, but a great deal of the music, movies, and television available to young people fosters an attitude of disrespect toward others. (Remember, even if you limit your child's exposure to media, he will undoubtedly encounter a great deal of it in the company of other children at his childcare center, the neighbor's house, and family get-togethers.) It is essential that you stay aware and that you actively teach the character values and skills you want your child to practice. How can you manage television and technology for your young child?

Monitor Your Own Habits
It is difficult to limit your child's exposure to television, video games, and the computer when you never turn them off yourself. In fact, most

adult relationships would improve if the television and computer were turned off more often. Be sure the television is off during family meals and conversations. (Consider recording the news so that adults can view disturbing events after children are in bed.)

If you rely on the computer to work at home, make an effort to do as much of that work as possible when your child is occupied elsewhere. You are your child's most important role model; be sure you practice the values you expect your child to learn.

Allow Televisions, Video Games, and Computers
Only in Common Areas of the House
We can think of no reason for a child younger than three to have a television in his room, yet we know many who do, complete with video recorder and DVD player. Your child does not yet have the ability to choose his own viewing material, no matter how well he operates the remote. Be sure that all screens are located where you can easily view them along with your child. Supervision is essential, especially at this age.

Screen time is addictive, and it isn't long before children (and adults) feed their addiction—especially when access to the addiction is so easy. A television located in a child's room encourages isolation instead of connection. When you combine addiction and isolation, you have a child who is developing habits of "life numbness" instead of "life enjoyment." In addition, a recent Stanford University study found that there is a direct correlation between low test scores at school and having a television in the bedroom—a fact that may not concern you now but that

> ### Dealing with Television, Video Games, and Technology
>
> - Monitor your own habits.
> - Allow televisions, video games, and computers only in common areas of the house where everyone can see them.
> - Limit time spent in front of the screen.
> - Watch or play *with* your child.
> - Actively teach the values you believe in.
> - Spend time developing a strong relationship with your child.

will become more important when your child starts school. When the TV is in a common room (such as the family room), family members have the opportunity to negotiate what to watch and when, so the television programming they do watch becomes a shared family experience, and adults remain aware of what children are seeing and hearing.

Limit Time Spent in Front of the Screen
The American Academy of Pediatrics recommends that children two years old and younger watch no television at all. There is increasing evidence that screen time before the age of eight can negatively influence brain development. You may choose to allow your child to watch a favorite program or video every now and then, but far too many children spend hours each day in front of the screen.

Your little one needs active play, time outdoors, conversation with you, and things to manipulate and explore far more than he needs the "educational" programs on television. Intellectual, emotional, and physical development all require activity and practice with other humans; the most important factor in healthy development is connection with parents and other caregivers. Children who feel connected to important others in their lives are less likely to engage in serious misbehavior. (We say "serious" because so much misbehavior is developmentally appropriate as part of the individuation process of testing and discovering boundaries.)

Watch or Play with *Your Child*
There is no better way to monitor the content of programs or videos (and to observe their effect on your child) than to watch or play with him. Invite your little one to teach you his favorite game; settle down next to him to watch his special cartoon. You can ask curiosity questions to learn more and to engage your child in exercising his thinking skills. Curiosity is a great parenting tool and may help you understand your child's fascination with what he sees. You will also know when material is inappropriate for your child—and will be able to turn it off.

Actively Teach the Values You Believe In

When parents don't teach, the culture will. Nature, it is said, abhors a vacuum, and the values and ideals of the mass culture will rush in to fill any empty space you leave in your child's education. Be sure you find opportunities to teach about respect, compassion, cooperation, and kindness. (Remember that during the first three years, you are planting seeds for the growth of lifelong habits. Children would never learn to talk if they didn't hear lots of language before they absorb and finally understand it. Early experiences prepare the brain for future mastery.)

When inappropriate behavior or attitudes occur in programs you are watching together, use them as teaching moments to help your child learn a better way. ("What would you have said to that boy?" "How would you feel if that happened to you?") When all else fails, pull the plug and find something better to do.

In fact, having the courage to pull the plug may be a good place to start. We know of one family that purchased a small TV that could be hidden with a toaster cover. They would bring it out only for special programs that they planned in advance to watch.

Spend Time Developing a Strong Relationship with Your Child

There is *so* much to do with young children. Your child craves real connection with you; when he has it, he is less likely to look for stimulation and company elsewhere. (And as mentioned above, he is less likely to misbehave.) As your child grows, his peers and the culture will become increasingly important. For now, you are his world. Be sure you take the time each day to connect with your little one and to explore the world you share.

WHAT ABOUT THE COMPUTER?

Much has been said and written about the importance of computer literacy. In a rapidly changing world, Americans are being urged to interest their children early in math, science, and technology in order to keep up with the rest of the world. It probably isn't necessary to start your child on the computer very early. Although none of the authors grew up in the computer age, we have all learned to use—and enjoy—them. (Well, at least most of the time.)

The choice is not between total abstinence or instant addiction; instead, consider creating a thoughtful balance. If your little one truly enjoys simple computer programs that help identify colors, letters, shapes, and numbers, some computer playtime every now and then may be fine. (Be sure you use passwords or otherwise protect your own important records and files; toddler curiosity and computer keyboards can be a volatile mixture!) But you should be aware that many experts believe screen time of any sort (including the computer) does more harm than good at this age.

You must find ways to protect your child, but you must do so within the context of the world around you. Your child will also be exposed to computer use at friends' homes, childcare centers, and eventually, school. You should begin early to teach your little one appropriate screen-use guidelines. True computer literacy will not be required until sometime after your child begins school. Don't push, and continue to limit time spent sitting in front of the screen. There will be plenty of time in the years ahead to master the keyboard.

DECIDE WHAT YOU WILL DO, BE KIND AND FIRM, THEN FOLLOW THROUGH

Television, computers, and the other trappings of modern life may not be a big issue during your child's first three years, but they will loom increasingly large as your child grows and moves into the world "out there." These early years are a good opportunity to practice the skills you will need as your child tests his limits and experiments with the world around him. Positive Discipline tools will help you remain calm, kind, and firm as you decide how to approach these complex issues in your own family. Educate yourself about the issues, then decide what *you* will do. Teach values and skills; say no when necessary. Then follow through with dignity and respect for yourself and your child. Like it or not, you and your child must learn to live in an increasingly complicated and challenging world. The lessons you teach now will build the foundation for the years to come.

17

WHO'S WATCHING THE KIDS? CHOOSING (AND LIVING WITH) CHILDCARE

No matter how capable and competent you are as a parent, it is unlikely you will care for your child entirely on your own. Most adults must work, either in the home or out of the home, and for most families childcare of some sort is just a fact of life.

In thousands and thousands of homes across this nation, each working day begins with the ritual of packing lunches, gathering backpacks and jackets, and driving the children to their childcare facility. Some children go to friends' or relatives' homes, while others spend the day in large centers with many other children. Some receive excellent care and opportunities to learn and grow, and have lots of fun, while others spend the hours bored, lonely, or neglected. And in thousands and thousands of homes, parents suffer confusion, regret, or doubt about the wisdom of leaving their children in someone else's care. For thousands of parents, childcare is a necessity, and choosing the best care for the available money is their main concern. Still other parents believe that only a parent should care for a young child and that childcare is always a poor substitute. Each family has unique needs and often conflicting beliefs to reconcile. Listen for a moment to the voices of two different parents.

Q. I have read that you feel that mothers who work do not have a negative effect on their children. Could you please expand on this? Radio programs, newspaper articles, and magazines offer such conflicting advice that I feel really confused. At the present time it is not possible for me to quit my job, because my husband is bedridden with a back injury. My son spends about nine hours a day at childcare. Will this have a negative impact on him? I feel terribly guilty. I love my son more than anything and want to be with him, but I can't be. Thank you.

Q. My neighbor just came by for a visit. Her son Joseph attends childcare three days a week while she works at a part-time job. Joseph is two months younger than my son, and yet Joseph can count and write his name and knows all his colors, while my son does none of these things. I am a full-time mom at home with our son all day. I feel really inadequate whenever my neighbor and her son visit. I am worried that my son will be behind when it is time for him to begin school. Our money is tight, but should I look into putting him in a preschool?

A. Most people hold strong opinions about who should care for young children. The authors believe that where or from whom a child receives care matters less than the quality of the care itself. "Quality" childcare supports the development of healthy self-esteem, emotional well-being, learning and brain growth, and the ability to form healthy relationships with other people.

Many mothers seem to feel guilty whether they stay at home or not. Feeling guilty does not do anyone the least bit of good. Neither does being judgmental. Everyone makes choices based on his or her own situation and beliefs. Young children love to be with their parents, and we know that the bond of mother, father, and child is vital. But this bond does not thrive only in isolation. Children can learn and grow in many different settings.

IS CHILDCARE HARMFUL?

Roslyn, one of the authors and the mother of four, shares her experiences as a stay-at-home mom with her first two children and then as a working mom with her two youngest children in childcare.

> *I stayed home with our two oldest children throughout their first three years. When our second child turned three, our family opened the Learning Tree, a Montessori childcare center. In many ways, our two youngest children had the best of both worlds. They were with their parents, since both their dad and I worked at the childcare center, and they also took part in a wonderful childcare program each day.*
>
> *All four of our children are thriving today. The center is, too; it's still operating more than twenty-six years later and even our grandchildren have attended it. Many of the other children we cared for in those early years of our center's existence are now young adults; some are parents themselves. They frequently stop by to visit and reminisce with us, and more than one has told us that their time at our center helped them experience subsequent successes in their lives. They are loving, capable, and responsible people and we are grateful our family played an important role in so many young lives.*

There are all kinds of conflicting studies, attitudes, and theories about childcare. Roslyn's experience offers a long-range perspective, one that includes raising children both in the home and out of the home. You may be thinking, "It isn't working outside the home when you are able to take your children with you." That is not the point. Roslyn's children still had challenges to deal with, such as sharing their parents with other children and being with large groups of children, often for long hours each day. Some parents work at home and must deal with constant interruptions. Parents who work away from the home and can't take their children with them find that life provides other challenges. The point is that every life situation presents challenges that can be dealt with successfully if you have effective attitudes and skills.

Being a stay-at-home parent offers many rewards for both parents and their youngsters. So do the experiences available in quality childcare programs. Neither one guarantees magical outcomes, positive or negative.

WORK AND CHILDCARE: WHAT ARE THEY?

People work in many different ways. Women work in the home and out of the home all the time. Beverly writes a column for a local newspaper and brings two-year-old Jason to a childcare center near her office. Mary Beth puts together the weekly church newsletter, spending two mornings a week at the church office while her son plays with other children during the women's Bible-study play group. Both of these moms "work" (volunteers are working moms too).

Childcare refers to more than just home- or center-based programs. Grandma takes care of baby Lori while Mom volunteers as a reading tutor at her oldest daughter's elementary school. Every morning when Elizabeth leaves for her job as a receptionist at a large hospital, she takes her infant to the neighbor's house, where her neighbor watches her own infant, Elizabeth's daughter, and several older children who arrive after school each day. Jean entertains her younger brother after she comes home from high school so their father can process tax returns in his home-based accountant's office upstairs. Childcare has many faces.

It seems that the definition of "working parent" often gets narrowed to include only people who are paid, who use childcare providers other than family members, or who work for more than a few hours each week. In fact, moms and dads do all kinds of work and their children have all kinds of childcare.

CHILDCARE: A GLOBAL PERSPECTIVE

It is normal to view situations through the lens of one's own culture and history. Over the course of time, however, few cultures have expected mothers to stay home all alone to care for tiny children. Most often children have been cared for by older siblings, aunts, and nearby or resident grandparents.

The popular phrase "it takes a village to raise a child" comes from rural Africa. In this context, the "village" is a child's blood relatives, neighbors, and community or tribal members. East Indian families typically contain several generations in one household. Some cultures in Africa or the Middle East allow a man to take more than one wife. These households might include several wives as well as stepbrothers and stepsisters, all of whom participate in caring for children. In many Asian countries, women move in with their husband's family when they marry. In Native American culture, it is traditional for children to be raised by many "aunties," some not related by blood at all. In all these cultures, children receive care from an extended family of friends and relatives. They might view our belief that mothers and fathers should raise children without outside advice or help as a form of insanity!

CHOICES

Take a moment to read the stories of some of the parents who bring their children to childcare facilities.

Stephanie is grateful that a childcare facility is located in the hospital where she works. Her son will be six months old next week and the proximity of the childcare center makes it possible for Stephanie to continue nursing him, something that is very important to her. She hurries downstairs on her breaks and lunch hour, eager to cuddle with her son. Stephanie was not married when she became pregnant, and the baby's father does not support her or their son, but Stephanie chose to continue her pregnancy and raise her son as a single parent. Divorce, single parenthood, and even welfare reform leave few options for a woman raising a child without outside financial support, but Stephanie is devoted to her son and works hard to provide him with a loving home.

Bernadette drops two-year-old Mitchell off at his childcare center just before eight o'clock each morning. Mitchell's dad works nights and sleeps during the day. Their combined incomes barely cover their living expenses. Even with subsidies from the city to help pay childcare costs, Bernadette must spend an extra two hours each day commuting to work on the bus, because a car and insurance payments would be beyond their limited budget. Bernadette is relieved to know that Mitchell is receiving loving care, being provided with nutritious meals each day, and being given opportunities to grow while she must be away from him.

Roger and Jennifer both hold well-paying jobs at the same hospital where Stephanie works. Jennifer tried staying home with three-year-old Todd but found she missed the stimulation of her job. The harder she tried to be a stay-at-home mom, the grumpier she became—and the angrier she became when Todd misbehaved. Perhaps, she worries, she just wasn't meant to be a full-time mom. She and Roger love Todd dearly; Jennifer has discovered, however, that she is a much better parent when she isn't cranky and irritable from being confined all day with an active toddler. She struggles with guilt, but she and Roger truly believe that Todd is happier and healthier at the childcare center, climbing on the equipment and playing with his many friends. Jennifer thrives at her job and can better enjoy Todd's delightful antics. She feels more confident in her new role of mother.

Vikki had looked forward to being at home with baby Alexandra, never dreaming her National Guard Unit would be activated. Instead of cuddling her daughter, cheering on her first steps, or feeling for new teeth, Vikki was carrying a machine gun, waging war half a world away. Alexandra's dad faced the task of getting little Alexandra up and ready and dropping her off at childcare each day before beginning his shift at a nearby factory.

Tyneesha, on the other hand, has two children who do not go to childcare. The children share a bedroom so that the spare room can be rented to a college student. The rental income makes it possible for Tyneesha to stay at home with four-month-old Erica and three-year-old Malcolm. Tyneesha's husband has a civilian job at the naval shipyard in town. His commute takes an hour each day, but homes located closer to the base are out of their price range. The long days wear Tyneesha out, and sometimes the demands of her two tiny youngsters make her want to scream. On other days, her heart melts just looking at them and she offers prayers of thanksgiving for the time she gets to spend with them.

Stay-at-home parents find that one-on-one daily contact with an infant, toddler, or preschooler includes magical moments of discovery, tender times of sharing, and precious memories for both parent and child. Staying home also means moments of despair when toilets overflow from being fed whole rolls of toilet paper by a curious toddler, episodes of hysterics when a preschooler's screeching wakes up his sleeping baby sister, or feeling helpless when a defiant toddler throws his blocks across the room after refusing to pick them up.

Many women want nothing more than to stay at home with their babies. In a perfect world, that choice would be possible for everyone—

but in the real world, harsh necessity intervenes. Parents who choose to stay at home to raise a child, to forgo career and financial rewards, or to accept a simpler lifestyle deserve recognition, respect, and support. Those who work deserve the same. The issue is not whether you agree with your neighbor's choice but whether you have made the best choice for yourself and for your children. Choosing to work or stay home is a complicated decision, and there is rarely a simple "right" or "wrong" answer. You must face your own reality and make the best decisions you can.

THE NEW EXTENDED FAMILY

For many of us, it has become increasingly rare to live near extended family who are willing and able to care for our children. In our book *Positive Discipline for Preschoolers*, we suggest that today's childcare programs may take on the role of the historic extended family, including such events as potluck dinners where parents can get to know one another and share stories. When this happens, it is childcare at its best.

Families need the support of many people when raising young children, and the staff of a quality childcare program can provide knowledge, experience, and information. When Ellen's daughter was diagnosed with asthma, the childcare teacher at her daughter's center provided reassurance and introduced Ellen to other families whose children had similar problems.

Janell has few friends with young children. Her own daughter, Hanna, arrived only a few weeks ago after more than a year of paperwork, delays, and waiting lists; Hanna turned four months old on her adoption day. Janell is a single parent who needs to work, and the childcare center has proven invaluable as a source of support for her newly formed family. Other families at the childcare center provide the sense of community, sibling-like relationships, and social gatherings that Janell and Hanna need. Several other children at the center were adopted, and one of them came from the same country as Hanna. This family quickly formed a close bond with Janell and Hanna, planning get-togethers and supporting one another as they and their new infants got to know one another.

Stay-at-home moms also need support. The common absence of a nearby extended family may create isolation for moms at home. Even if they have family nearby, moms need encouragement, social contact, and support. (We will discuss finding support and caring for yourself further in Chapter 18.)

SOME BENEFITS OF CHILDCARE: EARLY INTERVENTION AND CONSISTENCY

Quality childcare goes beyond simply providing a place for children to be cared for in their parents' absence. Early intervention, consistency during times of change, and support for families are wonderful ways in which childcare programs can enhance the quality of children's lives.

Bailey gets bused every afternoon to childcare. Each morning, he participates in a special program for youngsters with a variety of developmental delays. Bailey's mom, Shirley, had wondered why he seemed to have such a hard time learning new skills. Being a first-time mom, Shirley assumed her own lack of experience caused her to worry needlessly about Bailey, but only a few weeks after Bailey began attending his childcare, the director asked to meet with Shirley. The staff was concerned about Bailey's development. Together, the center and Shirley sought outside help. Shirley and the staff were right to feel concerned. Bailey was delayed in motor, speech, and other communication skills. Specific problems were identified, and a few months later Bailey was admitted to a special morning program at the university. Without the center's experienced staff, caring support, and knowledge, Shirley might not have gotten Bailey the early intervention he needed.

Early intervention is more effective in helping children with delays "catch up" than that provided to older children. The experience and training of skilled caregivers offers opportunities to identify children and families in need of special assistance. This type of identification might not happen in all centers, but if a caregiver expresses a concern about your child's development, it is wise to pursue the matter. Each caregiver has the experience of seeing many children and over time becomes better able to identify when things are amiss.

Kyle's parents have filed for divorce. He now sees his dad only on weekends. He and his mom have moved into an apartment, and Kyle's mom has to work longer hours than before. The only thing that remains unchanged in Kyle's life is his childcare center. Kyle sees the same faces every morning, recognizes the circle songs, and knows that snack time comes just after story time. With everything else in his life shifting like quicksand, he feels safe, secure, and reassured at his childcare center.

FINDING QUALITY CHILDCARE

We've talked about parents who work, by choice or necessity, and those who stay at home. But no matter their situation and choices, for almost all parents some form of childcare is a fact of life. We've discussed the benefits of quality childcare, but what about childcare that is less than ideal? What about all those horror stories in the newspapers and on the television news shows? Obviously, not all childcare is created equal—and not all of it benefits children. How can parents know that they're leaving their little ones in competent, qualified hands? What makes for *quality* childcare?

If you are one of the many parents who needs to find regular care for your child, you need to consider a number of factors. Don't be in a rush to choose: Take time to visit several different childcare programs. What do you see? Are the children happy? Do they move around the center confidently? Do the caregivers get down on the child's eye level to talk with him? Is the artwork displayed low enough for children to see it or is it only at adult eye level? Is the building clean? Are there visible safety hazards? Do the caregivers look cheerful or frazzled? (Do keep in mind that even the best teachers can have tough days!) Is there enough equipment to offer a variety of activities for art projects, role-playing, building, outdoor climbing, sand and water play? Does the equipment provided allow children to play freely, to dress up, to learn, and to be active? Or are children expected to be quiet, sit still, and "be good"? Are they confined to infant seats or parked in front of a television?

Find out if the program is licensed and by whom. Does the center pass city licensing requirements, health department codes, and fire safety requirements?

Some childcare programs offer "online monitoring." These programs allow centers to install cameras in several places throughout the building. Software is available for parents to install in their computer so they can see what is happening in the childcare program. Parents can "visit" occasionally during the day, see exactly what their child is doing, and watch their child in action. Other programs are moving to the Internet by designing home pages on which they post weekly information, share anecdotes, and scan in pictures of daily events, field trips, or special moments. Whatever the bells and whistles, trust your instincts before leaving your child in anyone else's care.

Choosing childcare should not involve bargain hunting—you're likely to get exactly what you pay for. Children—all children—are worth our investment.

WHY CARE ABOUT QUALITY CARE?

If you are a parent in a family that doesn't need outside care, you may feel that issues of establishing and funding quality childcare programs are not relevant to you. The truth is that the type of care, quality or otherwise, that any child receives affects everyone. The children who are cared for at home, the ones cared for in quality childcare programs, and the ones diminished in any way by spending time in poor-quality programs will all grow up to inhabit the same world.

In a remarkable longitudinal study, *The High/Scope Perry Preschool Study Through Age 40*, researchers examined the lives of a group of forty-year-old adults, all of whom had taken part in a test project during their preschool years. The project found that those adults who had participated in "quality" early-care programs went on to achieve higher school test scores and had higher rates of high school graduation than those children who had not received "quality" early-care experiences. The children in the programs identified as "quality" care also were less likely to be involved in crime as adults and averaged far more in annual earnings. School success, lowered crime rates, and workplace productivity are society-wide goals. Findings such as these remind us of how deep the roots of our early experiences are. What happens to children in and out of childcare affects the type of society and world all our children will someday share.

QUALITY CHILDCARE: HOW CAN I TELL?

Parents sometimes look at lists of qualities and requirements for quality childcare and feel overwhelmed. You may be wondering how you will ever know if the facility you are considering meets these standards. There is a relatively simple solution: *ask*. Childcare is an important decision, and your confidence as a parent will influence your child's comfort with and response to her new setting. Don't hesitate to ask for all the information you need to make an educated decision. If a center or provider seems reluctant to answer your questions or to allow you to observe personnel in action, it's wise to look elsewhere.

Childcare Checklist

Identify quality childcare using the following indicators:

1. The center or home has
   - Current licenses displayed
   - A low rate of staff turnover
   - Local, state, and/or national accreditation

2. The staff is
   - Well trained in early-childhood development and care
   - Working as a team
   - Staying up-to-date through training programs
   - Adequately paid

3. The curriculum emphasizes
   - Minimal academics
   - Social skills—lots of interaction with children and staff
   - Exploring through the senses
   - Problem-solving (with equipment and with other children)

4. Discipline is
   - Nonpunitive
   - Kind and firm at the same time
   - Designed to help children learn important life skills

5. Consistency shows
   - In the curriculum
   - In the way problems are handled
   - In routines the children can count on
   - In day-to-day center management

6. Safety is demonstrated by the
   - Physical setting
   - Program health policies
   - Preparedness for emergencies
   - Size of the group

Copy this checklist and take it with you when you visit prospective childcare facilities. We discuss each of the points in the following sections.

The Facility

Most states or cities require centers and homes to meet a variety of licensing requirements. Seeing licenses posted tells you the requirements were met. Check dates to be sure that licenses are current (although many states are so backlogged that long intervals between licenses are common).

Centers with low staff turnover indicate that staff members are well treated, receive fair compensation, enjoy their work, and feel supported by the center's administration. When staff members do not receive decent wages, they go elsewhere, often leaving the childcare field.

Look for special licensing. The best known is the NAEYC (National Association for the Education of Young Children, www.naeyc.org), which has a multifaceted approach. Centers spend several months doing self-assessments and correcting any weak areas and are then visited by independent accreditors, usually on several occasions. This accreditation is only valid for two years and then must be repeated. Programs displaying this type of accreditation truly have earned it.

The Staff

Training and experience make it more likely that caregivers will truly understand the needs of young children, provide activities that meet those needs, and have developmentally appropriate expectations. Some studies report that when childcare providers complete training, they give more sensitive and appropriate care. Education added to low turnover indicates experienced caregivers, a winning situation for everyone involved.

Look for the types of training staff members receive. Doctors, stock market analysts, childcare teachers—all must stay knowledgeable about current information in their fields. Do staff members at the center you're considering attend workshops? Are there in-house training programs, or are employees encouraged to take part in additional educational programs? Teachers deserve the opportunity to learn about new research, get inspired by and reminded of basic concepts, or feel encouraged when they hear others share solutions to common dilemmas. Are there special training requirements? Montessori and Waldorf programs have specialized training curriculum for their teachers. Community college, undergraduate, and master's level degree programs in early childhood studies exist in most states. Does the licensing board require continuing education on a regular basis?

Look for harmony. When there is discord at a center, the children feel it. Remember, young children can read the energy of the adults around them and they respond to what they sense. Centers that encourage cooperation—between children and staff members—model the value of teamwork. Look for regularly scheduled staff meetings, in-house communication tools, and camaraderie among staff members. (For more information on childcare, staff, and discipline, see *Positive Discipline for Childcare Providers*, Jane Nelsen and Cheryl Erwin [Roseville, Calif.: Prima, 2002].)

Discipline

Is there a written discipline policy? In what manner are problems handled? Are there texts on discipline recommended by the center? Ask what teachers do about a child who hits, bites, or grabs toys. Find out if teachers receive any training in how to deal with problems that arise.

Does the center condone spanking? Many states either allow corporal punishment or exempt some programs, especially church-based ones, from bans on corporal punishment. This is very important, especially in these vulnerable early years. Even if you approve of spanking (and by now you know we do not), please be aware of the extra fragility of very young children. Shaking a baby can lead to death, and an adult's strength can turn an intended swat from mild to bone-cracking in a heartbeat.

Is the attitude at the center positive or punitive? Are children being shown what to do more often than being reprimanded about what not to do? It is important to find childcare where discipline is neither punitive nor permissive. Trained childcare staff know how to deal with problems in a kind and firm manner that also teaches valuable life skills such as cooperation, problem-solving, and learning to "use your words."

Watch how teachers talk with children:

- Does the teacher get down to the child's eye level when talking to him or do teachers just yell instructions across the room?

- Do teachers speak to children in a respectful way?

- Are boundaries made clear, or does a teacher giggle uncomfortably when children run up and slam into her?

- Do teachers follow through? For instance, does a teacher call out to a child to "Put down that stick!" and then proceed to chat with a coworker while the child brandishes the stick overhead? Or does the teacher walk over and calmly remove the stick after giving the child a moment or two to put it down himself?

The best childcare emphasizes respect, kindness and firmness, and encouragement—just as you do at home.

Curriculum

There is a growing tendency for parents to seek childcare centers that offer academics such as reading, writing, and arithmetic. This a concern to most early childhood experts, and you should know why.

Kathy Hirsh-Pasek, director of the Temple University Infant Lab and coauthor of *Einstein Never Used Flash Cards: How Our Children Really Learn—and Why They Need to Play More and Memorize Less* (New York: Rodale, 2003), directed a research project where 120 four-year-olds in a middle-class Philadelphia suburb were followed as they progressed through kindergarten and first grade. The research confirmed that the children who attended academic preschools did know more numbers and letters than the children who went to play-oriented preschools. By age five, however, the kids from the play-oriented preschools had caught up, while those attending academic preschools felt less positive about school.

Parents mean well when they "push" their children to learn academics as soon as possible. They want their children to have every advantage and to feel successful. For this reason, it is important to know that pushing may do more damage than good. When children are pushed to excel in academics, they may miss out on ways for them to learn that are more developmentally appropriate.

Another point to consider might be to "get into the world" of your two- or three-year-old. How would you feel if you were pushed into learning something to make your parents proud rather than feeling accepted for who you are? How would you feel if these tasks were difficult (even though you could do them)? Might you have feelings of inadequacy? On the other hand, how would you feel if your parents followed your lead and allowed you to explore and experiment in a nurturing environment filled with enticing equipment that allowed you to feel capable with every accomplishment?

Does this mean academics should be eliminated entirely during the first three years? No, but the key is to follow the interests of your child. Some three-year-olds want to read and feel excited rather than pressured to learn. Some don't mind learning to sing the alphabet song (even though they don't have a clue what it means). Be aware of what your child is learning *and* how he feels about it. Your child may not have the words to tell you he is feeling pressured, but you will know if you are paying attention.

Consistency

Consistency in the curriculum means that certain activities are provided regularly. Show-and-Tell, daily story time, and singing are examples. Children thrive on routine, at their care facility as well as at home. Consistency also means that learning objectives exist and are implemented. Contrast a well-defined program with a place where children are given some old egg cartons to cut up, plopped down in front of the same container of blocks every morning, or left to watch endless videos and television programs. In the context of a clear curriculum, some of these activities may be fine. Just be sure that the program values hands-on learning, healthy activity, and developmental growth—not just silence and obedience.

Is there consistency from teacher to teacher or class to class in the way problems are handled? Does one teacher refuse to allow children to help prepare snacks while another turns snack time into a yogurt finger-painting free-for-all?

Centers with consistent programs encourage children to develop trust, initiative, and a healthy sense of autonomy. If these tasks are important at home, they must also be important where your child will spend so much of his time. Consistency begins with center management.

In addition, you should examine the way a childcare facility operates on a daily basis. Here are some questions to consider:

- Are expectations of the children, the staff, and parents made clear?

- Are events well organized?

- Do finances get handled in a businesslike manner?

Safety

Safety includes the physical setting, the program health policies, and the emergency preparedness of the center. A program with exposed electrical cords, unimpeded access to a laundry cupboard, or broken-down play equipment does not provide an environment safe for little ones. Leaving a tiny child in the care of other people each day requires faith *and* vigilance.

Watching a teacher spray the changing table with bleach solution after every diaper change reassures Keith that his son will not be exposed to dangerous bacteria. Seeing the center staff load the blocks into the dishwasher each evening gives Marnie peace of mind when she sees her toddler handling those same blocks the following morning. Mr. and Mrs. Jamison visit their daughter's center and see the staff and children participating in a fire drill. They are impressed with the level of competence shown at the center—and it even gets them thinking about the need to develop their own evacuation plan at home.

Find out if staff members have current CPR and first-aid training and HIV/AIDS training. Under what conditions will sick children be sent home? Look for fire safety procedures and earthquake or other emergency preparedness. Ask how injuries are handled. Reassure yourself that the adults in this place know how to care for your child under a variety of circumstances.

Group size is important for your child's safety as well. For children not yet mobile, Zero to Three recommends that childcare groups should be no larger than six; the caregiver/infant ratio should be no more than 1:3. For children crawling and up to eighteen months, the group size should be no more than nine, ratios no more than 1:3 (explorers are active and need a watchful eye). For children eighteen months to three years, group size should be no more than twelve and ratios, 1:4. Centers, group homes, and family childcare homes with mixed age groupings should never have more than two children under two years of age in a single group.

TRUST YOURSELF—AND GET INVOLVED!

Only you can decide what your needs as a family really are. If you decide there is a need for outside care, use the guidelines listed above to find the best possible place to entrust with the care of your little one. The best way to evaluate the quality of childcare your child will receive is to spend several hours visiting. That is the only way you can see if they practice what they preach. It is the only way you can observe how comfortable your child is in the environment. Of course, many children cling to their parents in a strange environment and do fine when their parents leave, but an extended visit lets you know how your child will be treated. Be sure to stay involved and tuned in; if at all possible, make occasional visits to the childcare center to reassure yourself that all is well.

No center or staff is ever perfect. If there are changes or improvements you would like to see made at your center, work toward bringing them about, support your program's efforts, and recognize the caregivers as a valuable extended family, part of your child-rearing team.

Above all, give up your guilt button. Whether you care for your infant or toddler at home or entrust her to a center, you are likely to have some mixed emotions. Pay attention, make choices as wisely as you can, then relax and trust your choice. Parents are all in the same boat when it comes to raising children. All children will inherit this earth—no matter where they took their naps, got cuddled, or first discovered *Curious George*. Knowledge and awareness will help you give your children everything they need during their important first three years of life.

18

GROWING AS A FAMILY: FINDING SUPPORT, RESOURCES, AND SANITY

No matter how sweet-tempered your new baby and no matter how delighted you are to be a parent, these first months and years can be a lonely experience. Mothers (or fathers) staying at home with a new baby often find that the job is tougher than they expected. Long nights punctuated by endless feedings and diaper changes can numb even the most devoted mom or dad. A spouse or partner may find blow-by-blow descriptions of your baby's bowel movements enthralling, but many people will not. After a while, most parents long for a real adult conversation, a movie, or an hour or two of solitude.

Many parents of young children are tempted to blurt out "Talk to me!" to anyone who wanders by, and with good reason. It is essential for new parents to seek out support through the early weeks and months of parenting. Connection with other adults nourishes new parents and, through them, their children and families.

LEARNING FROM THE WISDOM OF OTHERS

While people seldom agree on every detail of raising infants and children, building a support network, a circle of friends who've been there, provides an invaluable source of information about raising and living with children.

It can be helpful to have people to call when things happen that you weren't expecting. Make an effort to build relationships with folks who have children the same age as yours—or who have recently survived the stage you're going through. Don't be afraid to ask lots of questions; finding out that other people's children have done the same strange or appalling things that your child does can help you relax.

Some options include church or community-based mom-and-child groups, community college parent-child classes, La Leche League, and friendships with neighboring moms. One successful model is PEPS (the Program for Early Parent Support), a community-based program that began in the Northwest. "Save the Children Canada" now uses the PEPS program throughout the country. PEPS groups form right after a baby's birth and consist of people whose babies are born within days or weeks of one another. These families meet regularly in one another's homes or in family centers. There is also a special program for teen parents. The goal is to reduce isolation and create a network of support, resources, and encouragement. (PEPS can be contacted at www.pepsgroup.org.) Another popular group is Mothers of Preschoolers (www.mops.org), which offers get-togethers and parenting support through neighborhood churches. Look for similar programs in your area, or consider initiating one of your own.

Some parents have started "book study groups," where they get together and take turns discussing the concepts in this and other *Positive Discipline* books and work together on how to use Positive Discipline tools. Some moms have even attended the two-day "Teaching Parenting the Positive Discipline Way" workshop so they could learn to facilitate parenting classes, knowing that teaching (and having the courage to be imperfect) is the best way to learn.

If you live in an isolated area or have no new moms nearby, the magic of the Internet offers chat groups, question-and-answer boards, and lots of general information. You can receive information about Positive Discipline directly at www.positivediscipline.com or www.posdis.org, and there are many other groups you'll find if you look online. If you don't have home computer access, try your local library; many offer Internet access. In addition, *Exchange* magazine is a great resource for childcare providers and includes Roslyn's "From a Parent's Perspective" column. These articles can be used as handouts for a childcare center's families and staff.

Still, there's nothing like real, live people. If you can, find a parenting group for parents of young children. Perhaps your parenting group, with dinner out beforehand, can be part of a night out with your partner. However you arrange it, having a sympathetic group with whom to discuss problems, ask questions, and explore the mysteries of raising young children can make all the difference in the world. Consult your pediatrician too. Family doctors see and hear a great deal as they go about the business of helping young patients and parents. They can often provide support as well as practical information and advice.

No matter where you find support, however, remember that in the end you must decide what feels right for you and your child. Gather all the wisdom and advice you can, then listen to your heart before you choose what will work best for you.

REFILLING THE PITCHER

Q. I am a young mother with three children who are younger than five years of age. They are my greatest joy and I dearly love being a mother! Lately, though, I'm really overwhelmed. My husband works long hours and attends evening school. I do the housekeeping, work part-time, pay the bills, take care of business, and raise the children. They are smart, nice, talented kids (I'm a little subjective, of course!), but they are all, more or less, what you call strong-willed children. I feel like I'm pulled in so many directions, and no matter what I do, it's never enough.

From the minute I wake up until late at night, I never get more than a minute to myself. I'm always tired and sick, and I get terrible headaches. The bottom line is that I've been losing my temper a lot lately. Then I'm even more upset because I feel so guilty. I've read so many books and magazines, and I understand and agree with Positive Discipline in theory. No offense, but usually the examples and ideas seem so far removed from my real life that it just makes me more depressed.

A. What's wrong with the picture you describe? You are not working part-time or even full-time, but overtime! No one flies around wearing a supermom cape, but it sounds as though that is what you are trying to do. The person you are not taking care of is *you*—and everyone suffers because of it. It is easy to get so busy with all life's have-to's that your own needs get shoved not only to the back burner but completely off the stove. The best thing you can give to your family is a calm, rested you.

Consider getting a high school student to help with the housework. Be creative if money is short; perhaps you can barter something. Trade babysitting hours with someone else so you can go for a walk, take a yoga class, or get in a swim and sauna at the local Y once or twice a week. Your family will notice the difference, and of course, so will you.

Being a parent is a great deal like pouring water from a pitcher: You can only pour out so many glasses without refilling the pitcher. All too often, parents and other caregivers suddenly realize they've poured themselves dry for their children—the pitcher is empty. Effective, loving parenting takes a lot of time and energy. You can't do your best when your pitcher is empty, when you're tired, cranky, stressed out, and overwhelmed.

How do you refill the pitcher? Taking care of yourself—filling up your pitcher before it runs dry—can take any form. If you find yourself daydreaming in a quiet moment about all the things you'd like to do, that may be a clue that you should consider ways to take care of yourself. Here are a few suggestions:

Budget Time Wisely

Most parents find that they must adjust their priorities after the arrival of a child. It can be extremely helpful—and quite a revelation—to keep track for a few days of exactly how you spend your time. Some activities—such as work, school, or tasks directly related to raising your children—can't be changed much. But most parents spend much of their time on activities that are not truly among their top priorities.

For instance, if you're often up during the night with an infant or young child, make an effort to nap when your child naps. It is tempting to fly around the house doing all that "should" get done, but cleaning the bathroom and dusting the furniture will wait for you; you'll be happier and more effective if you get enough sleep.

Time is precious and all too short when you share your life with young children; be sure you're spending the time you do have as wisely as you can.

> **Caring for Yourself**
>
> It is important to take care of yourself as well as you take care of your child. Consider the following ideas:
>
> - Budget time wisely.
> - Make lists.
> - Make time for important relationships.
> - Do the things you enjoy—regularly.
> - Avoid overscheduling.

Make Lists

In a quiet moment, list all the things you'd like to do (or wish you could get around to). Then, when your child is napping or with a caregiver, spend those precious hours working your way down your list. Be sure you include not just chores and duties but activities that nurture you, like curling up with a good book, soaking in the tub, or having a cozy telephone chat with a friend.

Make Time for Important Relationships

It's amazing how therapeutic a simple cup of tea with a good friend can be, and sometimes a vigorous game of racquetball can restore a positive perspective on life. Conversation with caring adults can refresh you, especially when your world is populated with energetic little people. You and your partner may trade time watching the children so each of you has time for friends, or you may choose to spend special time together with other couples whose company you enjoy. A "date night" out together should be on your list as well. Meeting friends at the park can give parents and children time to rest and relax together. Keeping your world wide enough to include people outside your family can help you retain your health and balance.

Do the Things You Enjoy—Regularly

It is important that you find time for the things that make you feel alive and happy, whether it's riding your bicycle, playing softball, singing with a choir, tinkering with machinery, working in the garden, or designing a quilt. Hobbies and exercise are important for your mental and emotional health—and you'll be a far more patient and effective parent if you're investing time and energy in your own well-being. Yes, finding time for these things can be a problem, and it is tempting to tell yourself, "I'll get around to that later." All too often, though, "later" never arrives. Even twenty minutes a day for something you love is a good beginning. Self-care really isn't optional, because without it, *everyone* suffers. Parents often see taking time for themselves as "selfish." Nothing could be less true. Please, do not let yourself run on empty. Trust us: Your children will survive without constant attention from you. In fact, they'll thrive all the more with healthy, well-supported parents. Children sense emotional energy; exhaustion and resentment will not help your child grow and may drain the joy out of family life for all of you.

Avoid Overscheduling

Most parents do all they can to provide a rich and stimulating environment for their young children. After all, they're learning and developing important skills during these early years. Many young children find themselves enrolled in a surprising number of groups, often before the age of two. There are baby gymnastic groups and baby swim classes. There are preschools and play groups. There are even music and educational classes for toddlers. Parents often discover that they are living in their vehicles, rushing their children from one activity to another.

While these activities can be enjoyable and stimulating for a young child, it is wise to limit the number you sign up for. Researchers have noted that time for families to relax and just "hang out" together has become scarce; everyone is busy rushing off to the next important group, and relationships suffer as a result. Mothers and fathers are irritable and tired; children have little or no time to exercise their creativity, learn to entertain themselves, or simply play.

Remember, your child needs connection and time with you far more than she needs "stimulation." Time to cuddle, crawl around on the floor together, or read a book is far more valuable than even the most popular group.

LEARNING TO RECOGNIZE
—AND MANAGE—STRESS

Clenched teeth and fists, tight muscles, headaches, a sudden desire to burst into tears or lock yourself in the bathroom—these are the symptoms of parental stress and overload, and it's important to pay attention to them. Most parents—especially first-time parents—occasionally feel overwhelmed and exhausted and even angry or resentful. Because parents want so much to be "good" parents, they may find it difficult to discuss these troubling thoughts and feelings with others.

Kim had just managed to fall asleep when it started: the fretful, whining cry that told her that two-month-old Betsy was awake—again. Kim groaned, thought briefly about burying her head under her pillow, then heaved herself out of bed. Her husband had been out of town on business for more than a week, and this was the second time tonight that Betsy had awakened. Kim was exhausted.

She stumbled into the baby's room and began her night routine without even bothering to turn on the light. Half an hour later, Betsy had been fed, changed, and burped, but she was crying more loudly than ever. Kim settled the baby in her arms and began rocking in the old rocking chair, fighting the urge to cry herself. She felt helpless, completely at the mercy of this tiny person who couldn't even tell her what was wrong. She hadn't had time to do the laundry in a week, the house was cluttered, and she would have given her right arm for an hour at the hairdresser's. What had happened? This wasn't what she'd imagined when she was pregnant with Betsy.

Kim looked down at her daughter's face and suddenly saw not a beautiful, beloved baby but an ugly, demanding, noisy monster who wouldn't even let her get a decent night's sleep. What Kim really wanted was to put the baby down and simply leave.

It took almost two hours, but Betsy, soothed by the steady rocking, eventually fell asleep. It took her horrified mother a lot longer to deal with the unexpectedly strong emotions the encounter had created in her.

As we've mentioned before, there's a difference between a feeling and an action. It's not unusual for parents of infants and young children to be frustrated, overwhelmed, and exhausted, and most parents feel terribly guilty when they feel anger or resentment toward their children. The feelings are quite normal—but you need to be careful what you do with them.

If you find yourself wanting to snap or lash out at your children, accept those feelings as your cue to do something to care for yourself. Make sure your children are safely occupied and take a few minutes of time-out (it usually works better for parents than for kids anyway). Better yet, arrange for some time to do something to nurture yourself. Exhaustion and frustration can lead even the best parents to say and do things they later regret; it's far better to invest the time it takes to help yourself feel better.

EMERGENCY RELIEF

In the event you feel completely unable to cope, do not hesitate to seek help. Most communities offer a crisis line for immediate phone assistance. Some hospitals provide similar services; a few moments speaking to an understanding, reassuring adult may make a world of difference.

If you ever feel your child might be at risk, check to see if respite care is available in your community. It is not wrong or shameful to need help; it is true wisdom to ask for it.

IF YOUR CHILD HAS SPECIAL NEEDS

Every new parent counts toes and fingers and worries about anything that seems wrong. Sadly, sometimes these worries are founded. If you have concerns, take them seriously and ask your pediatrician or community health nurse to check them out. Identifying a child's special needs early promises the best results.

> *Rosemary noticed that her four-month-old daughter, Angela, did not wave at her crib mobile the way her friend's son did. She also thought that Angela seemed to turn her eyes inward at times. At first Rosemary told herself she was imagining things. Then she decided to have Angela's eyes checked at the local clinic, just for her own peace of mind. Rosemary doubted that it was possible to treat an infant's eyes, but to her surprise, Angela was diagnosed with strabismus, or crossed eyes, and within two weeks was fitted with special, tiny eyeglasses.*

This early intervention probably saved Angela's vision. Untreated, crossed eyes can result in a loss of vision in one of the eyes, but early intervention prevented that from happening. Angela, now in grade school, sees beautifully and no longer needs glasses of any kind. Other parents have discovered (after having the courage to insist on more thorough medical checkups) that what might have been dismissed as "colic" was in fact severe pain in the ears that could be corrected. One mother found that her infant stopped crying when she stopped putting him to bed in "footed" pajamas. As he grew older, it became apparent that he had sensory integration disorder, a condition that interferes with the brain's ability to "integrate" information from the senses and often leads to communication and behavioral problems; he benefited a great deal from occupational therapy.

Many special needs can be discovered by thorough medical exams or by parents experimenting with different possibilities. Many times babies *do* have colic that just takes time to outgrow, but sometimes it's something more serious. Be proactive in discovering if your child has special needs and getting him the support he requires.

Speech, hearing, and vision problems are all common in young children. These problems can and should be treated as soon as possible. A child with frequent ear infections does not hear sounds consistently, and his developing speech patterns may suffer. If you are unable to understand a child at all by the age of two and a half, consider getting a speech evaluation from a qualified speech therapist. Early speech therapy often provides excellent results.

The teachers at Aaron's preschool were frustrated. He did not seem to listen to them at all. One day his teacher tried an experiment. She stood behind Aaron, out of sight, and rang a small bell. All the other children turned in her direction. Aaron did not. Then she whispered his name. Again there was no response. The teacher urged Aaron's mom to seek a hearing evaluation. As it turned out, Aaron had a partial hearing impairment. He received treatment, and his teachers learned to make eye contact before speaking to him. Not surprisingly, his behavior improved at once.

One advantage of early-education programs for young children is routine screenings by public health nurses or other community or school personnel. Whatever the concern, parents need to trust their own instincts and seek help when worried about a child's health or development. The possibility of a child being less than perfect terrifies most parents, but early diagnosis and intervention will help you and your child feel better.

REACH OUT AND TOUCH SOMEONE

Beth looked back at the front window, where her friend Caroline held fourteen-month-old Gregory up to wave good-bye. As she slipped behind the wheel of the minivan, Beth looked at the two good friends who shared the back seat.

"Boy, am I ready for this," she said.

Anne and Joleen laughed. "Us too!" Joleen said. "And you'd better enjoy yourself—next week, the kids are all at your place."

Beth, Anne, Joleen, and Caroline had been sharing their "moms' day out" for about six months, and none could

Sharing the Attention

Q. I have three boys. My oldest turns six in March, the next will be four in February, and my youngest just turned two. The oldest and youngest of my boys are profoundly deaf. My problem, however, lies with my middle child. He is a very bright child who has been sandwiched between two siblings who require special attention. As a result he has taken on responsibilities beyond his age.

In the last month, however, he has become defiant. He whines all the time now when he doesn't get his way, and he has become somewhat withdrawn. I have racked my brain trying to find out what is different in our lives or daily routines, or anything that would account for this change. I know he receives a different type of attention than his brothers, but he does not receive any less attention.

Is there something I'm missing? Do you have any suggestions? Or is this just a phase, and it, too, shall pass? Please, any ideas would be greatly appreciated.

A. It takes a great deal of patience and sensitivity to raise children with special needs, particularly when you have more than one. Children are wonderful perceivers (they notice everything) but they are not good interpreters, and children often believe that the special therapies, doctor's appointments, and treatment that their special-needs siblings receive indicate more parental love and attention. Attention isn't just a matter of quantity—it's a matter of the beliefs and feelings that children form about how much they (and their siblings) receive and what that tells them about their special place in the family.

It's also wise to remember that while children develop at different paces emotionally as well as physically, three- and four-year-olds are often experimenting with what we call "initiative"—

imagine how they'd survived without it. Each Saturday morning, one of the four women cared for the group's six children. Lunches were packed, activities were planned—and the three moms who had the day off had four blissful hours to shop, play tennis, take a walk, or just share conversation and a cup of coffee. All had felt a bit guilty at first, but they quickly learned to wave bye-bye and drive away, knowing their chil-

forming their own plans, wanting to do things their own way, and occasionally practicing that by becoming defiant, whining, and so on.

You're probably right that some of this will pass, but here are some suggestions to try in the meantime:

- If you don't already have them, create routines for morning, evening, off to school, and so on. Each child can have special tasks that he performs, and once the routine is in place (a big chart can help), the routine becomes the "boss." It's wonderful that your middle son wants to help and be responsible, but children sometimes make themselves overresponsible in an effort to earn love and belonging.

- Because your son is bright and all children are naturally egocentric at that age, he may feel responsible somehow for being the only hearing child in his family; he may feel guilty for being able to hear. Make sure he knows it's okay just to be a kid and that his brothers' deafness is not about him.

- It may help to set aside special time with each child, time that you spend just with him. This doesn't mean spending money or huge chunks of time—fifteen minutes to go for a walk, throw the ball, or to read a story is usually all it takes. One dad used bath time as his chance to sit and visit with each of his twin sons, one at a time. During your special time, ask your middle son to share his happiest and saddest times of the day; be prepared to listen well and to share your own. The keys to his behavior lie in what he believes about himself and his place in the family. Let your children know how much you value this time with them and be sure you set aside time in your busy week for special moments to happen.

dren were well cared for—and would be happy to have a calm, cheerful mother pick them up. Because the women were careful always to return at the designated time, no one felt taken advantage of.

Support comes packaged in different ways. Whatever works for you and wherever you find it, accept it with gratitude. Parenting is too big a job to tackle alone. Children and their families need a community of support. The face that community wears may be that of a familiar relative, a parenting class, good friends, or even words floating through cyberspace. The important thing is that it is there. Use it—for everyone's sake.

CONCLUSION

It sometimes seems as though the first three years last forever. You live with the endless succession of diapers and bottles—and sometimes the equally endless nights—and you can hardly wait to get on to the next stage of your child's life. And then you enter the toddler years and you rush around childproofing your home, trying to remain calm and patient, doing your best to cope with your active, challenging little person and his occasional tantrums and misbehaviors. You collapse, exhausted, at the end of another hectic day—and you can hardly wait to get on to the next stage of your child's life.

And so it goes. Ask parents whose children are older, whose children are busy with school and friends, whose children are independent teenagers, or whose children have grown up and begun a family of their own, and they will tell you: The first three years go by too fast, far more quickly than you realize when you're in the midst of them.

In only an instant, the darling little outfits will have been outgrown, the binkies and blankies cast aside. The favorite toys will lie untouched in the closet while their formerly devoted owner busies himself with

new activities and new friends. It may be incomprehensible now, but the day will come when you watch your confident, eager child run to meet his friends and find yourself longing for exactly what you have now: the sweet, cuddly baby who needs you so desperately, the busy toddler who can turn your world upside down and still capture your heart with a single glance, the child who tests your patience and perseverance one moment, then runs to hug you and plant a sticky kiss on your cheek the next.

There is a great deal to learn and remember when you're raising a young child. You'll ponder feeding schedules, toilet training, eating habits, and various methods of discipline. You'll wonder if you are competent enough, loving enough, or just plain good enough at this awesome task. Often you'll get caught up in your responsibilities and duties (and you certainly do have many of them, all of them important). Sometimes you'll long for peace, quiet, and time to yourself.

But if there's one lesson, we, as authors and as parents of children now well beyond their first three years, want to share with you, it is this: Cherish these moments while they are yours. Stop to wonder at the miracle of a sleeping infant, the marvel of a curious toddler. Take a slow, deep breath and savor the joy of watching your child learn, grow, and discover his place in this world. Take lots of photographs; make time to laugh, to play, to simply enjoy. These first years will be gone before you know it.

It is our hope that in these pages you have found information you can use as you and your little one navigate these critical first months and years together. It is a vitally important time; both of you are learning a lot, and both of you will make lots of mistakes. Always remember that mistakes are merely opportunities to learn and grow together and that the hugs and tears that sometimes follow mistakes may actually draw you closer to those you love.

The best gifts you have to offer your children are not things they can touch, hold, or play with. In fact, they may not recognize or appreciate these nontangible gifts for years. They are, nonetheless, priceless. You can offer your children trust, dignity, and respect. You can believe in them, encourage them, and teach them. You can bestow on them the gifts of confidence, responsibility, and competence. And you can show them how to love and appreciate life by sharing it with them, every step of the way.

Learn as much as you can; ask for help when you need it. Forget about that fantasy child. Watch, listen, and learn to understand the child you have. Most important of all, have the courage to trust your own wisdom and knowledge of your child. There is no greater challenge than parenting—and no job more rewarding.

SUGGESTED READINGS

Adler, Alfred. *What Life Could Mean to You.* New edition. One World Pub., 1992.

———. *Social Interest.* New edition. One World Pub., 1998.

Chess, Stella, M.D., and Alexander Thomas, M.D. *Know Your Child.* New York: Basic Books, 1987.

Dreikurs, Rudolf, and V. Soltz. *Children: The Challenge.* New York: Plume Books, 1991.

Duffy, Roslyn. *Top Ten Preschool Parenting Problems.* Redmond, Wash.: Exchange Press, 2007.

Erikson, Erik H. *Childhood and Society.* New York: Norton, 1993.

Erwin, Cheryl. *The Everything Parents' Guide to Raising Boys.* New York: Adams, 2006.

Frieden, Wayne S., and Marie Hartwell Walker. *Family Songs.* Available as downloadable MP3 files at www.focusingonsolutions.com.

Garcia, Joseph. *Sign with Your Baby.* Seattle: Northlight Communications, 2005. See www.sign2me.com.

Glenn, H. Stephen, and Michael L. Brock. *7 Strategies for Developing Capable Students.* New York: Three Rivers Press, 1998.

Glenn, H. Stephen, and J. Nelsen. *Raising Self-Reliant Children in a Self-Indulgent World.* New York: Three Rivers Press, 2000.

Greenman, Jim, and Anne Stonehouse. *What Happened to the World?: Helping Children Cope in Turbulent Times.* New South Wales, Australia: Pademelon Press, 2002.

Greenspan, Stanley I., M.D., and Wieder, Serena, Ph.D. *The Child with Special Needs: Encouraging Intellectual and Emotional Growth.* Cambridge, Mass.: Perseus Publishing, 1998.

Harlow, Harry F. *Learning to Love*. New York: Ballantine, 1973.

Healy, Jane M. *Endangered Minds: Why Children Don't Think and What We Can Do About It*. New York: Simon & Schuster, 1990.

Kohn, Alfie. *Punished by Rewards*. New York: Houghton Mifflin, 1999.

Kvols, K. *Redirecting Children's Misbehavior*. Seattle: Parenting Press, 1997.

Lott, Lynn, and Jane Nelsen. *Teaching Parenting the Positive Discipline Way: A Manual for Parent Education Groups*. Lehi, Utah: Empowering People, www.empoweringpeople.com.

Nelsen, Jane. *Positive Time-Out and Over 50 Ways to Avoid Power Struggles in the Home and the Classroom*. New York: Three Rivers Press, 1999.

———. *Serenity: Eliminating Stress and Finding Joy and Peace in Life and Relationships*. Lehi, Utah: Empowering People, 2005. An e-book is available at www.positivediscipline.com.

Nelsen, Jane, and Cheryl Erwin. *Parents Who Love Too Much*. New York: Three Rivers Press, 2000.

———. *Positive Discipline for Childcare Providers*. New York: Three Rivers Press, 2002.

———. *Positive Discipline for Your Stepfamily*. Lehi, Utah: Empowering People, 2005. An e-book is available at www.positivediscipline.com.

Nelsen, Jane, C. Erwin, and C. Delzer. *Positive Discipline for Single Parents,* 2nd edition. New York: Three Rivers Press, 1999.

Nelsen, Jane, C. Erwin, and R. Duffy. *Positive Discipline for Preschoolers,* 3rd edition. New York: Three Rivers Press, 2007.

Nelsen, J., C. Erwin, M. Hughes, and M. Brock. *Positive Discipline for Christian Families*. Lehi, Utah: Empowering People, 2005. An e-book is available at www.positivediscipline.com.

Nelsen, Jane, Linda Escobar, Kate Ortolano, Roslyn Duffy, and Deborah Owens-Sohocki. *Positive Discipline: A Teacher's A–Z Guide*. New York: Three Rivers Press, 2001.

Nelsen, Jane, R. Intner, and L. Lott. *Positive Discipline for Parents in Recovery*. Lehi, Utah: Empowering People, 2005. An e-book is available at www.positivediscipline.com.

Nelsen, Jane, and Lisa Larson. *Positive Discipline for Working Parents*. New York: Three Rivers Press, 2003.

Nelsen, Jane, and Lynn Lott. *Positive Discipline in the Classroom: A Teacher's Guide.* Lehi, Utah: Empowering People, www.empoweringpeople.com.

———. *Positive Discipline for Teenagers.* New York: Three Rivers Press, 1997.

Nelsen, Jane, L. Lott, and H. S. Glenn. *Positive Discipline in the Classroom,* 3rd edition. New York: Three Rivers Press, 2000.

———. *Positive Discipline A–Z,* 3rd edition. New York: Three Rivers Press, 2007.

Piaget, Jean. *The Origins of Intelligence in Children.* New York: International Universities Press, 1952.

Sammons, William, and T. Berry Brazelton. *The Self-Calmed Baby.* New York: St. Martin's Press, 1991.

Shore, Rima. *Rethinking the Brain: Research and Implications of Brain Development in Young Children.* New York: Families and Work Institute, 1997.

Siegel, Daniel J., M.D., and Mary Hartzell, M.Ed. *Parenting from the Inside Out: How a Deeper Self-Understanding Can Help You Raise Children Who Thrive.* New York: Tarcher Putnam, 2003.

Singer, Dorothy G., and Tracey A. Revenson. *A Piaget Primer: How a Child Thinks.* New York: Plume, 1996.

ADDITIONAL RESOURCES

CCFC: Campaign for a Commercial-Free Childhood. c/o Judge Baker Children's Center, 53 Parker Hill Avenue, Boston, MA 02120-3225. Ongoing information is available at www.commercialfreechildhood.org.

Duffy, Roslyn Ann. "From a Parent's Perspective" (bimonthly column), *Exchange* magazine, Exchange Press, Redmond, WA 98073-3249, (800) 221-2864. Information for parents and childcare programs is at www.ChildCareExchange.com.

La Leche League. 1400 N. Meacham Road, Schaumburg, IL 60173-4808, (847) 519-7730. See http://www.lalecheleague.org.

Mothers of Preschoolers. www.mops.org.

PEPS: Program for Early Parent Support. http://www.pepsgroup.org.

T.R.U.C.E.: Teachers Resisting Unhealthy Children's Entertainment. P.O. Box 441261, West Somerville, MA 02144. More information at www.truceteachers.org.

FOR MORE INFORMATION

The authors are popular speakers and workshop presenters for parents, elementary school teachers, preschool teachers, and childcare providers. They are also available for parent and teacher coaching by phone.

Contact Jane Nelsen by going to www.positivediscipline.com or jane@positivediscipline.com.

Contact Cheryl Erwin at www.posdis.org, cheryl.erwin@sbcglobal.net, or (775) 331-6723.

Contact Roslyn Duffy at www.RoslynDuffy.com, or (206) 527-9728.

ACKNOWLEDGMENTS

We are often asked, "Where do you get your stories?" We get them from so many people, and without them this book could not have been written. We want to note that names and details throughout this book have been changed to protect the privacy of the families who shared them with us; some are composites of several families. And that makes sense: Parents and children everywhere experience many of the same challenges as they grow together. We can all learn from one another.

We owe our biggest thanks to our children. They have provided us with personal family "laboratories." As you will learn, we believe that "mistakes are wonderful opportunities to learn." Our children have put up with our mistakes—and have helped us learn from them. We love them and appreciate them.

We also have had many opportunities to learn from parents in our parenting classes and in our counseling offices. It is easy to play the "expert" with other people, but in truth, *you* are the only expert on your own children. After all, no one knows your children as well as you do. This book offers solid information and good suggestions, but in the end, you must trust your own wisdom and knowledge of your children to help you decide what to do. It isn't always easy. We often tell parents in our classes, "You help me when I get emotionally hooked, and I'll help you when you are emotionally hooked." Parents often tell us how much we help them; we want them to know how much we have learned from them—and how grateful we are.

Each of us has had the opportunity to answer questions on www. positivediscipline.com as well as other venues, from radio call-in programs to parent and teacher groups; to audiences at our various talks around the country and internationally. Such questions, and our answers, provided excellent material for this book.

We appreciate all of those who care enough about raising children to read parenting books and to take parenting classes; we also appreciate our colleagues and friends who continue to work tirelessly to create more respectful families, schools, and communities. You might not think parenting has changed much in recent years, but we continue to learn new ways of understanding both our children and ourselves. Much of the information in this book has been contributed to and enhanced by other Adlerian professionals. We are grateful for them and for the work they do.

We have had excellent editorial help. We gratefully acknowledge Lindsey Moore, our project editor at Three Rivers Press. Lindsey truly understands the concepts of Positive Discipline; her insight and eye for detail have helped us immeasurably to communicate our message more clearly.

A special thanks to the Learning Tree Montessori Childcare for much of the background material for the chapter on finding quality childcare. Such insights helped bring deeper meaning to this work.

We will always be grateful to Alfred Adler and Rudolf Dreikurs, the originators of the philosophy upon which Positive Discipline is based. These pioneers left a legacy that has changed the lives of thousands—including our own. We feel honored to continue their legacy by sharing their ideas with others.

One extra loud hurrah goes to Paula Gray, the person responsible for the inspired artwork throughout this book. Paula has contributed her talent, her energy, and her patience to this and several other Positive Discipline books, and we continue to be very grateful for her contributions.

And oh, how we love our families. Instead of complaining about the time it takes for us to write books, they support and encourage us. They constantly demonstrate how capable they are of being self-sufficient instead of demanding. They are proud of us for sharing concepts that have helped us all enjoy each other so much. Although our own children are grown now and busy living their own independent lives, we continue to love spending every moment we can with them and with the next generation, our grandchildren. May this book make the world a healthier and happier place for them, their peers, and the children they will one day parent.

INDEX

ABOUT THE AUTHORS

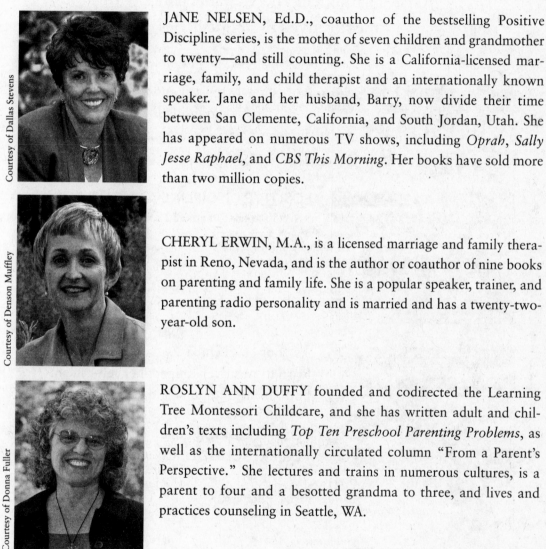

JANE NELSEN, Ed.D., coauthor of the bestselling Positive Discipline series, is the mother of seven children and grandmother to twenty—and still counting. She is a California-licensed marriage, family, and child therapist and an internationally known speaker. Jane and her husband, Barry, now divide their time between San Clemente, California, and South Jordan, Utah. She has appeared on numerous TV shows, including *Oprah*, *Sally Jesse Raphael*, and *CBS This Morning*. Her books have sold more than two million copies.

CHERYL ERWIN, M.A., is a licensed marriage and family therapist in Reno, Nevada, and is the author or coauthor of nine books on parenting and family life. She is a popular speaker, trainer, and parenting radio personality and is married and has a twenty-two-year-old son.

ROSLYN ANN DUFFY founded and codirected the Learning Tree Montessori Childcare, and she has written adult and children's texts including *Top Ten Preschool Parenting Problems*, as well as the internationally circulated column "From a Parent's Perspective." She lectures and trains in numerous cultures, is a parent to four and a besotted grandma to three, and lives and practices counseling in Seattle, WA.

Also by Jane Nelsen, Ed.D.

Raise a Confident and Capable Child with the Positive Discipline Series

In this newly revised and updated edition of the classic parenting handbook, you'll discover positive solutions for every parenting challenge.

POSITIVE DISCIPLINE A–Z, 3rd Edition
$16.95 paper (Canada: $21.95)
978-0-307-34557-8

As your child embarks on her school years, learn to positively impact her self-esteem both inside and outside the home.

POSITIVE DISCIPLINE FOR PRESCHOOLERS
$16.95 paper (Canada: $21.95)
978-0-307-34160-0